Solo Traveler

Tales and Tips for Great Trips

by Lea Lane

Fodor's

Fodor's Travel Publications
New York | Toronto | London | Sydney | Auckland
www.fodors.com

Solo Traveler: Tales and Tips for Great Trips
By Lea Lane

Editor: Paul Eisenberg
Editorial Production: David Downing
Design: Tina Malaney
Cover Illustration: Allison Schulnik
Production/Manufacturing: Robert B. Shields

First Edition

ISBN 1–4000–1400–X

Library of Congress Cataloging-in-Publication Data available upon request.

SPECIAL SALES

This book is available for special discounts for bulk purchases for sales promotions or premiums. Special editions, including personalized covers, excerpts of existing books, and corporate imprints, can be created in large quantities for special needs. For more information, write to Special Markets/ Premium Sales, 1745 Broadway, MD 6-2, New York, New York 10019, or e-mail specialmarkets@randomhouse.com.

PRINTED IN THE UNITED STATES OF AMERICA

10 9 8 7 6 5 4 3 2

For Sabrina Rose Lane

May you become an intrepid solo traveler, exploring
a welcoming world, and beyond.

Contents

Acknowledgments

So many people offered special attention and effort. Paul Eisenberg, my editor at Fodor's, nurtured this breakthrough book with enthusiasm, patience, and skill. I am indebted to him for his gentle guidance and our mutual respect and friendship.

Special thanks to my supportive research associate Dian Larkin, who has worked with me on several travel books, and is an independent woman with a lawyer's eye and a writer's soul.

I am grateful to Fodor's designer Tina Malaney for her thoughtfulness, and for giving this book its distinctive look and feel. Also at Fodor's, Robert Fisher, a prodigiously creative editor, has always encouraged me, and I thank him now for his exemplary work through the years.

Associates in the Society of American Travel Writers and other fellow journalists and editors who helped along the way, include Cheryl Andrews, "The Joans"—Bloom and Brower, Alys Bohn, Gayle Conran, Karen Weiner Escalera, Glenn Faria, Derek Fell, Maebeth Fenton, Arhlene Flowers, Nancy Friedman, Bigitta Kroon-Fiorita, Debbie Geiger, Lois Gerber, Steven Gordon, Lucille Hoshabjian, Valerie Kidney, Alice Marshall, Nancy Marshall, Liliane Opsomer, Beth Preddy, Janet Rodgers, Deborah Roker, Bob Sehlinger, Virginia Sheridan, Judy and Gordon Thorne, and Jane Wooldridge.

I appreciate for varied reasons: Elizabeth Beach, Peter Berg, George Berger, Barbara Bisno, Judy Bluth, Stuart and Deb Bussey, Barry Diamond, Cathy Dreilinger, Laurel Dunn, Phyllis and Stuart Edelson, Sylvia Erlich, Merle Frank, Bob Frost, Lana Gelb, Alex German, Bob German, Alan Jacobs, Judy and Stan Jacobs, Susan Kaye, Dovia Lerrick, Carol and Steve Levy, Erica Levy, Rachel Levy, Liana Perel, Kevin Reed, Jess and Brian Santucci, and Penny Thurer.

I'm blessed with special sons, Randall and Cary Lane, a lovely, talented daughter-in-law, Jennifer Reingold, and my darling granddaughter, Sabrina, to whom this book is dedicated. A special tribute also to my late husband Chaim Stern, who was so proud of my independence, and for whom I gave up going solo for too short a time.

And last, two solo travelers most inspired me: my glamorous Berlin-born aunt, Hilda Schacht, who was an independent role-model for life in general. I called her "Auntie Mame." And my brilliant and beautiful grandmother, Katinka David Schacht. Her stories of life abroad whetted my appetite for travel, and her one solo trip, as a young girl crossing the Atlantic to settle in America in the late 19th century, was more meaningful than any I have made, or ever will.

Introduction

A few years ago I was on a three-month odyssey in Russia and Eastern Europe, sizing up hotels for a travel publication. Friends would join me every now and then for a week or so, but there were gaps when I'd be on my own. Several friends worried about me being "lonely."

When they read this book they'll find out that those were the best times of all.

I got to do what I wanted, meet and talk to locals, relax, and feel the intensity of the experience and the thrill of the unexpected. One time in Erfurt, a German city where Martin Luther lived and preached, I was staring at a painting at a local museum when a nice-looking guy came over. Turns out he was the director of a European travel show, and was so delighted to find an American tourist on her own that he decided to shoot the show around me, on the spot. So there I was, exploring the city followed by a crew who interviewed and fussed over me, doing takes and angles, laughing with a whole new set of friends, and winding up as guest of honor at a merry dinner at a medieval castle.

Traveling alone isn't only a different travel experience. It can be the *ultimate* travel experience.

A few years ago, when I was interviewed by the *New York Times*, here's part of what I said (even before I knew I would be writing this book!):

"There's a difference between being a tourist and . . . a traveler. Tourists do what makes them comfortable. . . .Travelers seek discovery. They take more risks. They get pleasure in overcoming difficulties and discomforts, and they seek out the people.

"I've traveled in different ways. I've traveled alone, I've traveled with family, with friends. I think *most of all I enjoy being alone* with the people if I had to choose one—and I know that sounds unusual but *you're not alone when you travel alone. If you're open-minded you will find very much the opposite. You become a part of the scene. And to me that's the best part of travel.*"

Sure, as part of a happy couple, for many years I traveled with a compatible partner. When it works, it's great. But often—very often, it doesn't. I'm on my own again, and a basic premise keeps me going: If you're alone anyway, why not travel?

Who Are We?

Almost half of adult Americans are single, divorced, or widowed. The Travel Industry Association (TIA) recently reported that solo travelers account for 15.9 million traveling households in the United States, and for 21.8 percent of all travelers. More and more, solo travelers are an established segment of the industry. But when the TIA recently asked travelers about their plans for the longest trip of the summer, they predicted only 4 percent of these trips would be taken solo. This gap between plans and reality is probably due to the worn-out stigma that traveling by yourself is not desirable.

That's a shame, and this book will change that perception.

Solo travelers tend to travel for fun rather than business (63 percent of all trips are for pleasure). We travel by trains, planes (26 percent), and automobiles.

Some of us prefer going it all alone, but individuals who want company have increasing options. Tours, activities, and cruises focus on all ages, often at holidays, when solitude can be difficult. Groups match travel roommates of either sex—for friendship, or maybe, romance.

All types take to the road on their own, but most single travelers are women, tired of waiting for friends and significant others. There's a rapid increase of women travelers in their forties and fifties, and tour companies are expanding women-only trips, as well as other niche segments.

You don't have to be single to travel solo. More and more, members of couples and families are avoiding tiffs and boredom, and setting out on their own—breaking away—for trips, or parts of trips.

You may be single, or you may be married or attached, but want to go it alone sometimes. You may be a regular solo traveler, on business, vacations, or family gatherings. You may have tried it a bit—a weekend or a business trip, but want to do more.

Or you may be—ta-da—a Virgin Soloist. Even if you think you never have traveled alone, think again. Have you traveled on business? Even an overnighter? Have you traveled on your own to a family gathering: reunion, wedding, funeral, or celebration? What about holidays? Visits to friends? And, at a minimum, have you spent some time on your own while traveling with others—a breakaway meal, or an afternoon in a museum while your friend is at the beach?

Whatever your situation, I just want you to solo, or solo more, and do it the best way possible. I'm going to try to help. When you've tried it, trust me, you won't want to stop.

The difficulties of traveling by yourself are obvious. There are challenges. But you can simplify, make some choices, learn some skills, and do just fine on your own, or with a group.

Aspects of soloing are better and more special than any other way of traveling, including meeting people easily and getting in touch with where you are, and who you are. Prolific New Yorker writer A. J. Liebling put it beautifully, when as a young man he traveled solo to France: "I liked the sensation of immersion in a foreign element, as if floating in a summer sea, only my face out of water, and a pleasant buzzing in my ears. . . .I was often alone, but seldom lonely."

About This Book

Solo Traveler is a guide, but it's not a conventional guidebook. I'll share some of my favorite things to see and do, but in the end my job is to guide *you,* to help you make good choices and avoid wrong turns. This book will help you see that you can add dimension to your life through traveling by yourself. It will help you conquer negativity, fears, and all that keeps you from traveling on your own. And it will open up the world to you, whenever you want it. No more waiting around for somebody to join you. No more sad excuses, no more dwelling on loneliness and "I can't travel alone."

You'll be amazed how solo traveling can be eased with some guidance, encouragement, and support. Think of me as a good friend who prods you, nudging gently to help you make the most of your travel life. Or as a sassy big sister or aunt or girlfriend who's been around the block, a lot—to more than 110 countries, many more than once, and many on my own. But who's counting!

I've set up this book to be an easy, enjoyable read. The tone is personal, humorous (well, I think it is), and empathic. You'll find many specific tips, and if you only read these points, you'll be ahead of the game. But there's more. Resource sections and boxes dispense practical information. And in essays and stories from my travels (the "tales" part of this volume) I open up my own life and experiences to help you understand the emotions and challenges involved in this meaningful lifestyle.

My goal is for you to discover the wonders of traveling on your own and show you how it can enrich your life in countless ways. My hope is that you read and enjoy this book, plan a trip, join the growing numbers of satisfied, intrepid, delighted solo travelers—and go!

chapter 1

Joys, Ploys & What Annoys

I love traveling on my own and want you to experience it as I do. And I really do understand that with all the joys of solo travel come some discouragements and soul-dampening misperceptions that can foil the trip before it begins.

Let's start with the joys. Read the list on page 3 slowly—aloud if possible. Concentrate on each item, think about each statement and what makes it true. You may have already thought of these joyful free-thought statements during your pre-trip-planning process. If you have doubts, you'll have to work a bit to change the concept of traveling alone from negative to positive. But it will happen, I promise, by the end of the book—and forever, once you experience a solo trip.

Refer to this list often while you read the book.

What Soloists Think Will Annoy Them

Most negatives about solo travel are misperceptions. Here are some commonly cited issues—and the realities surrounding them.

I'll feel lonely. Sometimes you will. But sometimes you'll be lonely—or lonelier—when traveling with others. The worst trips I've ever had were with people who were incompatible. Not only did I feel lonely, I felt frustrated, angry, and several other unprintable adjectives. "Alone" does not mean lonely. Separate these two words.

I don't like being by myself. You don't have to be by yourself. You can join a group and be with people all day and night, and you can even find roommates through companies, clubs, and Web sites. And it's up to you whether all, some, or none of your time is really solo.

I'll be in danger. These days we realize more than ever that the world is not always a friendly place. We've adjusted to this heightened sense of vulnerability with an equally heightened vigilance. Women are more vulnerable than men, so if you want to avoid a problem, keep a really low profile, dress down, and remain sensible about situations at all times. Just as there are ways to call attention to yourself, there are ways to stay practically invisible. The sexier you look, and the younger you are, the harder you'll have to work on this. But even if you're so beautiful that you have to wear a mask and a body suit, you'll figure something out (see Chapter 14, Safety & Health).

I'll be in trouble if I get sick. Being sick is especially difficult when you're alone. So, build yourself up before you leave, take sanitary precautions, bring extra meds, get adequate insurance coverage and at the first sign of illness, consult a doctor. Again, see Chapter 14 for further advice.

Eating alone is no fun. Sometimes it isn't. But remember: eating with an incompatible companion can be worse. Alone, you can eat an entire pepperoni pizza with no judgments about carbs or portion size—and you can be sure you won't have an argument or a boring conversation. You can pack a doggy bag with no shame. And eating solo is faster! In Chapter 10, Eating Alone, I offer many ways to brighten this sometimes anxious side of soloing.

I'll have to do everything myself. Not really. People are prone to helping single travelers (the "White Knight" syndrome—just

JOYS OF SOLO TRAVEL

Freedom   New friends

Confidence   Possibilities

Becoming a traveler rather than a tourist

Solitude   Competence

Succeeding on your own

Understanding better who you are   Romance

Discovery   Independence

Silence

Experiencing where you are

Resourcefulness

Appreciating your own impressions and opinions

Spirit   Approachability

Pleasure

Confronting and conquering fears

Unlimited experiences

Fantasies

Change   Lingering

Using instinct and common sense

Acceptance

Adventure

Self-esteem

Simplicity

Doing what you want, when you want, for as long as you want

The offbeat

Opportunity   The unpredictable

make sure to seek out likely knights, not nasty knaves). And if they don't volunteer, all you need to do is ask. Concierges and other lodging staff and travel personnel are trained to go out of their way to help solo travelers. It's their job, so let them do it. Problem areas are public places, such as restrooms, where you can't easily leave your bags with strangers, and times when you're rushing. We'll work on solutions.

People will feel sorry for me. Actually, if you have a positive attitude and a warm smile, people will admire your independence. But don't worry about what others may think. Concentrate on how you feel about yourself, and project confidence.

I don't trust my judgment. Traveling on your own forces you to make choices and decisions all the time. You will learn to trust those choices as you succeed. That is one of the nicest by-products of solo travel.

I'll miss my support system and routine. You might, sometimes, just as you might if you travel with others. But the busier and more interested you are in what you're doing, the less you'll miss your routine.

I won't have anyone to share the wonderful moments. Not at the exact moment, maybe, but later you can share your photos, journals, and memories. And if sharing the moment means a lot, you can always join a group, or get a cell phone and talk immediately to a friend—even narrate what is going on, sometimes with images as well. The tech world is becoming the solo traveler's best ally.

I'll be afraid. You might be at times. Traveling alone is a major achievement, filled with unknowns that can breed fears, whether warranted or not. If you conquer your fears, you will feel courageous. The more you do it, the easier it becomes. If you have a problem, you can work on it.

I'll get lost. Count on it, so don't be too hard on yourself. Prepare well. Read maps ahead of time, and mark them, and put important directions in written form as well. Don't leave for

SOLO TRAVELERS: IN THEIR OWN WORDS

You may be thinking, "Sure, Lea's a travel writer. It's easier for her to go around on her own." But travel Web sites reveal hundreds of soloists extolling the joys of traveling on their own. Read what one solo traveler says:

I had always dreamed about traveling to Europe. So when I got a good job that would allow me to travel, I was ready to go. Unfortunately none of my friends had jobs that would allow them to travel with me. I decided solo travel was an option. I was so scared on the day I left, I considered taking the shuttle back home and just studying about Spain and Italy for three weeks and faking that I went.

I ended up going and had the time of my life and came back as a completely different person. Braver, more adventurous and more confident. Don't let the thought of solo travel hold you back. Life's too short.

Name and address withheld
La Mesa, CA 10/28/03

your next destination without having an idea of the route, and leave extra time to get lost without panic. When in doubt, ask for directions. And remember that sometimes, getting lost leads to the best experiences of a trip (see Chapter 8, Getting There, Getting Around).

I won't have anything to do in the evening. Join night tours, or do whatever you might do on your own at home—a movie, museum, a concert, or just chilling out. The good news is that you can often find single-ticket availability to even the hottest event. Just ensure you budget for a taxi back to your lodging. Select your hotel, in part, based on its proximity to nightlife (see Chapter 3, Where to Go, What to Do On Your Own and Chapter 9, Successful Solo Lodging).

I'll have to handle all the money. Use one or two credit cards and an ATM machine and you should be fine. If you prefer traveler's checks, they are safe as well. Just don't walk around with a lot of cash, and be cautious about hiding your loot.

Pay for priorities but skimp on things that matter less. Spend fewer dollars on a room you won't be in much, more on film if you love to take photos. Eat in cafés to save for a local painting. If costs add up anyway, remember that time and opportunity are most precious, so compensate by being thriftier when you return from the trip. If you've never budgeted, I'll show you how (see Chapter 2, Planning & Saving).

I'll have to make all the plans. That's a wonderful aspect of solo travel. No bickering, whining, disappointments or grudges. You get to do exactly what you want. Both planning and spontaneity are important when you solo. If you plan ahead, studying history, geography, language and customs, you will be able to make the most of the many surprise opportunities you'll find (see Chapter 2).

I'll be tired. Yes, you tend to be more wiped out when you have to do it all yourself. But you can get as much sleep as you like—whenever you want. Schedule according to how you feel, and don't push yourself beyond what's comfortable for you.

I'll have no one to talk to. Not so. You'll have a world of people to talk to—in lines, in restaurants, on the street, in museums, while shopping—in fact, so many people that you may find yourself happily hoarse at the end of the day! Stay interested in what and who is around you, and ask questions. The easiest is "Where are you from?" Then follow up, and be sure you answer with warmth and enthusiasm. A smile alone may start a whole conversation (see Chapter 13, Meeting People).

Solo travel will be too expensive. Sure, taking a trip alone is normally more expensive for one than for half of a pair. You may have to pay a single supplement—a surcharge for occupying a room alone—or a full double-occupancy rate, but there are ways around this (see Chapter 2). And remember, you can spend exactly what you want—cutting back on some things and splurging on others, to make up for these extra fees.

Unforeseen problems will come up. They always do. A trip, after all, is just a part of life. You'll manage just fine if you take your time, trust your instincts, and, if needed, request help. Don't focus on negative possibilities. So far you've gotten through life most of the time on your own. You'll surprise yourself, and be delighted how the same resourcefulness you use in daily life will manifest itself on the road.

I feel weird about ditching the group. Why is it that people who happily go their separate ways most of the time seem conjoined when they travel together? The thought process seems to be, "Go to a movie while my friend takes a walk? No way. We'll be apart for two hours!" I address this attitude in Chapter 16, Breaking Away.

I don't care what you say, Lea, I don't like the idea of traveling solo. So don't totally go it alone. Join a tour group of likeminded people. Select an interest, like sculpting or architecture or tennis or wine or bird-watching. Chances are there's a group that is traveling somewhere to enjoy that interest (see Chapter 5, Soloing with Others).

Ploys for Successful Soloing

You may have all the following characteristics, or you may have to work on some of them. All have helped me enjoy going it alone, and I try to develop and maintain them whenever I can.

MOTIVATION

You really, really want to visit somewhere. Maybe to attend your nephew's graduation in London. Or see the gorges in China before they get flooded. Or meet a famous speaker at a conference. This is the sort of thing that will get you out, alone. At the front of your yearly calendar, list in order of preference where you really want to go and what you really want to do, in this year—and in your lifetime. Then start crossing these things off!

Baby Steps

My first trip alone was brief. I was about seven, and I ran away from home for an hour or so, to 41st Street in Miami Beach. I lived on 31st Street. I had packed my little Samsonite cosmetic suitcase pretty well, as I recall. A toothbrush (no toothpaste, but hey, I got it half right), a dress (no underwear), *Heidi* (I was already reading travel books), and pennies from my piggy bank. Nobody seemed to notice I was gone, and all was forgotten and forgiven when I arrived back at my door.

But wanderlust had begun.

My first *real* solo trip was embarking at age 19 on the Silver Meteor train from Miami to New York. I was president of my college sorority, attending a national convention. What joy that mid-20th century day, to lug that same Samsonite cosmetic case to my closet-sized "couchette" compartment, with its pull-down bed and tiny steel sink. I looked out from the grimy window, my young reflection overlaid on the passing fields and towns. People bustled onto the train with steam rising and hissing, and crossing bells clanged and the engine hooted through the night. How I loved it: the clacking rails, the porters with their Southern accents, the iron smell of the tracks, the heavy creamers on linen-covered tables in the dining car. Maybe it was the movies I'd seen, but I felt I had been riding the rails all my life, by myself.

I was a fledgling woman traveling to an unrequited love, the exciting sophisticate adored by many, unaware of me, but often in my dreams: Manhattan. It was visceral; I felt butterflies.

I had usually visited with my younger brother Stuie in tow. We stayed with Aunt Hilda, on East End Avenue, across from Gracie Mansion, the mayor's residence, and if we went out on her balcony at a certain time, Mayor Lindsay, handsome as any movie star, might wave to us, or rather wave to the air; he always knew someone was looking down on him.

Aunt Hilda would take us to the requisite attractions, and through the years we had watched the United Nations Building arising floor by floor on the East River, climbed high into the Statue of Liberty's arm, and had been amazed at the Rockettes, high-kicking at Radio City. Auntie took us to the new Four Seasons restaurant, where Stuie ordered pheasant under glass, and Coney Island, where the hot dogs sputtered, and compressed air at the fun house blew your dress up into your face.

New York was bursting with success, and Auntie's building seemed to reflect that glamour. Bill Cullen, host of many television game shows at that time, threw his garbage down the chute like the rest of us mortals. And I once entered the elevator occupied by Paul Simon, who was shorter than I was, and wore a Yankee cap. I said, "You're him." He said, "I am." And then we looked at the floor.

But on that long-ago, still-innocent day when I arrived on my own for the conference at the Waldorf-Astoria, I could not know I would interact many times with that hotel: 20 years later bring my family there for a weekend, and five years after that, tryst there with a new love. I would meet editors and friends there, and attend banquets through the decades. And I did not know that I would critique that very hotel in print, many times, as the writer I would become.

I stayed with Aunt Hilda for a couple of days after that sorority conference, and I still remember the late afternoon she sent me to the movies by the Plaza hotel, while she "cooked meatballs" for her boyfriend, the Greek doctor. I was naïve enough to believe her. I didn't smoke, but bought a pack of cigarettes and held one, unlighted in my fingers after the movie, which was Swedish and gloomy.

I took the crosstown bus to my aunt's apartment, and not sure that she wanted me back yet—meatballs took time to digest, I figured, I walked a bit in the twilight past brownstones and neighborhood shops. I could just about imagine myself on my own, as my aunt was, and it felt exhilarating. It was too much then to think about traveling anywhere else. The city was quite enough.

I still loved New York, although, as usual, it paid me little heed. But after that train trip on my own, I felt like it just might love me back, a bit. ❧

RESOURCEFULNESS

If you get knocked down, you can figure a way to get up. If you lose your keys, you can trace your way back to where they are, and if you don't find them, you call a locksmith. You know to bring a book or a journal with you so that you spend waiting time productively. If this is not you, spend some time thinking about possible problem situations and how best to handle them. You can divide travel categories: transportation, lodging, eating, and so forth. Keep a list of problems and solutions and you'll see that most things are simply solved—if you don't panic, and you're willing to accept some help.

CURIOSITY

You'll find out about something and check it out, and that leads to other discoveries, and before long, you find something or someplace you would love to experience. And as you go, you keep discovering more and more things. Curiosity keeps your mind busy and that keeps you from feeling bored and alone. It helps to read about a place and jot down things that you don't want to miss. As a bonus, asking questions when you're really interested is the best way to meet others.

RISK-TAKING ATTITUDE

You can travel stand-by and not feel anxiety. If a change happens, and you face an unknown, you look forward to the opportunities ahead. If you drink tap water and you're not sure if it's ok, you don't panic. You ask, and then you act, if necessary, to minimize the problem. Calculated risk is the key here. If your gut tells you no, don't talk yourself into something. Think it out; then, still, trust your gut. If a group is hang gliding and begging you to join them and you're afraid of heights, be firm. "No way" is a term to practice and use without guilt. Just be sure you don't use it all the time.

PASSION

You love something or someone so much that you'll do anything to get to it/them. You adore glass, so you want to visit Murano, in Italy and Washington State, too, for Chihuly's art-glass bridge. Caviar's your thing, so Russia beckons. Pretty obvious, and pretty similar to motivation—only more directed. Passions can lead you to the great places of the world. I have friends who use their passions as excuses to travel and splurge—otherwise they probably would be vacationing on their couches. I know golfers who intend to visit the top 100 golf resorts during their lifetime, divers who fly all the way to Palau, climbers who want to summit the Big Seven peaks. If passion is what it takes, find one!

SENSE OF SELF

You enjoy your own company. You trust your decisions. You like yourself, and feel good about others liking you. Since you'll be spending a great deal of time on your own, this is mighty important.

STRENGTH OF MIND & BODY

You're in good shape, both mentally and physically. You're ready to roll. If not, work on it. (This, too, would be a good idea whether or not you travel.)

SENSE OF HUMOR

You can laugh at yourself. You enjoy the ludicrous and the absurd—not for being different, just for being funny. Life will throw rocks in the road and the wind may be blowing against you, but if you can find a chuckle even in adversity, you'll be a fine soloist.

OPENNESS

Strange customs don't turn you off. You can ask others for favors, and answer their questions without undo difficulty. You're willing to eat what is put before you, unless, maybe, it's moving. You respect all creatures. Without openness, you might look upon the different with disdain, and spiral into negativity. Be as open as possible to what the world has to offer, and learn and grow from it.

CONNECTION

You are aware of caring family, friends, and associates no matter where you wander. And you aren't afraid to stay in touch and call on them, if needed. You carry their photos, and their notes and mementos.

STUBBORNNESS

You don't give up easily. You'll check around for a room without a single supplement. You'll insist on a table with the view of

Can I Be Your Photographer?

Can I be your photographer . . . carry your bags . . . be your lover?"
Wry questions pop up when I mention that I'm a travel writer, often
on my own. "I'll leave everything and everyone I care about and go off
with you," people jokingly plead. "I'll be your Sancho Panza, your Robin,
your Scarecrow . . . your stud."

"Ah yes," I say looking off. "You think it's all fun. Get in line."

I know what I do may seem like an ideal living. What could be bad?
The perquisites, the comped lifestyle. After all, "travel journalist" came in
second (after "movie star"!) on the top-10 best-career list on an A&E
cable TV poll.

People don't think about low pay, gained poundage, long separations,
rip-offs, last-minute changes, killed stories. Or trips in flying buses with
rusty propellers and a pilot who scratches his head while opening a map
and scanning the desert below. Or tse-tse flies biting your face on a 10-
hour drive on rutted, dusty roads in a jeep without springs.

Or the month I hole up alone, writing about a one-week trip. And the
three months I wait for the pay.

Those who wish to become my traveling pilates trainer or valet or
research assistant or driver usually regale me with their own travel stories, almost as a defense or challenge. "So what if you have a good life,
traveling," they seem to think, eyes glazed in a travel reverie. "You'll pay
for it dearly right now. My turn to one-up you with my special trips, in
painstaking detail: Barbados last December when the only solar eclipse in
this century was perfect in a clear sky. The last-minute weekend deal I
got to London, with tickets to the award-winning musical, which may
come to Broadway next year, but not with the original cast. The first-
class upgrades, e-v-e-r-y one of them. The B&B in Anchorage with a view
of Denali (totally visible to us, although usually cloud-covered) where
they served us fresh-brewed Guatemalan coffee, free-range organic eggs
with smoked, just-spawned salmon, and fresh Yukon apple butter, which
the former Miss-Alaska owner canned herself from her own orchard, and
carried to our featherbed—included in the price."

Help.

Thoughts of travel light up people's eyes and loosen their tongues. In
an airplane or some other captive spot, I endure hours of travel talk. And

in a group, travel tales spread in geometric progression, 'til I want to tip-toe out the door, the talkers unaware that I have left, or perhaps that I was ever there at all.

That's why I write about travel. Not only a chance to pass something on to you, but a chance to tell you my own stories for a change.

Long ago I opted for a freelance life over a traditional career. I interned on the *Miami Herald* when I was 18, and could have gone that way. I've run a corporate company and worked as an editor in an office with a window. But this bird needs to spread her wings and leave even a gilded cage.

And despite the temptation of traveling with a bag-carrying boy-toy-massage-therapist-bouncer-researcher, I seem to like—really like—being a free spirit, on my own. ᣰ

Mount Rushmore rather than the one by the kitchen. Traveling alone takes effort and determination, but is worth every bit of it.

KEEN OBSERVATION

All your senses are sharp, not just sight and sound. You are fasci-nated by the scent of a lavender field, and the feel of that field beneath you. You look at faces and hands and remember the details of places you have visited. You notice the tops of build-ings and the bottoms of ponds. When a guide speaks, you look around, not just at the guide. Observe carefully, take notes, and you won't be bored.

PATIENCE

You realize that doing things on your own often requires spend-ing more time dealing with details than you may be used to. You can wait . . . and wait . . . and wait, if something is worth it. And the joys of solo traveling are worth waiting for!

Solo Traveler Quick-Start Tips

You know that cheat sheet that came with your printer and spared you from reading the manual? This is it, sort of. But I hope you'll read the rest of this book.

Reach out. Communicate regularly with your family and friends. E-mail, download photos, phone, mail—keeping in touch makes you feel especially good when you're on your own. That way you can share the day's activities immediately with those who care.

Use contacts. Before you leave, see if you can find friends or relatives of friends, or shopkeepers who know someone, or someplace special where you're going. Bring a note as your calling card—this can make for a special get-together or evening on a trip, and you might even build a trip around these contacts (see Chapter 13).

Blend. Learn a bit of the language and customs before you leave, and bring a phrase book. This is a smart way to gain good will, as well as communicate (see Chapter 12).

Capture. Bring a Polaroid camera, take lots of photos—and leave them as gifts for helpful people and new friends. Take loads of photos or video on a digital camera or camcorder—this will give you a fun activity, and lots of memories to reflect on.

Try a threesome. For travel, that is, if you have a good relationship with a couple. Some of my best times were with compatible people who happened to be together and who both enjoyed my company. Most important: split all bills three ways—all the time—and make that clear from the start.

Relax your routine. Play-act at a restaurant, where you'll never see anyone again, and you want to feel amused. Walk in a city instead of on a treadmill. Let grooming go—a bit. No need to shave your legs or wash your hair every night. Enjoy this break, just because you can. (But stay healthy and clean!)

Break away. Once in a while, when traveling with others, go off on your own (see Chapter 16).

Compensate. Let the concierge map out your route. Carry a phrasebook, and use it. Ask that burly dude to help lift your suitcase onto the train (he'll usually volunteer if you struggle a bit). It's amazing how resourceful we can be, especially on the road. And what's even more heartening is how willing folks are to assist.

Finesse nights and meals. Stay in a small property, sit in the parlor, and others probably will join you. Exercise at night—in a fitness room, or even aerobic dancing en suite to local music. Movies are always an option. If museums are open, evenings are great times to gaze about. Most European shops close late, and malls everywhere are hubs of activity. Shopping fills the night exceptionally well (and your luggage). Magic word for singles: courier. Another: taxis.

I like to relax after a busy day on my own. A good book, or maybe a movie on PayTV. I often connect with friends and family by phone or e-mail and share my experiences, or maybe write in a journal. I indulge in the solitude, and then start out early the next day, refreshed.

As for eating alone (see Chapter 10), staring at that paperback or listening in on conversations are the standard time-killers. More and more restaurants cater to single diners at a bar setting, but otherwise, some suggestions: choose casual places, like diners or pubs. Eat sushi and interact with the chefs. Take your fancy meals at lunch, when more diners are solo. Come early. Stay at inns where meals are served communally. And don't count out room service, especially if you have a balcony to complement the indulgence.

Or be creative. One night I wore sunglasses and an outrageous blouse, and the waiters catered to me as if I were a movie star. Another time, I tipped my dependable driver in Kuala Lumpur (from a reputable company) by asking him to join me at meals. He hardly spoke a word of English, but it wasn't the first time I'd been with an incomprehensible dinner companion.

Savor. Okay, so you won't be whispering to someone special, "Does this sunset put you in the mood for anything?" But you might say to yourself, "Magnificent!" and think of past setting suns. Lasting memories require focus and contemplation, and when you travel alone you have time for that.

Be confident. Most of the world may seem hand-in-hand when you're not, but please don't let that stop you. Opportunities and options multiply when you're soloing, so venture forth. As for getting approached, the usual safety precautions are doubly important. Don't call attention to yourself if you don't want attention—a good rule, in general.

Take baby steps. Start with an overnight or a weekend, in a place with lots to do. Revisit a favorite museum in the next state. Enjoy a nearby town. Snorkle in the Keys. Weekend in NYC. Even just a spa day on your own will give you an idea of how it feels to be a solo traveler. Consider a cruise or resort spa where the settings, breadth of activities, and presence of other soloists can easily eclipse any awkwardness you may feel (see Chapter 4, One-Stop Soloing).

Planning & Saving

Think of the many processes that divide easily into three parts: Warm up, exercise, cool down; appetizer, main course, dessert; organizing, writing, editing; foreplay, lovemaking, cuddling. You could think of dozens more in a lively parlor game.

Let's add another trio: planning, traveling, remembering. Planning is key to most anything, and, ironically, it leads the way to spontaneity. It whets your travel appetite, dispels anxieties, and is as much a part of the process as the travel itself, or the journals, photos, or videos that stem from it.

As a seasoned travel writer, I'm sometimes given a couple of days notice and a fixed itinerary crammed with activities, and a get-there-and-get-it done, seat-of-the-pants shove to somewhere, where I make do by instinct and savvy. But I remember as a novice when I'd just be going for the joy of it—and I really miss the enthusiasm of planning those earliest travels. I'd start months ahead, calling travel boards and collecting packets of brochures, which spilled out all over the floor and usually stayed there until I departed. I'd study the photos and read the over-hyped, purple prose, and daydream of rooms overlooking blue Alpine lakes and imagine climbing fortress towers and gazing at landmark monuments, and enjoy every minute of the reverie. The planning was so pleasurable most of the time I probably could have skipped the trip.

To add to the anticipation, as I created the itinerary I'd play local music, cook regional specialties, and check out famous writers from areas I'd be visiting, and read their novels and memoirs set in those places. That's how I discovered many of my all-time favorite books, including *The Magic Mountain* by Thomas Mann, and *Bitter Lemons* by Laurence Durrell. This kind of absorption is useful in its imaginative way, and lends a positive intensity to conceiving and planning your trip.

DECIDING WHAT YOU WANT

Because you'll be busy covering so many details on your own during your trip, you want to forestall avoidable mistakes and— key to any trip—avoid wasting time. The more you clarify in advance—what you want to do, how you want to do it, and where to find it, the better your plans, and your travels, will be.

If you're traveling with a specific goal, such as a college reunion, or if you're on a planned itinerary, then you can move on to the "gathering information" phase. But otherwise, set aside some time to think what you might like best.

A Standard List

You might ask yourself these questions, think about them, and jot some notes to analyze your ideal travel experience:

☞ Do I want relaxation, stimulation, or both?

☞ Do I prefer city or country atmosphere?

☞ Do I want to be challenged physically?

☞ Do I feel seasoned enough to handle just about anything?

☞ Do I want to enjoy previous interests, or develop new ones?

☞ Do I want to spend lots of time in one area, or would I prefer moving around?

QUICK SAVING TIPS

Set a budget. Figure the max you're willing or able to pay. Whether it's $10,000 or $1,000, know your means and stay within them. Be conservative, as travel budgets usually runneth over. Prepay when possible to stick to your value objectives.

Prioritize. What's important? Eating at Michelin 3-star restaurants? A cruise cabin with a balcony? Or maybe you enjoy hot dogs and prefer a tent. Write down what you won't give up without a fight. For all other things, strive to cut costs.

Compromise. If you savor staying at a Four Seasons, consider booking a minimal room and you'll still enjoy the public spaces. Also, you might fly business class going—there are some great deals out there now—and economy back.

Use ATMs. You'll need to take some cash, but nowadays ATMs are everywhere, and you'll get a better exchange rate than at a bank or hotel. Get some currency at an airport ATM when you arrive, and learn the exchange rate ASAP; if you don't see a chart at the airport, ask at your lodging—even before paying the taxi.

Be careful with your plastic. Bring a couple of credit cards, but no need for more. Of course, avoid carrying wads of cash, or even wads of traveler's checks. Using a debit card might help you spend more sanely (and avoid getting hit later with a huge credit-card bill). Downside: you could clean out your checking account if you're not paying attention, and you don't get bonus points. But it might be preferable to getting a panic attack when the bill comes.

☞ Do I care about climate?

☞ How important are food and lodging?

☞ Do I want to be totally alone most of the time, or with others?

☞ Do I want to venture on my own, or with a guide or driver, or other support? Or do I prefer a group?

► How much do I want to shop, sightsee, socialize, or participate in other aspects of travel?

► Am I spontaneous, or do I prefer an organized itinerary?

► Do I have a tight budget, or is money not an issue?

► How much cultural change or enrichment would I like?

► Do I feel the need to speak a bit of the language? Can I?

► How much time do I have?

► Is safety a major concern?

► Do I want to travel with a pet?

► Do I want an active social life?

A More Personal List

Instead of, or in addition to the previous list, you might prefer to start with the words "On my trip I want to . . ." and just fill in whatever comes to mind, without analyzing. Your wants may include specific names or general ideas, and they may be inter-related or not, contradictory or not. Just free write whatever travel goals you desire. Add entries as you think of them, delete others as you wish, and put the list away for a while to refresh your thought process. For example: "On my trip I want to . . ."

► travel alone

► travel with others, in a group under 10 people

► meet friends

► meet more than friends

► feel I've accomplished something that helps the world

► veg out on a beach with sand dunes

► eat great desserts every night

► get healthy, and lose five pounds

► lose my virginity (not on my list, but may be on yours)

▶ learn something new—preferably sculpting or drawing

▶ find myself

▶ see lots of paintings by van Gogh

▶ get an all-over tan

▶ spend quality time with my whippet, Rover

▶ do just about anything that seems interesting

To begin your travel plans, try to set up a trip that includes at least one of the desires from your list, or maybe even several of them. Some combos are naturals: if you want to meet friends and get healthy, you could easily choose a spa trip or a health-theme cruise (see Chapter 4, One-Stop Soloing). To lie on a beach and be with others, you might look at a Club Med–type place. Some wants will be difficult to accomplish without lots of time and money, but that shouldn't stop you from wanting them, or even sometimes splurging to accomplish them.

Using the above list, some combinations appear difficult, but don't give up too fast. At first glance it may seem impossible to see lots of van Gogh's near a clothes-optional beach, and get an overall tan, but a bit of research will show that the Netherlands has some (cool and windy) nude beaches—not that far from Amsterdam's definitive van Gogh museum.

This brainstorming list is a fun way to start planning your trip. To save time next time you're off to somewhere, keep your current list, and refer to it again, starting with the "I want to's" that remain.

How Do I Feel?

You might want to create yet another brainstorming list to clarify your feelings about your trip, which will be especially important when you're traveling alone. Do this ahead of time. Jot down any travel anxieties. What makes you uncomfortable? Are you intimidated by any aspects of travel? Do you have fears about places you're visiting? Allow time to think, and be willing to put down what you feel; again, this is *your* list.

Maybe your "feeling" list will be empty—no potential problems. But if you're traveling to Antarctica and have nightmares about icebergs and Emperor penguins, you might want to talk about your anxieties with a friend who's been there, or with a therapist (maybe you're projecting about your mother!). Planning can avoid emotional dips associated with solo travel.

Ways to Plan

Research and gather information to plan effectively and sensibly, and create at least a basic itinerary. But do try to avoid overscheduling—leave room for the magic of surprise and the joy of the unexpected, inevitable bonuses of traveling solo.

Ask around. Family, friends, work associates and their circle definitely have first-hand opinions and experiences, and usually enjoy sharing them. Local people from countries you're visiting, or recent visitors can be especially helpful.

Take notes and gather info, especially word of mouth, but keep in mind that your tastes and interests may differ from others. Uncle Saul may travel regularly to the Caribbean and have the best intentions, but if he loves to salsa in Puerto Rico and you enjoy dawn digs in Belize and lights out at nine, there's an info disconnect.

You also have solo-specific outlooks and needs. Packing lightly, avoiding single supplements, and eating on your own are issues that others may not care or know much about.

Refer to files and notes. Clip articles, or copy material from Web sites. Keep a file on your computer marked "Travel." Study and note and print out—and weed out. And if you haven't been keeping files, you might want to start.

Refer to guidebooks. A well-researched, up-to-date guidebook is like a best friend full of helpful information. Seek a bookstore with an extensive travel section. Read several books relating to your particular travel needs and destinations. You can photocopy relevant pages, then mark them up and bring them on your trip so that you won't load your luggage with heavy books—a no-no for a solo.

Rediscover the library. That old-fashioned repository of information now provides not only books and periodicals but videos, DVDs, computers, computer software, and book clubs and lecture series. Leave time to dig deep for information filed by subject matter and country, and augment this data with literature and videos: England comes to life in *Jane Eyre* more than with a guidebook alone.

Search the Web. Scan bookseller sites for a quick take on travel-related literature and visit the "Travel Talk" area at www.fodors. com. Throw a specific question out there and you'll get loads of answers. Write a snappy head, and be specific: "What's the best waterfront restaurant in Sydney, with local specialties and moderate prices?" or "Solo traveler needs advice today about dining solo in Morocco!" You get the idea.

Use a travel agent. These travel pros used to monopolize transportation and lodging sites, and we didn't have to pay them—airlines, hotels, cruise and car companies gave them a percentage. But in an era of Internet reservations and do-it-yourself research, agents have had to scramble and adjust, specialize and study, and many now need to charge you.

Instead of just being reservationists, many travel agents are experts in specific areas, such as adventure cruising, or Eastern Europe, and their input and advice can help immensely. But choose carefully. You don't need a specialist in New Zealand when you're going to Helsinki. And you want to be sure your agent stays up to speed.

One New York–area agent I lovingly call "Snobby Man," deals only in "ultraluxury travel." He's so exclusive he has an unlisted phone number. Over drinks one evening he admitted that he often uses information from a trade publication I used to write for; it provides detailed hotel and cruise reviews—right down to the carpet stains. Agents buy this expensive reference tool because it's impossible to be an expert and up-to-date on everywhere. Trouble is, entries for this excellent publication are usually updated every two years. The carpets might be changed, the chef fired, and the rooms rewired for cable, and you'd never

know. So traveler beware, because even super-expensive Snobby
Man isn't always in the loop.

Suggestions for working with your travel agent:

☞ Be clear about what you want, and interact to achieve it.

☞ Do you need a rental car? Do you want to stay in town? Is the
booked room too expensive for your budget? Ask all the questions you want, preferably in person—and don't be afraid to
suggest changes.

☞ Ask for receipts and invoices for all monies you pay—you may
need them later to prove your payment or reservation.

☞ When you see the finished itinerary, be honest, and if you have
a problem, change it; if needed, research a bit yourself.

☞ You may also be working with tour operators, or agents and contacts at your destinations—so find out about them.

☞ Get all info on visas and other documentation, shots, vouchers,
and forms—including insurance.

☞ Leave with a satisfactory, detailed itinerary.

☞ Pick up tour brochures that focus on your destination and solo
excursions.

Before You Go

Get your house in order. Find someone who'll take care of your
residence while you're away: pick up your mail and newspaper
(or have the post office or carrier hold it), water your plants, feed
your pets, check on frozen pipes (and, likewise, periodically start
your car), and cover day-to-day happenings. Thwart theft by
having lights, the TV, or radio go on and off by timer. And if you
travel lots, consider an alarm system (it also lowers home insurance payments).

Pay bills before you leave. For any bills that may arrive while
you're gone, leave checks with the person taking care of your
mail; write them out as much as possible, and provide pre-
addressed stamped envelopes. Pay ahead, by months if neces-

sary, and think about automatic withdrawals and payment by phone or Web.

Also: get your hair cut and your nails polished, your body waxed and your face peeled *before* you leave (unless, of course, you're headed for a spa for just such pampering). You'll have enough to do traveling on your own, and time is precious.

Anticipate bad weather. Check the Internet or watch the Weather Channel to plan your packing, and bring layers and foul-weather gear to cover any possibilities. Most important, relax: If snow has fouled up your plans, make snow angels. In Manila I opened the windows one morning to what sounded like a train wreck—it was a typhoon, and I had no idea it was coming. I actually had to go about my business, amid the fallen trees and downed lines—not suggested.

Get current. Bring needed converters, adapters, and plugs and learn how to use them. North and Central America use 120 volts; the rest of the world uses 220–240. Ask first before plugging into any strange outlet! I fried a computer following bad advice in Rio.

Prune your itinerary. Build in free time and wiggle room throughout your trip. If there's a detour you'd prefer, take it. I did that in the Greek islands, staying extra days on islands I especially liked, skipping the over-touristed ones. If this change of course leads to your losing a deposit, weigh this against sticking to the plan while you're bored or exhausted.

Prepare for culture shock. Even though we're wired globally and can learn about different cultures, you'll still want to brace yourself for the sometimes profound differences you'll find as you travel on your own. I still remember the pungent smell of New Delhi as I disembarked from the jet, the burning smog and littered streets of Cairo, and the swarming crowds in Tokyo, where half the people wore face masks and I felt dropped into a world of Michael Jacksons.

No matter how much you read and hear, the sensual smack in the face of a new place will remind you once again of the wonders of travel, and how we are all the same, yet different. Read up to gain insight about the differences, remain open-minded, and expect anything. I still find bull-fighting gruesome, but I do at least understand it holds a higher meaning for Spanish aficionados.

And when you return home, you may be surprised at the culture shock of our own insulated world of SUVs and superstores, obesity and fast food; our obsession with pop stars and pop guns, cosmetic surgery and body odor, terror alerts and reality TV. Your perspective will have broadened, and you will hopefully return a wiser, kinder person—and more observant and considerate of our own culture, due largely to the flexibility you enjoyed as a solo traveler.

HOW TO SAVE

Favorable exchange rates, economic downturns, slow travel seasons, public transportation, inexpensive lodgings—all tactics for any budget-minded traveler, but what happens when you're on your own and trying to save a buck? How does the dynamic shift? And what about that most vexing of all lodging issues for soloists—the dreaded single supplement? Read on.

Minimize the Single Supplement

Most rooms are designed and priced for two people, and if a hotel or cruise line charges only half for one occupant, it's not getting expected revenue. The "single supplement" adds back some of the cost of a double room, and often adds lost revenue from drinks, food, or other expenses a second traveler would have paid beyond the package price. Solo travelers may wind up paying as much as three times the per-person double rate.

Is it a hopeless situation? No way. Look for specials when suppliers waive or discount their single supplements. Be resourceful; travel off-season, when rooms are cheaper, and try to bargain with the property for other perks (meal vouchers, waived health-club usage fees, etc.) that may not cost the property very much, but could make a difference to you.

Some of the usual suspects also have some of the more reasonable deals. Club Med has a special week for singles, and charges a reasonable single supplement. Also look for cruise lines offering sailings with lower—or cancelled—single supplements. Several of the smaller or more upscale cruise lines, and many river vessels offer reduced or eliminated supplements.

Share a Room

A guaranteed-share program, in which you can request a provided roommate, is offered by many cruise lines and tour companies. If you agree to share a room and the company cannot pair you with someone, you don't have to pay the single supplement. Ask your agent, or check with each company directly about restrictions.

Cruise lines, tour operators, and other companies may match up individuals of the same gender, but typically limit compatibility checks to smoking preference, so you have to deal with finding out as much as possible.

Just remember, saving money is great, but not if you don't get along with someone. Check carefully. Proceed cautiously! Even with people you know, sharing a room can become a horror story of sleepless nights and bickering over everything from temperature to light to air. I once shared a room with a lovely lady who needed the lights on all night, and made at least three trips a night to the bathroom.

Although most of these services don't aim to match romantic partners, many members seek or are willing to travel with opposite-sex companions. This is up to you, but you need to be up front. I've had problems through the years traveling with male "friends" who ran me around the room when they arrived at our destinations. Nothing is worse than a rejected travel partner, especially one with too much testosterone—but you should never compromise your feelings. Get it in writing, to remind each other of your agreement, or just avoid the situation.

Learn Key Phrases for Saving

Deals. To get people traveling, suppliers dish out big deals. (Be sure to ask about packages, special discounts, club rates—like those offered for AAA members). Check out Web sites for bargains. Hotels undergoing construction, or new or partly refurbished hotels or ships often cut their rates. Ask them to waive the surcharge.

Close-to-home. Beaches in Hawaii and Australia are sublime, but beaches in the Caribbean or Bermuda are lovely, too, and so, in fact are those on Key Biscayne or Hilton Head or San Diego. If you save on the long haul, you could upgrade the rest. For value, think Montreal, not Paris; Mexico City, not Madrid. Eliminating overseas airfare and using ground transport can save you big-time, important for savvy soloists.

Off-peak. The close-to-home rule can be negated by the off-peak rule. Travel is time-sensitive, so in less-well-traveled periods, costs are down. And by traveling solo, you have the flexibility to take advantage of such deals. Shoulder or low seasons offer best value, as do early-bird specials and last-minute tickets. And as a bonus, most destinations are especially wonderful at off-times: more real, less crowded, with better service. You can probably get to Europe cheaper than you can visit your Mom in Topeka, with airlines offering fares under $400 round-trip. And hotel rates in Florida, the Bahamas, and the Caribbean can be half in summer what they cost in winter.

Rates at hotels and cruise lines usually have three seasons: high, shoulder, and low. Also good bets are many destinations the week after New Year's, midweek travel to Las Vegas and resort areas, and weekend travel to big cities where business travelers dominate weekdays and hotels are empty on Friday and Saturday nights. But fantastic savings may also reflect fantastically lousy weather (a Caribbean cruise in the fall, hurricane season). Or, low season may not be convenient to travel.

Prepaid. Cruises, tours, packages, all-inclusives—even day trips show most costs up front, helping curtail nasty end-of-the-trip surprises. But read your agreement carefully: meals, beverages, excursions, tips, and taxes can quietly take the form of add-ons; don't be shy about also having a friend peruse the fine print before you sign.

Packages. A cost-effective, high-volume-based travel package can be a top value, and some are tailored for independent travel. In fact, travelers often sign up for the overall value, skip some parts—and still save money. I jettisoned a cheapie bus tour right after landing in Rome and caught up with the group as we boarded the plane in Milan—and I wasn't the only one!

Frequent-flier miles. Flying isn't the only way to rack up miles. Credit cards that earn frequent-flier points, long-distance telephone deals that earn miles, and even the airlines' own bonus offers can give you free flights faster than you might imagine. However, you may have to book months in advance and be flexible about your dates. Again, flying solo gives you this freedom.

Also, look at the price of buying a ticket before you trade in miles. It hardly makes sense to give up 40,000 miles for a ticket to Europe that's selling for $400, but it might be worth it to give up 25,000 miles for an Alaska ticket priced over $600.

Luxe for less. Rather than leave luxury rooms empty, hotel managers offer great deals. Pay for the lowest priced room, and then, last-minute, request an upgrade. Mentioning a special occasion can't hurt—for instance, telling the rep that you're taking this trip for your 45th birthday. You just might be sleeping in a lavish suite, if you proceed gently.

Devalued currency. Japan, South Africa, Argentina, and Canada are destinations where, as of this writing, the dollar is strong, and buys more than at home. (Variables change quickly, so stay alert.) Check out currency valuations on the Internet, on TV, in newspaper business sections, or at airport or hotel exchanges.

Discover America. Cut costs when traveling in the good ol' U. S. of A. If you do head for metropolitan lights, stay in the suburbs close to public transportation that will take you into town. Stick with neighborhood eateries, and try out early-bird specials and pre-fixe menus that won't erode your solo budget. All-suite motels that include breakfast can be especially cost-saving. State and national parks are still a bargain—though you may need to reserve well in advance. And generally, the countryside is a better bargain than any place near a major attraction. If saving is a priority, avoid destinations during "hot" festivals and events, when hotel prices often skyrocket. (Although once you read about festivals in Chapter 3, Where to Go, What to Do on Your Own, they may be hard to resist.)

Undiscovered. Less touristed areas can yield lower costs. Many U.S. states offer unexplored events and historic and cultural sites, combined with familiar comforts as you solo. Even in more popular regions, find less-visited cities, and in cities, seek undiscovered places. On a trip to Canton, Ohio, I skipped the Football Hall of Fame, but found a nearby Amish village, a low-cost gentle excursion; the area was hardly changed by tourism, as some other Amish sites can be. Abroad, too, consider less-touristed regions in Eastern Europe, Africa, and Central America, which offer good bang for the buck.

Bad rep. Some cruise ships offer discounts long after they have virus problems, as one incident can cause a major falloff in tourism, and a falloff in prices. And even after the State Department or another authority declares that a destination or travel venue's diciest problems are dormant, perception might still keep tourists away—and that's when you can travel for big savings.

When you're traveling in "iffy" areas, basic precautions can protect you. Don't hang around tourist spots. Stay in small hotels, eat where locals do, skip crowded, public venues. Calling attention to yourself is not good, so be conservative.

Edgy atmosphere isn't for everyone, especially on your own, but a small risk may deliver the world at a bargain. I enjoyed Northern Ireland, drove around Egypt for a month, visited Peru during the time of the Shining Path. And I'm still here.

Public transportation. Getting around takes a big rip out of your travel buck. Public transportation is the best way to save. Hop ferries in Alaska rather than taking a cruise. Instead of taxis, use trolleys, subways, trains, buses, waterbuses, camels, or pedi-bikes, which often reflect local creativity: the brightly colored jeepney of Manila, the open-air thuk-thuks of Thailand, and the crowded jeepneys of Panama remain indelible experiences in themselves. These less-expensive transportation modes are great ways to meet people, see sights, and have fun.

Live like a local. As in short-term studio apartment, not hotel suite. Use the local food market. Eat simple meals. Bring your laundry to a laundromat. Shun minibars—buy candy and drinks at machines. Frequent neighborhood watering holes; seek free fun such as festivals and parades. If you stay away from the tourist (inflated) side of town, you can find value.

Creativity/flexibility. Consider house swaps or time-shares. Study, work, volunteer—what you have to offer may cover your travel or your room and board. Create a group of 10 and get your trip paid for. I wrote my master's thesis on a comparison of British and American automotive terms, which got me to travel around Great Britain as a student. And then I wrote an update for an academic journal 10 years later—two trips!

Clean and basic. Posh may be preferable, but not being able to afford the Ritz is no reason to stay home. Look for lodgings that are inexpensive, clean, safe, and well located (see Chapter 9, Successful Solo Lodging).

EIGHT VALUE DESTINATIONS

A little money goes a long way at these places, and the mood is right for a solo traveler.

Italy's Amalfi Coast

This stretch from Sorrento to Salerno is heavily discounted in winter and early spring. Temperatures can be cool then, but the reason to go remains beauty—whether from off-road belvederes, or amid gardens in Ravello. The road from Positano to Amalfi is the most dramatic, with limestone cliffs plunging to aquamarine waters. The bus system along the coast is so extensive (and the driving so extreme) that you might prefer inexpensive public transport, even if you can afford a driver. A charming alternate is by fishing boat from village to village; haggle on the price.

Good deal: SITA blue line buses from Sorrento to Salerno. Purchase tickets in advance, at cafés or newsstands. Drivers will stop anywhere along the drive. Schedules are available, buses are frequent, and you'll meet lots of friendly locals, all of whom seem to have an Uncle Sal in Brooklyn.

Canada

Our northern neighbor is one big-discount destination, because our dollar is worth more than the Canadian one. And some of the more unfamiliar provinces offer some of the best deals—great for summer getaways.

If you like Maine and bargains, you'll love the Canadian province of New Brunswick, just to the north. I enjoyed sweet scallops and even sweeter strawberries, and experienced the highest tides in the world in the Bay of Fundy. Sea kayaking in Newfoundland, the northernmost province of Eastern Canada, is outstanding, and Gros Morne National Park, on the west coast, is a starkly beautiful terrain of unusual geology and glacier-carved fjords. I find Canadians extremely kind and helpful. And when you're soloing, it's especially nice to be traveling in a foreign country where you can speak the language.

Greek Islands

An odyssey through this ancient archipelago can be inexpensive, if you travel the way locals do, by ferry—a minicruise of fresh Aegean breezes. Longer hauls, such as Piraeus (the Athens harbor) to Crete, include overnight accommodations with private baths. Guest-room owners meet the ferries and you can check premises before committing; nightly prices for a simple room start as low as $25. Among my favorite value islands are two in the unspoiled Sporades: Alonnissos, with a haunting hilltop town, and a marine national park protecting the rare Mediterranean monk seal; and craggy Skyros, with isolated beaches, a white-on-white main village, and a tradition of craftsmanship.

Good deal: On Alonnissos, guide Chris Browne offers lunch and a snorkel, and leads hikers to monasteries, and through the steep countryside covered in sage, heather, and rock roses. *www. alonnissoswalksco.uk*

Northern England

The former giants of the 19th-century Industrial Revolution have transformed glum factories into museums, galleries, and restaurants. Music, theater, and ballet companies abound—super-solo friendly. In Leeds, the Royal Armouries display the collection formerly kept in the Tower of London, and the Henry Moore Institute is the largest sculpture gallery in Europe. Liverpool is proud of more than the Beatles Museum. The Walker Art Gallery, Merseyside Maritime Museum, and Tate Liverpool are among other highlights.

Hold the coal, because Newcastle is hot right now, with a new music center on the river, next to the Baltic, the largest contemporary art gallery outside London. Manchester's City Art Galleries have a fine exhibit of Pre-Raphaelite paintings, and the ornate Victorian Cotton Exchange is home to the renowned Royal Exchange Theatre.

Thailand

Never colonized, Thailand has unusual rituals that date to the 13th century. Thailand remains exotic and inexpensive. Bargain at the vast Weekend Market for handicrafts and silk fabric. Some of the world's greatest hotels are in busy Bangkok and fine rooms can be under $100. Sukhothai, the ancient capital, is Thailand's most lovely and traditional city; Chiang Mai, in the northern Golden Triangle, near Laos and Cambodia, is known for its hilltop temple and lively night market. A highlight is an elephant trek in the jungle nearby.

South Africa

South Africa offers excellent value, but security is an issue—take taxis at night and avoid wearing expensive clothing and jewelry. Along with the sophistication of Cape Town and the beauty of the beaches, South Africa offers some of the least-expensive safaris in Africa.

Good deal: United Touring Company has an eight-day trip to Cape Town including air from Atlanta or New York. A great opportunity to solo with others. *www.unitedtour.com*

New Zealand

The New Zealand dollar's good exchange rate makes up for the long flight (12 hours from Los Angeles). And once you try kayaking in the South Island's fjords, hiking among the North Island's volcanoes, or bungee jumping into a chasm, you'll forget about the distance.

New Zealand's lure goes beyond Lord-of-the-Rings scenery and games you can play amid all this natural wonder. Most enchanting, perhaps, are the warm people, who cheerfully welcome you into their homes on farm stays—most tempting for a solo traveler. Highlights include the volcanoes at Tongariro National Park and the wine country outside Wellington on the North Island. On the South Island, check out the wine country near Blenheim, wildlife at Kaikoura, Abel Tasman National Park; Glacier Country on the west coast; Mount Cook and Fiordland.

Good deals: New Zealand tourism's Web site lists specials from the United States, including air from Los Angeles, rental car, and accommodations. *www.purenz.com*

Bali

Bali's tourism has suffered because of the bombing in Kuta Beach a few years ago. Savings remain huge. Even small, inexpensive inns are charmers, filled with teak furniture and hand-printed batiks. People are graceful, and gracious, and caring about soloists. Skip the touristy coast; Bali's beaches aren't what's special about this gentle, artful Hindu island. Where the locals live, in the quiet, central area, is the traditional Bali of sinuous rice paddies, exquisite tropical gorges, lotus blossoms, and temples.

Good deal: Having been suddenly "undiscovered," prices are stunningly cheap. For example, hotel rooms that went for $400 have dropped to almost $100.

3

Where to Go, What to Do
on Your Own

Where and what is best when you are truly blessed by being an independent traveler? Well, first I can think of just a few places *not* to seek out—family resorts, couples resorts, or "romantic" islands where dancing under the moonlight isn't much fun alone. I made that mistake once—newly separated from my first husband. We had previously booked a trip to a Caribbean island. Anxious to prove "I will survive," as Gloria Gaynor's voice blared from every radio, I said to myself, "Girl, get going, pack up that bathing suit and pareo, and fly down on to that island on your own!"

I'll admit, I was petrified, as the song says, and my instincts were right. It's one thing to travel alone and hold your own. But when everyone else is holding hands, holding your own—anything—looks pretty funny. As it turned out, after a night or so of eating by myself and feeling like the unpopular girl in a lunchroom full of Heathers, I was adopted by a group that was filming some underwater footage for a TV show. I had a great time with them, as a sort of gofer and mascot. So I learned something else: Even in the worst circumstances, there are people who will help you out if you give off a friendly vibe—or just plain beg! (I'm kidding. I don't beg. Ever.)

Choosing a Place

Where do soloists solo? And what should you do if you want a really great travel experience, really, *really* on your own? The power to choose is one of the joys of single travel, but leaven your choices with doses of pragmatism: consider places where there's plenty to do, and a variety of people doing it. Where you can be busy if you want to be, and do what you enjoy, or do nothing much, and you can fit in without feeling odd or uncomfortable. Choosing a destination comprises thinking about what you want, and starting with some possible ideas. I touched on some of these ideas in Chapter 2, but remember:

- Keep files of articles and recommendations for solo travel

- Consult all available sources: travel agents, the Internet, guidebooks, and word of mouth from people you know and trust

- Think of your favorite things, starting maybe by visualizing an ideal day alone

A great day in the city (for me) might include breakfast on a terrace, visiting a museum, walking, lunch at a great local restaurant, more museums or shopping at local boutiques, and a cultural event after a light dinner. Likewise, a great day in the country might include a walk, shopping at an outdoor market, enjoying scenery and local sites, lunch outside if possible, or by a view, wandering around the beauty spots, early dinner, and a cozy room with a deck where I can relax under the stars.

Depending on where I am and the availability of these activities, I try to find things that will match my ideal. I don't always find an exact fit, but I usually come close—and often when I get to a place, I change my plans anyway! I've traveled to Brussels to check out art nouveau buildings and wound up visiting Waterloo battlefields, and planned on snorkeling in Puerto Rico and spelunked in caves instead. Remember, in all phases of your planning and actual trip, flexibility is key. Your freedom to deviate from or ditch the entire plan on a whim is what makes soloing the ultimate way to go.

Monuments

Visiting a natural or man-made monument on your own intensifies and distills the experience. You can always join a group, but being alone in the moment is special. I remember standing at Bryce and Zion canyons, and looking up at the spires and colored cliffs, and practically feeling a part of the canyons themselves. I know that sounds wildly New Age, but I was able to hear the wind, and smell the rock—my senses were that acute. Others were busy talking, or taking photos—I just absorbed the moments. I recommend getting to these popular places early or late, before the crowds arrive. The experience changes when people overrun a place.

Monuments and cherry blossoms. Step on the stones of history; tour the White House; visit our monuments to Democracy; watch the Senate in action; enjoy culture, art, and pure *energy*—the essence that makes Washington, D.C., a critical tourist destination. The Cherry Blossom Festival, an annual commemoration of Tokyo's 1912 gift of 3,000 cherry trees, is certainly one of the best times to explore our nation's capital. I prefer the suburbs that aren't crowded—where some streets are canopied in blossoms; a solo gawker won't cause Neighborhood Watch to go ballistic. Ask locals for the prettiest locales. *202/ 661–7599, www.nationalcherryblossom.com*

Monuments and wine. In France, of course. Visit Versailles (*yes,* people really *lived* here!); Monet's house, gardens, and the charming village of Giverny, last week in May, when the gardens are at their showiest; the Eiffel Tower; the walled city of Avignon; sit in the sanctity of Notre Dame or the Basilique du Sacré Coeur in Montmarte; revere art at the Louvre Palace; study La Defense and its Grand Arche; and pass in triumph under the Arc de Triomphe. Who needs anybody else?

Ancient monuments and tea. Stonehenge, an enigmatic prehistoric circle of bluestones, is the world's best-known Megalith-Age stone monument, and symbolizes mystery, power, and endurance. I came upon it suddenly, rising mysteriously out of the morning mist; Avebury is the world's largest and most complex Megalith-Age monument; the Stanton Drew stone circles are less studied and well preserved; and Silbury, a grass covered chalk mound in the shape of a flat-topped cone, is the largest prehistoric artificial mound in Europe. Study up and enjoy the solitude.

National Parks

Hawaii Volcanoes National Park. This place is hot, as in red-hot burning lava. Home to Kilauea, the world's most active volcano, the park offers the thrill of regular volcanic eruptions and sizzling rivers of lava, as well as nearly 330,000 acres of other "cool" stuff: hiking trails carved out of lava rock; distinctive wildlife, flora, and fauna; and exceptional ecological history. Enjoy on your own. I did—from a helicopter! *808/985–6000, www.hawaii.volcanoes.national-park.com*

Mount Rushmore, Yellowstone, Sequoia, and Grand Canyon. Gaze in wonder at the "Shrine to Democracy"; set your watch to the Geyser in Yellowstone National Park; measure up to a Giant Redwood in Sequoia National Park, or gaze into the Grand Canyon for a deeper perspective on life. Each national park offers a special connection to the great outdoors—hard to come by in today's world. Visitors from every perspective can find agreeable "in park" or "near park" accommodations from campsites to resorts and everything in between, and although crowds may be there, you don't need company to enjoy any of it. In fact, viewing the Grand Canyon once with others and once alone, there was no comparison. Solo was better! *Mount Rushmore, 605/574–2523 or 605/574–3171, www.nps.gov/moru; Yellowstone National Park, 307/344–7381, www.nps.gov/yell; Sequoia/Kings Canyon National Parks, 866/646–0388 or 559/565–3341, www.nps.gov/seki; Grand Canyon National Park, 928/638–7888, www.nps.gov/grca*

Festivals

Most solo travelers tend to gloss over festivals, but these celebrations swirl you right into the action, offering vivid local color, and often history and pageantry. People are friendlier during festivals and events. At the Palio in Siena, Italy, an ancient horse race of flags and ritual is still held around the main piazza. I spent the afternoon with a delightful local couple who afterward invited me for pasta and chianti classico in their urban apartment overlooking the Tuscan hills.

I remember Loi Kathong, a night festival of the harvest season in Thailand, when offerings of candles on decorated banana leaves float and sparkle throughout the country's waterways. An enchanting experience, and free. I joined a bunch of Thais on a boat—one of hundreds in the harbor, and deposited my meagerly decorated leaf into the clusters of candlelight. I felt a part of the people, and the place, far more than on any other day there.

Here are other festivals you might enjoy; for details, see Resources at the end of the chapter.

Art festivals. Living art is literal at the Festival of the Arts and Pageant of the Masters, an annual Laguna Beach, California, event, including a juried art show and *tableaux vivants* of famous paintings. Art and art festivals are literally everywhere you want to be: with workshops and with young artists; folk-art festivals; craft and artisan events; historic-arts festivals; wellness and harmony arts; the list is as exhaustive and imaginative as the arts themselves.

Cowboys and rodeos. The Wyoming Tourism folks say that Rodeo is America's first sport, and that the Cowboy State provides daily summer rodeo entertainment. Cheyenne Frontier Days, a nine-day celebration of the West, claims to have the world's largest outdoor rodeo; Cody Nite Rodeo professional rodeos have performed for 75 years. And, perhaps surprisingly, Hawaiian rodeos are roping audiences in *Ka' Aina O Ka Paniolo*, "Home of the Hawaiian cowboy." Sounds like a chance to meet a cowpoke!

Dance Festivals. "Let's meet again . . . in the stillness of the night." Finland is passionate about the Tango, and the Seinäjoki Tango Festival happily proves that "tango is dance therapy for the soul." Enjoy professional-level performances and join in the dance with the rest of the tango-phile Finns. It may take "two to tango," but solo travelers can learn, dine on reindeer and salmon—and find a partner. Dance events and festivals happen all year long, all over the world, in every major city.

Drama festivals. The Firefly Festival in South Bend, Indiana, has it all, including workshops and classes. When in Rome, the Off-Night Repertory Theatre Company and the Miracle Players are English-speaking favorites. In Juneau, enjoy uniquely Alaskan interpretations from Shakespeare to Eskimo cultural plays. London's New Globe Theatre—a circular replica of the original co-owned by Shakespeare—is one of many curtains opening on the Bard. I sat comfortably in the seats there as it rained, and the groundlings standing in the open-air stuck it out and got muddy-wet, just like they would have in the 17th century.

Film festivals. Cannes and Sundance film festivals are red-carpet events, but aficionados maintain that newer festivals are more edgy, and better opportunities to catch celebrities in their acts, so to speak. The Flanders Film Festival attracts celebs and composers; the Hamptons International Film Festival is a tony upstart; and the Bangkok International Film Festival secured a thumbs-up right out of the box office. There's obviously no pressing need for company when you're sitting in the dark, but lots of chance for discussion after.

Flower festivals. Nature's artistry, healing aromatherapy, romance—I love flowers. Visit Michigan's Tulip Time Festival, a blooming favorite "Small Town Festival in America," or enjoy an abundant English country garden at the London Chelsea Flower Show. In Ottawa, 5 million tulips anchor an extensive festival and concert series. Walks among peonies and pansies are perfect solo activities.

Harvest festivals. *La Tomatina*—the world's largest food fight—is an infamous moment in a historic festival in tiny Buñol, Spain. Participants gather in the town square to squish and throw ripe tomatoes at each other, and wind up looking like chips in salsa. Reserve accommodations early, this is one hot-tamale ticket. Other wine-and-food extravaganzas preserve cultural heritage, still others serve dinner in service of charity.

Hot-air balloon festivals. Down Under gears up each year for the World Hot-Air Balloon Championship. The Victorian riverside city of Mildura, Australia, committed to providing a world-class festival, polishes its unique heritage and outback sophistication for an influx of bloomin' balloonin' visitors. There's no better way for a solo traveler to meet someone than in one of those tiny balloon baskets.

Literary festivals. They're not all that sexy, but literary festivals are critical to those who live to read, write, or both, and great for solitary souls. The Mountain High Writer's Workshop helps struggling writers, the Derbyshire Literary Festival applauds authors, and the Adelaide Writer's Week is one of the world's largest literary festivals. Or, follow your favorite author: in Canterbury they celebrate Chaucer; Spain hosts a party for Cervantes; and Shakespeare inspires festivities everywhere.

Music festivals. Music festivals are travel—and solo—favorites. Don't miss: the "washer-woman" at the Appalachian Washboard Music Festival; the yachts moored at the edge of the Newport Jazz Festival; Music and Markets (and Mozart) in Prague; or the ambitious new International Music Festival in Sevilla. I love the World Creole Music Festival, a grand show the last weekend of October; the Creole world congregates in Dominica for three nights of pulsating Caribbean rhythms. Revelers will insist you join in the dance—just move your hips and swing your arms.

Sacred festivals. The Day of the Dead honors spirits who visit the Earth on this day each year; to this tradition San Antonio adds the "New World of Wine and Food Festival," "Haunted River Festival," and "Coffins on Parade." Ancient, beautiful pilgrimage festivals include the Perfume Pagoda Festival in Vietnam, and the Incan Sun Festival in Peru. Alone, you'll have a chance for pensive thoughts, if not profound. I've celebrated

No Fair

Generally, it's a couples world, and you'd better get used to it, because you'll notice it more than ever as you solo travel. I remember dropping my son Cary off to college in upstate New York, and on the way back, passing the New York State Fair. I had always wanted to see the livestock, hear the faded rock groups, and eat the sweet, sticky stuff that always appears at these venues. So I parked, and entered, and what I found—because believe me, I was looking— was that among the thousands of people milling around the New York State Fair that fine late-summer day, I was the only person on my own!

Impossible? Not that day. Oh, I saw an occasional man or woman waiting outside a toilet area, and a frazzled mom or dad dragging a baby in tow, but otherwise, everybody was with somebody or somebodies they could talk to. I could have been in a science fiction movie from the 1950s where a strange creature is dropped onto Earth, and tries to fit in, but something isn't quite right and everyone can kind of tell. I was that odd creature! I was . . . a solo Conehead!

And you know what? I ate the sticky stuff, and touched a rooster comb for the first and only time in my life (felt like a big Gummy-Bear), and listened to country music, and I thought about all the singles who may not have gone to the fair by themselves just because they were alone, and who missed a rewarding, once-a-year experience. It was shocking. It was sad. It was reality. ❧

Mardi Gras in New Orleans, and aside from the beer cans and beads, you can enjoy floats, parties, and the sensuous city.

State fairs. State fairs remain an American tradition, and the Texas State Fair is one of the biggest and braggin'est. Catch popular music acts, a Broadway show, a ride on America's tallest Ferris Wheel, and Big Tex—America's tallest cowboy at 52 feet. The Wyoming State Fair & Rodeo's been ropin''em in since 1905, and somewhere in Pennsylvania there's a fair every night of the summer. Just 'cause you're on your own, don't stay away. Jump in!

Unique festivals. For a hot-doggin' good time, try the Lowell Winterfest Human Dog Sled Championship; or chalk this on your calendar: the Absolut Chalk Street Painting Festival—with original art literally at your feet. For something completely different, judge an array of carefully cultivated and groomed facial hair (and their men) at the World Beard and Mustache Championships (great place to meet a hirsute guy), or catch the wind and head for the Kite Festival.

Winter festivals. A month-long Anchorage festival offers outhouse races, a masquerade ball, and the Iditarod Sled Dog Race. Nearby, the Northern Lights are a wondrous backdrop for the World Ice Art Championships. Visitors to Lapland's Snow Castle hotel can add "The Snow Show" art exhibit to their itinerary, and Iceland's Blue Lagoon visitors can "chill" at the Food & Fun Festival, or winter camp with a private guide. All cool for soloists.

Special-Interest Things to Do Alone

Air shows/military performances. The mystery of flight fascinates us grounded humans, and our natures love precision. Perhaps this combination explains the appeal of synchronized air shows—but many of us wish we could *just do it.* Fighter Combat International, an outfit with locations in Arizona and Canada grants applicants that exact wish. It's you alone—and a veteran fighter pilot—in the cockpit of a German-built Extra 300L world-class acrobatic aircraft. *480/279-1881, www. fightercombat.com*

Garden and botanical garden tours. Self-guided garden tours take the passionate gardener beyond flower festivals and into the orbits of fellow passionate gardeners. Why not schedule a trip around other people's gardens—a larger, grander version of the small town fund-raising garden tour? If you decide to tour gardens instead of museums or castles, you won't be alone.

Sculpture gardens. Love art, gardens, and walking? Consider planning a sculpture-garden tour, a combination garden/walking/museum ramble. Easier than you might think, you can string together fabulous destinations and unusual experiences.

Meet the artists, tour studios and workshops, attend a workshop yourself, visit wonderful communities and, of course, get an eyeful of sculpture. In Oslo, the Vigeland Sculpture Park draws visitors from around the world. I especially enjoyed the workshops, where the sculptor created the works we admire. In Storm King, New York, I've spent sweet, solitary summer days with a book and a diet soda amid the Nevelsons, Moores, and mountain backdrops.

Sporting events. What's your pleasure—baseball, gymnastics, diving, ice-skating, NASCAR? Sports-tour coordinators provide complete solo or group tours for travel, accommodations, and attendance at the Olympics, the Daytona 500, the Super Bowl, the World Cup, NBA events, the World Series—any game you enjoy. Or, if you're a baseball fan, consider the time-honored practice of visiting major-league, spring-training baseball camps, or getting farm-team game tickets, which can often be picked up at the last minute. And I love the Westminster Dog Show at Madison Square Garden—quasi sport, but loads of fun to watch trainers run pampered, pedigreed pooches around the ring.

GET OUT AND STAY OUT

Hiking, trekking, and kayaking all can be enjoyed on your own. Really. My colleague Jack, a happily-married travel writer, camped alone by Victoria Falls on the border of Zambia, and experienced one of the most profound experiences of his life. My friend Dena—a great athlete to be sure—made it to a basecamp on Mount Everest in the Himalayas with a sherpa guide, and no one else. I'm more the "soft-adventure" type—a long walk and a three-star hotel is adventure enough for me—but if you're in shape physically and mentally, an adventure on your own is an enticing, exhilarating challenge.

Soloists in growing numbers are taking to cross-country bicycling. Possibly the simplest New Millennium face-off against the elements, solo cycling offers flexible adventure levels in a relatively low-risk, low-cost touring package. You can visit multiple destinations quickly, meet people, and have time alone. Deb, a, busy corporate manager, swears by semi-slow barge and bike tours, where you can hop off the river vessel and bike or walk, or just barge along—a bit slow for impatient me, but heavenly for Deb—who met a younger biker on one of her solo trips and bikes with him now on a permanent basis! Adventure Cycling runs bike tours and provides detailed maps showing campsites, hostels, hotels, bike routes, as well as bike-repair shops, and alas, even hospitals. *Adventure Cycling Association. 800/755–2453 or 406/721–1776, www.adventurecycling.org*

Fishing provides near-perfect, pensive moments regardless of whether you're angling solo on a dock or beach, or on a charter or party boat. I've tried everything (once) from sail fishing off the Mexican coast to fly-fishing in Chile, and I'll stick to snorkeling, thank you very much. But closer to home, fisherfolk know that from Montauk Point to the Keys, the eastern seaboard also yields terrific fishing.

Urban trekking is a hot new pastime, and most major cities offer self-guided walking tours. Step into comfortable shoes and get trekking through history, architecture, nightlife, high-end shopping, or restaurant row—it's up to you! I don't know what it is about cities, but I walk for hours without feeling tired— maybe it's the people-watching. Or, trek back roads. Discover France coordinates the details of solo countryside *tours de France. 800/960–2221, www.discoverfrance.com*

Observing Animals

Whether you travel with Fido (see Chapter 6, Traveling with Pets), leave him at home, or hail from a petless household, you can easily enjoy animals, in their own settings and soak up some terrific scenery while you're at it. The solo traveler has the best opportunity to view and interact, and you feel anything but alone; rather, you can achieve a quiet, sometimes profound connection, quite difficult with others around.

Alone, you can concentrate on creatures for hours without boredom, taking notes, photographing, or just observing. Animals may perceive us more as a curiosity than a threat, with our

continued on p. 47

Close Encounters of the Brrr-d Kind

At times during my travels I seemed to actually cross the divide between species (and no, I wasn't dreaming of elephants on the ceiling; I was sober). Some examples:

The almost-freezing waters of the Bay of Fundy off the east coast of Canada provide one of the great feeding and breeding grounds for whales. But boy it's nippy out on the boats—I wore four layers, a hat and gloves, and stayed under a wool blanket, and I was still chilled. And it was *August*. The experience was worth every shiver. The endangered Right Whale remains here—about 400 left on the Earth. And on the day I went out, we saw about 20 percent of them! Some days none appear. A thrill, indeed.

In Lapland, I shared a sledge with a fellow journalist, dogsledding across the Finnish fells. The speed was surprising, but more so was how the dogs were wired to work. At our lunch break of hot reindeer soup in the snow, the dogs ate heartily, and after only maybe half an hour they barked and yelped and howled, ready to get back to their heavy task. We were tired, and wanted to laze a bit, and I watched their keen eyes and forceful bodies. One dog kept barking at me, as if begging, "Get back on the sledge, dummy, and let me pull you across the snow again." When we finally got going, I swear he smiled at me.

Cruising the Inside Passage of Alaska, animals were teeming as if in a nature documentary: otters gamboled in the icy waters, seal colonies sprawled over rocks, haughty bulls overlooking their barking harems of blubbery females. Eagles swooped from towering pines to talon wriggling fish.

But my favorite moments were on shore, in an evergreen forest along a river. Some friendly passengers had invited me to join them (remember, invitations happen, if you smile); I opted for a solo ramble. The river flashed silver with salmon leaping toward their spawning ground. I walked a mile or so and stood on a bridge as hundreds of the intrepid fish lay gasping along the river bottom, draining color and form as I watched. Muscled and forceful a few miles before, they were now deflated as balloons, littering the river bottom.

As I absorbed this drama, couples and groups passed by, chatting away about the stock market and totem poles, not noticing the solemn, life-cycle event right there beside them, just under the water. 🦅

two spindly legs and big thumbs. They'll go about their business—eating, feeding, mating, even killing—if you keep a minimum distance, usually a few meters away, and stay quiet. (Safety tip: If they're about to kill, stay even farther away.)

Crowds, loud noises, and unexpected movements put animals off. Near a logging road, on a lake in northern Maine, I kayaked by a heavily racked moose, nibbling in the water a couple hundred feet away. I stopped paddling, and remained still. The moose continued eating, with an occasional come-hither glance; more likely, "Not another stupid human watching me eat!" All was well until I sneezed. The moose bounded away into the woods.

Even if you're with a group, try to break away from the herd at least for a while—unless you're instructed not to, or it feels wrong. Be patient, respectful, still, and alert.

The unexpected is part of the animal experience. For years I enjoyed walking by myself in a nature preserve in Westchester County, New York. The land abuts a dairy farm, and I often stopped to watch the black-and-white cows—fascinated by everything from their tagged ears to their pink udders. One day in the field across the cinder trail from the bovines, separated from me by a crumbly fieldstone wall and a bit of barbed wire, a massive bull glowered for a minute or so, and pawed the ground, as if pondering a tryst or a charge. I couldn't move, and he kept staring. I backed away, slowly, down a hill, and never returned. And that was just a walk by a pasture. So pay attention, because you never know.

SAFARIS

If you travel to Africa, I suggest experiencing four types of safaris for the complete experience. Try to join as small a group as possible, or hire a private guide and take all the time you can afford.

By day. A daytime safari by jeep moves you quickly to track cape buffalo, rhino, lion, and leopard—and other large land animals, from zebra to elephant. My thrill was observing two lion cubs, about a week old, and finding a lion couple resting, exhausted, after many days of copulation. My other favorite experience was driving through a forest of giraffes, maybe 20 of them, nibbling the tops of acacia trees on either side of the road.

By night. On a night safari by jeep, you can find hyenas, civets, anteaters, and smaller nocturnal animals and birds, as well as the larger animals, especially by salt licks and water holes. Your armed guide will shine his light into the dark plains, and suddenly you'll see eyes gleaming back, and notice rustlings in the brush. Eerie, and wonderful.

On foot. During a walking safari, you can closely observe smaller critters and plants, and sometimes, from afar and downwind, a herd of elephants, or other larger beasts. When you walk you feel the danger and the wonder—and you'll need an armed sharpshooter guide. I asked mine if he ever used his gun. "Yes," he replied, "but I have only one bullet. That's all I have time for."

On water. A river safari introduces you to crocodiles, hippos, and glorious birds, as well as the big animals that come to drink and play and get-it-on, down by the riverside. Gliding along next to crocs is a safe thrill, if you keep your appendages in the boat.

In Malawi Africa, in a camp by a river, our safari group was warned not to walk alone in the evening. Hippos come ashore then to nibble at the foliage, and when a hippo gets hyper, no animal is more dangerous. But the guard with the rifle never came to my tent to escort me to dinner, and I was hungry. After about a half hour of waiting, I ventured out gingerly, staying on the path and walking fast. I wasn't alone. Ahead of me in the dark I made out a hefty woman, bending over. She must be on her way to dinner, too, I figured. But as I got closer I realized that it wasn't a hippy lady.

It was a lady hippo.

I ran, screaming (silently), into the closest tent, where three women who had also encountered the hippo were huddled together. We were all scared, and all hungry. Finally someone noticed we weren't at dinner, and the man with the rifle rescued us. The hippo had returned to the river, its dinner over. I took warnings more seriously after that.

SNORKELING & DIVING

Fish are fascinating, darting in iridescent schools or poking around the coral, but I cherish my watery encounters with larger creatures. In Homosassa Springs, on the west coast of Florida, I snorkeled alone in warm, crystal waters, and spied a manatee and her calf swimming ahead. Manatees are clumsy-looking mammals, imposing up close, like water-elephants, but surprisingly gentle. I remained still, and Big Momma circled me a couple of times and finally brushed her hairy, wrinkly skin right past me, experiencing what a strange-looking creature with a tube in its mouth felt like. I felt loofahed.

Perhaps the manatee decided I was worth investigating, even with her calf beside her. Or she may have been threatening me with her formidable bulk, and I was just too dumb to realize it. In either case, if anyone else had been snorkeling alongside me, my literal brush with nature probably wouldn't have occurred.

My favorite one-on-one animal connection was on the Sea of Cortez, in Baja, California, where sea lions live in and about the craggy rocks. I was on a nature cruise in a yacht that carried only 17 passengers. Cold as the water was, most of us participated in hopes that the sea lions would slither down from the rocks and play with us.

They did, circling and teasing and even jumping out of the water and onto the back of one of the passengers. They seemed genuinely happy to be cavorting with us after the long winter hiatus.

I broke away from the crowd, snorkeling, along with one guide. The other cruisers complained of the cold and went back onboard. I was soon rewarded, remarkably. A lone sea lion, eyes as big and dark as checkers, tread in the waves a few feet away, staring at me—I should say, through me. We were both mostly underwater, and I stared back through my goggles, just under the surface. Neither of us moved much for a minute or more. I think we were communicating, but in any case, it was one of the most thrilling experiences I've ever had. And I don't think it would have happened had I been in a group.

Bull by the Horns

My son Rand is an avid traveler, who lives on the edge despite my protests. I introduce him here as a guest speaker about a singular solo experience:

Hemingway introduced himself to me in the form of steer's head. It was Pamplona, Spain, and I was participating in the running of the bulls at the Festival of San Fermin. At the time, I didn't grasp the full extent of Hemingway's involvement ("a friend of this town and admirer of its fiestas," read a monument I saw later on Pamplona's Paseo Hemingway, "which he discovered and made famous"). I just knew that the run was stupid and crazy, and for whatever reason, my life wouldn't be complete without doing it.

The steer came into the picture during the "free-for-all," a kind of after-party for those who spend their early mornings darting in front of 1,300-pound, sharp-horned creatures. Dressed in the traditional all-white with a red sash and red kerchief to give the bulls a target, I had completed the run itself without a scratch, not bad, considering that the half-dozen bulls had gored two locals and trampled 20 others.

Feeling my oats, I had decided to stay in the giant Plaza de Toros, the run's endpoint, to again tempt fate. Three smaller, faster bulls were set loose, one at a time, to wreak havoc upon anyone in their way, for the amusement of a throng of 20,000.

While a few people were knocked unconscious, I handled the first bull properly, grabbing its horns and dodging out of his way. The second bull proved trickier. Most participants jumped up against the ring's 5-foot-high outer wall whenever a bull came looking for trouble, but this bruiser had figured that trick out, and took to the nifty crunching sound he could make using his head to sandwich people against the wall. Most unfortunately, he had this revelation 10 feet from where I was standing. I had two options: up-and-over, or run.

I chose to sprint, at which point my horned friend abandoned the wall and bore down directly on me. I felt 40,000 eyes on my back as I ran furiously, looking back in disbelief. Then, suddenly, I was on the ground, listening to a tremendous roar from the crowd, the kind you hear at a car race when some sorry sap crashes brilliantly.

I had run head-on into a castrated steer, which had been dispatched to calm the bull down. And I could barely move my left arm, which had taken the brunt of the hit and would remain black-and-blue for a month.

Yet I felt no pain. "To be gored was honorable," Hemingway once wrote. And sitting later that morning at the Iruna Café in the Plaza del Castillo, the same café Hemingway's Jake Barnes, Brett Ashley, and Robert Cohn loved and quarreled in, with a beer in my hand and a large ice pack on my forearm, I felt very honorable. No, more than that: alive.

Most of my friends had judged me crazy for attempting to run with the bulls, my girlfriend tried to beg me out of it; my mom threatened to disown me. But I had flirted with dangers and taken away the revelations that come with it: the actual thick, vibrating "fear in the air" I've heard veterans talk about, as well as the literal experience of running for my life. It was, as Hemingway once wrote to a friend, "the godamdest wild time and fun you ever saw."

That's actually how I discovered Hemingway. His work had been on neither my high school nor college syllabi (such was P.C. academia in the 1980s), and I had found more contemporary reading on my own time. When I travel, I like to tote along some corresponding literature, and my Pamplona trip naturally called for *The Sun Also Rises* and his lesser-known paean to bull-fighting, *Death in the Afternoon*.

As I came across new places in Pamplona, I would invariably find out Hemingway had been there, seven decades prior. The bullfighters still stay at the Hotel Yoldi. Las Pocholas still serves a fine chorizo. The Txoco Bar continues to look out over the Plaza del Castillo, where people still dance arm-in-arm all night. As much as it deflated the thrill of discovery, I had found a kindred spirit. Hemingway had become my travel buddy. ❧

BIRD-WATCHING

Bird-watching, or simply, birding is the number-one hobby in the world. The pastime requires time and stillness—a perfect match for the solo traveler.

I remember puffins, neat little aquatic avians, orange-beaked, spiffy in black and white. On their protected rock off the coast of New Brunswick, Canada, they played and went about their puffin business as we observed from blinds, peeping toms, all.

In Punto Tumbo, Argentina, a tiny peninsula where Magellen penguins have colonized, I sidled and sidestepped among thousands of bobbing, tuxedoed Charlie Chaplins, and after a couple of spellbinding hours, decided I was in love with all of them.

Penguins have notable personal behavior. Some ran into the Pacific, some dabbled their webbed feet and decided otherwise; some lounged in their hole-in-the-ground nests, some lazed on the beach. Penguin couples necked (literally) or squabbled and squawked (literally). The month was January, and the chicks were going through adolescence, gray and molting, as awkward as middle schoolers.

In the midst of all this activity, a wayward bull sea lion lay beached, far from his rocks, and would inevitably perish. The penguins left the huge creature alone. His brown, haunting eyes looked soulful, and I half expected to hear a voiceover. But this was not the Discovery Channel. It was the raw, real thing, mysterious and frightening.

The experience ended on a cheerful note. When I returned to the car, there was a little penguin, waiting patiently to hop in.

ZOOS & OTHER ANIMAL FUN

Animals amuse me so, as I'm sure I do them. I love the way monkeys scratch and groom, so unaware that they act—and look— like us. Monkeys that hang around palaces and gardens get wise, and delicately select peanuts, diverting you while their hidden accomplice snatches the whole bag. Elephants can be tricky too, selecting a banana, then stealthily grabbing the bunch by their trunk, like a thief, and popping it into their mouth.

In Wales, I laughed my way through a stage production at a sheep farm, where a variety of rams ran out, one by one through a noisy door, to a scripted narration, and then just stood there in tiers, individually penned, staring at us on our wooden benches, staring at them. It was existential, really, with nothing happening, like *Waiting for Godot*. In fact, the show had more energy, and a larger cast, than some road productions I've endured.

But among the saddest sights I've seen have been animals in captivity. I remember a bat in Malaysia, its wings spread in the sun, pinned to a stake at a busy crossroads. The captor was hoping to make a few cents. And I remember with sorrow the many mangy animals—elephants, bears, donkeys, monkeys—chained and solitary in make-shift menageries throughout the world. When a zoological exhibit is humane and enlightening, you can truly enjoy it as a solo activity—bringing to you the wildlife you would have to otherwise travel far to see.

RESOURCES

Art Festivals

Apr. Art Crawl Month, self-guided tours, St. Paul, Minnesota. *651/265–4908; www.stpaul-artcrawl.org*

June. Annual Art & Design Walk, Melrose Ave., Los Angeles. *800/368–6020 or 310/289 2525; www.visitwesthollywood.com*

July. Laguna Beach Festival of Arts. *800/487–3378; www. lagunafestivalofarts.com*

Birding Festivals

Jan. Wings Over Wilcox, Wilcox, Arizona, celebrating the vacationing sandhill cranes. *602/364–3697; www.arizonaguide.com*

May. Great River Birding Festival, Wabasha, Minnesota. *877/525–3248; www.mississippi-river.org/birding*

Aug. British Birdwatching Fair, Oakham, Rutland, England. *01572/771079; www.birdingfair.org.uk*

Nov. Space Coast Birding and Wildlife Festival, Brevard County, Florida. *321/268–5224; www.nddb.com*

Cowboys & Rodeos

July. Cheyenne Frontier Days, "The Daddy of 'em All." *800/227–6336; www.cfdrodeo.com*
Festival of the American West, Logan (Wellsville), Utah. *800/225–3378 or 435/ 245–6050; www.utah.com*

Hawaii Professional Championship Rodeo. *808/885–7311 or 808/966–5416; www.rodeohawaii.com*
Parker Ranch Rodeo on the Big Island of Hawaii. *808/885–7311 or 800/648–2441; www.parkerranch.com*

Dance Festivals
June. Jacob's Pillow Dance Festival, the Berkshires, Lee, Massachusetts. *415/637–1322; www.jacobspillow.org*

July. Seinäjoki Tango Festival, Finland. *09/420–1111; www.tangomarkkinat.fi*

Drama Festivals
The Firefly Festival, South Bend, Indiana, weekends throughout the summer. *574/288–3472; www.fireflyfestival.com*

The Juneau Perseverance Theatre, Juneau, Alaska. *907/364–2421; www.perseverancetheatre.org*

The New Globe Theatre, Southward, England. *02079/021400; www.shakespeares-globe.org*

The Off-Night Repertory Theatre Company (year-round), and the Miracle Players (summer), Rome, Italy. *39/0670393427; www.miracleplayers.org*

Film Festivals
Jan. Bangkok International Film Festival, Thailand. *662/250–5500;* www.bangkokfilm.org
Sundance Film Festival, Park City, Utah. *310/360—1981; www.festival.sundance.org*

May. Cannes Film Festival. *310/209–1200; www.festival-cannes.fr*
Tribeca Film Festival, New York City. *212/941–2400; www.tribecafilmfestival.org*

Oct. Flanders Film Festival, Gent, Belgium. *09/242–8060; www.filmfestival.be*

Hamptons Film Festival, Long Island, New York. *631/324–4600; www.hamptonsfest.org*
New York Film Festival, New York City. *212/875–5600; www. filmlinc.com*

Flower Festivals
Apr. Oregon Wildflower Festival, Glide, Oregon. *541/677–3797; www.sunnywalter.com*
Skagit Valley Tulip Festival, Vancouver, British Columbia. *360/428–5959; www.tulipfestival.org*

May. Canadian Tulip Festival, Ottawa, Canada. *613/567–5757; www.festivaldestulipes.ca*
Chelsea Flower Show, London, England. *0207/834–4333; www. rhs.org.uk*
Tulip Time Festival, Holland, Michigan. *800/822–2770; www. tuliptime.com*

Harvest Festivals
Mar. Boca Bacchanal, Boca Raton, Florida. *561/395–6766 or 800/331–7213; www.bocabacchanal.com*

Apr. Annual Taste of Vail, Colorado. *303/665–4200; www. tasteofvail.com*

June. La Jolla Festival of the Arts and Food Faire, California. *858/456–1268; www.lajollaartfestival.org*

Aug. Ayuntamiento de Buñol, Spain. *96/398–6422; www. cyberspain.com*

Hot-Air Balloon Festivals
May. Village by the Sea Hot Air Balloon Race, Delray Beach, Florida. *561/279–1380; www.launch.net*

June. Hot Air Balloon Championship, Mildura, Australia. *03/9596–8744 or 03/5021–1320; www.2004worldsballoons.com*

Sept. Gatineau Hot Air Balloon Festival, Canada. *819/595–2002; www.ville.gatineau.qc.ca*

Literary Festivals

Mar. Adelaide Festival, Adelaide, Australia. *08/8216–4444; www.adelaidefestival.org.au*
Tennessee Williams/New Orleans Literary Festival. *504/522–2081; www.tennesseewilliams.net*

May. Mountain High Writer's Conference, Denver, Colorado. *303/745–6655; www.mountainhighwriters.com*

Music Festivals

May. Prague Spring Music Festival, Czech Republic. *257/312547; www.festival.cz*

June. Washboard Music Festival, Logan, Ohio. *800/462–5464; www.1800hocking.com*

Aug. Newport Jazz Festival, Fort Adams State Park, Rhode Island. *866/468–7619; www.festivalproductions.net*

Sept. Sevilla International Music Festival, Spain. *95/450–6610; www.sevillafestival.org*

Oct. World Creole Music Festival, Dominica. *www.worldcreolemusicfestival.net*

Sacred Festivals

Feb. Mardi Gras Festivals and Carnivals, New Orleans. *800/672–6124 or 504/566–5011; www.neworleanscvb.com*
Perfume Pagoda Festival, Chua Huong (near Hanoi), Vietnam. *04/826–4154; www.vietnamtourism.com*

June. Incan Festival of Inti Raymi (Sun Festival), Cusco, Peru. *888/671–2852; www.peru-explorer.com*

Nov. The Day of the Dead, San Antonio, Texas. *800/843–2526; www.sanantonio.com*

State Fairs
Aug. Wyoming State Fair and Rodeo, Douglas, Wyoming. *800/ 426–5009; www.wyomingtourism.org*

Sept. Texas State Fair, Dallas. *214/565–9931; www.bigtex.com*

Year-round. Pennsylvania State Association of County Fairs. *717/365–3922; www.pafairs.org*

Unique Festivals
Feb. Lowell Winterfest Celebration, Lowell, Massachusetts . *800/443–3332; www.lowell.org*

June. Absolut Chalk Street Painting Festival, Pasadena, California. *626/440–7379; www.absolutchalk.com*

Oct. Kite Festival, Nova Scotia, Canada. *800/565–0000; www. nsinns.com*

Nov. World Beard and Mustache Championships, Carson City, Nevada. *530/581–3940; www.worldbeardchampionships.com*

Winter Festivals
Feb. Iditarod and Fur Rendezvous, Anchorage, Alaska. *907/ 257–2331; www.iditarod.com*
World Ice Art Championships, Fairbanks, Alaska. *907/459– 3282; www.explorefairbanks.com*
The Snow Show, The Snow Castle, Kemi, Finland. *212/885– 9710; www.gofinland.org*

4

One-Stop Soloing: Cruises & Spas

Comfort is one of my favorite words, along with family, love, health, gelato, friends, pets, flowers, travel, and others I prefer to keep to myself. Ease, and balance are also wonderful words, especially when you're going it alone. And to achieve these ideal concepts on your solo vacation, what could be better than unpacking just once? Cruises and spas offer convenience, relaxation, stimulation, and simplicity, especially because of their largely all-inclusive pricing. And they offer ample chances to be alone or part of a group.

CRUISES

You might consider cruising as a form of transportation, but I think of it mainly as a moving destination, a delicious excursion to places you may not get to otherwise, in a way unlike any other. Besides unpacking just once and settling in, other benefits include an already-budgeted experience, and an exciting, planned itinerary with lots of options for discovery, entertainment, or relaxation.

Most ships cater to solo travelers, either subtly or not, with "singles" cruises, "singles" get-togethers, and carefully arranged

Who Needs a Valentine?

I once joined a Princess Cruise Line Valentine excursion where everyone onboard—except for a handful of us—were couples renewing their vows. Because we were thrown together in one place for several days, the soloist group had time to get acquainted, and we seemed to have more fun than most of the couples. One of our group, Rue McLanahan, who played an oversexed middle-aged woman named Blanche on *The Golden Girls*, was just as gossipy as the character she played on TV. Gavin McCloud, Capt. Stubing of *Love Boat*, fame, was also onboard, and since we both had lived in the same Westchester town, we had lots of conversations. When I met him on another cruise we felt like old friends. 🎬

table placements. If you want to dance, there may be regular dance partners on board, and a crew member will usually oblige. Some men serve as escorts, hired by the cruise lines to dance with as many ladies as possible—favoring none! Typically these are mature, well-groomed, and well-spoken men (despite the wicked send-up portrayed in *Out to Sea,* with Jack Lemmon and Walter Matthau).

Hiking (and I do mean hiking) the decks of *Queen Mary II,* the largest, longest, tallest, grandest, "mostest" ship ever, I reflected on "grand" versus "grandiose." I've enjoyed every cruise I've ever taken whether for the itinerary, which often drives my choices, or for the ambience. But when it comes to solo cruising, for me, less is more, especially with a fabulous itinerary. If you're "not a cruiser," or you're tired of the same old, same old, check out my picks and see if you're tempted to grab your passport and come aboard.

Lea's Five Favorite Cruises

IN DARWIN'S STEPS

For eight days I sailed among tiny volcanic islands, off the Ecuador coast, in Darwin's path when he researched *The Origin of the Species.* Our yacht, *The Letty,* held 20 (but—lucky us:

only 9 were on board, plus a staff of 10!). Meals were plentiful and tasty, and the cabins paneled and air-conditioned, with private bath. Galapagos creatures still live without much human interference, and if they choose, you can interact. Guides led us on a couple of hikes and snorkels a day (the water's cool; wetsuits are a good idea). We swam and splashed among sea lions and penguins, rays and sharks, and stepped gingerly amid nursing seals. Nearby albatross danced a mating duo like Fred and Ginger. Blue-footed boobies let us nose around their nests, and we followed giant lumbering tortoises, watched whales, and crouched among marine iguanas (who despite their savage looks appeared insatiably romantic). *Inca Floats, 510/420–1550; www.incafloats.com*

THEME LOVER

With fewer than 150 passengers aboard, the award-winning Star Clippers' four- and five-masted tall sailing ships are able to dock at private harbors and lush anchorages on volcanic isles. I took the Leewards itinerary, sailing from St. Maartan. My favorites were Dominica, with its profusion of waterfalls, bamboo groves, and vanilla orchids, and Iles de Saintes, totally French—sassy, stylish, and beautiful. Other hedonistic voyages focus on the British Virgin Islands and European waters, the Far East, and across the Atlantic. Days we lazed or explored, and at night, requested piano favorites with cocktails, dined haute in slacks and tees, and strolled under sail on an empty top deck. Themed cruises are a special option. Pilates under the Pliades? Then Health and Well Being was the theme to choose. You could have danced the Zouk and Soca on Caribbean Discovery, or brought an instrument and jammed during Jazz & Blues. Who knows what awaits in future winters? *Star Clippers, 800/442–0551; www.starclippers.com*

RIVERS RUN THROUGH IT

My best meals in France—ever—were during a weeklong cruise on the Rhone and Saone rivers, round-trip from Lyon aboard the *Princesse de Provence*. We anchored at rolling Burgundy and Beaujolais wine regions and history-drenched towns, including

Avignon and Arles. Peter Deilmann, a European-based cruise line, navigates the major rivers of Europe, spring through summer. The smallish riverboats gleam with rich woods, original artworks, Meissen porcelain, and Tiffany glass. I requested an upper-deck stateroom, and my French doors framed the verdant shoreline. Dockside, I walked, relaxed in cafés, people-watched, shopped, and checked out the sites. Excursions are well-guided and reasonably priced, and because the vessel is small, ports didn't seem overrun with tourists. The experience was delicious and stress-free, and happily there are lots of European rivers left. The line also cruises in Asia. *Peter Deilmann Cruises, 800/ 348–8287; www.deilmann-cruises.com*

CRUISING IN THE SEA OF CORTEZ

Fly into Cabo San Lucas to the Sea of Cortez, off Baja California, where turquoise, inland waters lap against desert sands, a starkly beautiful, surprising contrast. On the *Safari Quest*, a yacht with 17 other lucky passengers, hundreds of bottle-nosed dolphins jumped and dived in our wake. I snorkeled, eye to eye, with a sea lion, crossing a species divide in a humbling, unblinking connection. And far off, I spied the world's largest creature— the (truly) awesome blue whale! Informative discussions, Sunfish sails, gourmet cuisine, comfortable cabins with private baths, shelling, stops to isolated, primitive fishing islands, kayaking, and nature walks and picnics in a blooming desert are only part of what I enjoyed. The yachts also sail in Alaska, the Columbia and Snake rivers, and the Pacific Northwest. *American Safari Cruises, 888/862–8881; www.amsafari.com*

ON THE MED, FROM ROME TO NICE

Windstar Cruises positions itself as a decidedly unordinary cruising experience, and indeed, cruising under five-sails, with fewer than 300 passengers, is the far side of mainstream. My weeklong Mediterranean itinerary on the sleek, casual vessel out of Rome included Corsica, with its rocky villages and wild scenery. I enjoyed an on-board massage off Elba, where Napoleon made the best of his 10-month exile. I hiked the sea-and-sky coastal paths of Cinque Terre's isolated villages and vineyards and tarried amid Portofino's tony pastel shops in that glam Italian harbor. I gambled and gamboled in Monte Carlo, sunned in St. Tropez, and ended in Nice, at the Matisse and Chagall museums, and the narrow lanes of shops and cafés in the old town. *Windstar Cruises, 800/258-7245; www.windstarcruises.com*

SPAS

Ah, yes, the spa experience. In the name of relaxation and beauty I've been rubbed, massaged, abraded, twisted, pummeled, saunaed, loofahed, hosed, pinched, soaked, creamed, bathed, steamed, plucked, vibrated, waxed, tweezed, lasered, peeled, buffed, bronzed, brined, and kneaded. Products touching my skin in the name of therapy have included mud, honey, chocolate, sand, brown sugar, birch limbs, pineapple, sea weed, yogurt, turmeric (yellow), river pebbles, hot rocks, cold fish, olive oil, steam, sea salt, marigolds, and roses. I've emerged from treatments the color and texture of a tandoori chicken, and come away smelling more like soil than petals, but truly I've enjoyed the promising pitch of each treatment and (usually overpriced and overpackaged) product, the soft and calloused hands of masseuses and masseurs, and I remain hopeful that every experience has enriched me. The one sure thing is that New Age music!

Spa memories inevitably focus on touch and smell, senses often understimulated in other situations. In Mexico, I luxuriated in a "moon massage" with oatmeal, jasmine, and rosemary—a Mayan twilight experience in the Caribbean Sea. But although we often concentrate on the luxury of a spa experience, many go for the clinical aspect. Outside of Santiago, Chile, I visited a tiny, antiseptic room in a wellness clinic near a thoroughbred horse farm run by snobby Chileans who wouldn't let my driver in to see the rooms.

History sometimes combines with pampering, as taking the waters goes back thousands of years, where settlements grew around hot springs. Bath in England, built originally by the

continued on p. 65

Steerage & the Klipfisk Lady

Since writing a book on "the world's most exciting cruises," I have experienced delightful adventures on the water, alone and with others. Where did I go? Cruising through the Panama Canal, and along the Yucatan Peninsula of Mexico, and to offshore islands of the Philippines and Brazil. I gazed at calving glaciers and the shifting green curtains of the aurora borealis in Alaskan bays, and stood on the rails of a liner in Southhampton, England, where the Titanic embarked for the first and last time.

No problems on that voyage, but not all has been smooth sailing. The low point was cruising third-class on an about-to-be mothballed Turkish ship, from Haifa to Istanbul. The itinerary was glorious, with stops in Cyprus and Izmir, Turkey, near the ruins of Ephesus. My cabin was triangular, about as big as a closet, and right next to the anchor; the room shook and screeched every time we entered or left a port. The mattress seemed sooty, at best, so I slept in my clothes, and I'm sure I heard something smaller than a sailor scurrying behind the wall. The toilets were public, with holes beneath your feet where you could see the sea, wa-ay below. When I tried to upgrade in desperation I ran into a heavy chain, barring the stairs to the second-class deck. All that was missing was a whip to keep us third-classers below. But I was young and strong and made lemonade from lemons with this story—I've told it for years!

I was once on a Norwegian mailboat delivering its goods along the coast. One morning we stopped at a fishing village known for its dried cod—klipfisk—sold to the Portuguese, who regard it as a diet staple. Leaving the boat, I must have still been bleary, as I read that we had eight hours at the port rather than we were due back at 8 AM—an hour away. So I took my time, wandering around the town, when I suddenly heard a blast of the boat's horn. Why? I heard it again! The boat was leaving, and I wasn't going to make it. On instinct, I ran into the middle of the street and hijacked a suburban mom and her toddler in a Volvo, screaming, "Take me please, or I'll miss the boat!" The mom didn't want to run me over, and with true Scandinavian social welfare, sped me to the boat, just as the gangplank was rising. ᕗ

Romans, and adored by the English, is still a favorite. Pamukale, in Turkey, is a wondrous hillside of natural limestone pools, and I cleaned up pretty good in a Turkish hamam, where the tile is cool and people still carry silver soap holders. I strolled among vivid flower beds at Baden Baden, Germany, but didn't like the look of the baths, so I just skipped them.

If weight loss and detoxifications are goals, you can find spas with a tough regimen and not much to chomp on. In Berkeley Springs, West Virginia, where George Washington once lolled and presumably soaked between wars, politics, and tooth-sanding, I stepped into a steam box that looked like a freezer, with only my head sticking out, and came out crimson as a poppy, except for my face. At the Homestead resort, in Virginia, I was hosed as if I were on fire, and I later changed into a paper bathing suit and splashed in the same warm enclosed pool where Jefferson once swam—I hope not in a paper Speedo. While on a press trip in Finland, I heated up in a sauna with other journalists—not a pretty sight.

Destination & Resort Spas

Relentless pampering can be jarring if you're unaccustomed to either the indulgence or the price tag, but if you want to be spoiled, explore these properties.

Lea's Picks. Cal-A-Vie, Vista, California. *866/772–4283, www.cal-a-vie.com*; Canyon Ranch, Tucson, Arizona. *800/742–9000, www. canyonranch.com*; Cap Juluca, Leeward Islands, BWI. *888/227– 5858, www.capjuluca.com*; Delphi Mountain Resort & Spa, Leenane, Co. Galway, Ireland. *095/42987, www.delphiescape. com*; El Santuario, Valle de Bravo Edo., Mexico, *866/896–7727, www.elsantuario.com*; Miraval, Catalina, Arizona. *800/232–3969, www.miravalresort.com*

SPA-SECTIONS OF RESORTS/HOTELS

Romantic resorts and glam hotels, previously off-putting for soloists, are opening elaborate spas and health centers, often with adjoining accommodations. These special sections are

continued on p. 69

Tea for Two

I had been nursing the end of a long relationship with "the CEO." He was supposed to have joined me on a two-week summer cruise from St. Petersburg to Moscow, but we bailed out right before, and this solo voyage became an opportunity to get as far away from him as possible.

In St. Petersburg, where the voyage began, I languished on a bench watching a woman push a twig broom in front of pastel buildings reflected in the Volga, and the scene seemed as dismal as my mood, a seedier Stockholm. In those early post-Glastnost years, millionaires were created daily, speeding in Mercedes past neatly dressed people selling off their best clothes along the streets, and an overload of scientists and teachers were left practically starving, making maybe $50 a month when bread cost a dollar a loaf.

The Hermitage needed air-conditioning, but then, as often happens as I travel alone, I found joy: the paintings and malachite-topped chests and new-to-me van Goghs and Rembrandts lifted my heart.

"Is this city really beautiful?" one of the Russian tourists onboard asked as we were about to embark on our cruise.

"Oh, yes," I answered, knowing she had not seen many great cities, and probably never would. And I was surprised to find that I meant it.

The first night on the boat I made friends with Ludmilla, a cherry-lipped, platinum blonde teacher from the Ukraine, newly divorced with two little girls. We dined together and shared discussions of life and loves and politics, and fears. Each night she lectured about Russian history and culture, coiffed and made up like a movie star from the 1940s, but she wore the same two dresses for two weeks. By the end of the cruise, most of us left our extra sweaters and scarves and shirts in anonymous bags outside her room.

The sluggish boats of Russia ply their ways along the rivers and canals back and forth between the two great cities. Stalin artificially connected this beeline in the 1930s, flooding villages and anything else in its path. We were told that many thousands of people lost their lives, somehow, in creating this lock-filled water highway, and one of the saddest sights in my life was a steeple, like the mast of a sunken ship, sticking out from the water close enough to touch as our boat floated by.

On our daily port stop along the way, we'd peek inside rival riverboats to compare the disappointing accommodations. That summer in 1995 our boat was boxy, seedy, still decorated in Soviet chic with large, plain dining areas, ornate overstuffed chairs, worn carpeting in small public spaces, and a couple of floors of tiny, paneled cabins. The heads had showers with water flowing right onto the floor, and little towels, which I first mistook for napkins.

Grandmas with babushkas covering most of their gray hair prepared the modest meals—tan meat, potatoes, and maybe the climactic thrill of a fresh orange for dessert. This was a spa cruise—without meaning to be.

Mid-journey, our boat docked at a pretty village lined with towering trees, and a band played a vivacious, off-beat "Dixie" as we disembarked. I walked along on my own, past a flea market spread around the dock, a jumble of tables and blankets laid out with a mix of schlock and family treasures: oval black pins with flowered paintings, enameled watches, worn household items. There was so little to sell, and I observed the modest goods and the ill-dressed people with need and pride mixed on their faces. Nearby, men hammered on the roof of an old Orthodox church, returning it to religious purposes after years of neglect.

I felt a tap on my shoulder. A lady smiled, a huge version of the stacked doll-within-a-dolls offered on tables in front of me. She was weathered, and gap-toothed but was probably younger than I was. Her face was kind, and lined, and humbly beautiful.

"Come with me," she gestured, pointing to a bunch of cottages on a nearby rise, and despite some doubts—the boat embarked in about an hour—my gut said "Yes," and I followed her.

Her tiny home seemed out of a storybook, fronted by a neat garden of purple cabbages, green onions, and other hardy crops. At the door, a slender teenage girl in T-shirt and jeans greeted me. "Hello, lady. I'm Irina. My mother would like you to have tea with us. I will practice my English."

Of course! I was entranced, and when I complimented her on her language skills, the girl blushed, her pale face presenting the same broad smile as her mother's.

In the cottage entryway, a bench covered several pairs of neatly placed shoes and boots. Hooks held clothing, and a hanging cloth, patterned with red roses, delineated a sleeping alcove beyond. Naïve prints of kittens and puppies covered the walls, and the windows were trimmed with handmade lace curtains, matching the tablecloth that covered a table in the middle of the main room.

A samovar was flanked by tea cups and lace napkins, a cut-glass plate held a puddle of purple jam, sugar cubes filled a glass jar, and a cake the color of lemons was already sliced. I figured that this woman, who seemed to have no husband, probably extended this gracious invitation every time the boat docked, looking for someone to converse with her child.

She poured tea, placing the brew before me, and then served her daughter and herself. For a half hour or so, she sat and served and smiled, while I talked with Irina, as best I could, about Checkhov, dating customs, and America.

When this unexpected interlude ended, the lady presented me with a hand-stitched tea towel. I insisted on giving her something, but she was adamant: she did not want her photo taken, and she did not want money. Her daughter's conversation had been what she sought.

Already the cruise had transported me far from my miseries. Back into the sunshine, I followed the deep harmonies of men's voices, and I entered the half-repaired church by the harbor, the rich sounds reverberating through me. The darkness was tinged by primitive frescoes and silver-and-black icons. As I stood among the locals, I inhaled the smoky spices, incensed in the truest sense of the word—inundated sensually, happy as could be in that moment.

A woman pulled at my arm, and I half-expected another invitation to tea, but it was a cruise-mate, barking in a whisper. "Gotta go! The boat's leaving."

Then and there, I wouldn't have minded being left.

In Moscow, our final stop, we were warned about the high rate of crime by paranoid Americans who insisted that we needed bodyguards. Funny, but Russians thought the same about the streets of New York City. One of the waiters on the boat guided me through the maze of subway stations, some ornate with dripping crystal chandeliers, others modern and sleek. I thrilled him by treating him to a $5 hamburger lunch at Moscow's most popular restaurant, where lines formed for blocks: McDonald's.

Later, I ventured out by myself. Past the Kremlin, St. Basil's Cathedral, and Lenin's tomb, where a crew was filming a gum commercial, and into a park where I watched people strolling by as they do in any city greenspace. I had arranged to meet Boris, a scientist acquaintance of a Russian engineer who had moved to New York. Boris's life was a tragedy of wrong place, wrong time: a baby during the siege of Leningrad when his father was killed; a Jew growing up in a country where anti-Semitism remained official, and communist sanctions were stringent. And now, in his middle age, Boris was an overeducated remnent of Soviet schooling, barely able to survive without his safety net of socialism.

My engineer friend suggested that I pack a bag of useful items like shaving equipment, soap, gadgets, and packaged foods, and I handed the bag to Boris without a word as we met, transferred as stealthily as contraband. He spent the day showing me around his favorite parts of the city. Amazingly, touchingly, he insisted on paying for a cab ride back to the boat—an expensive gesture I was terribly sorry about, but he seemed to need to do, and I thought of the lady who had invited me to tea.

By the time he came onboard our docked riverboat as my guest for dinner, Boris was famished but too proud to even take an extra roll. I put them in his bag, and kicked a fellow passenger in the shins for complaining about his declining stock portfolio.

The heartache and hope, generosity and spirit of the Russian people took me away from my own small miseries, and I appreciated my good fortune as never before. Now when I feel sorry for myself for stupid things, I often think of pretty Ludmilla and brilliant Boris, and Irina and her mother in the cottage. I give tribute to them, and to the many fine people I have met through the years as a solo traveler, throughout the world, who live their lives with dignity and courage. 🐚

filled with splurging solo friends you've yet to meet, and the pampering is comparable to some of the better destination spas.

Lea's picks. Arizona Biltmore Resort & Spa, Phoenix, Arizona. *800/950–0086, www.arizonabiltmore.com*; Gurney's Inn & Spa, Montauk, New York. *800/848–7639, www.gurneys-inn.com*; Lighthouse Hotel & Spa, Galle, Sri Lanka. *94/924017, www.slh.*

com/lighthouse; Victoria Jungfrau Grand Hotel, Interlaken, Switzerland. *033/8282828, www.victoria-junfrau.com*

RETREATS

Take time away from it all. Drop out for a week, a month, or a day and drop into a solo creative retreat, a quiet wellness center, or simply time alone for new perspective. Become reacquainted with yourself—what you discover may surprise you.

Lea's Picks. Alaska Native Heritage Center, Anchorage, Alaska. *907/330–8002, www.alaskanative.net*; Antelope Retreat and Educational Center, Savery, Wyoming. *888/268–2732, www.anteloperetreat.org*; The Golden Door, Escondido, California. *760/744–5777, www.goldendoor.com*; Green Valley Fitness Resort & Spa, St. George, Utah. *800/237–1068, www.greenvalleyspa.com*; Raj Ayurveda Health Spa, Vedic City, Iowa; *800/248–9050, www.theraj.com*; Tara Mandala Private Retreat Cabins, Pagosa Springs, Colorado. *970/264–6177, www.taramandala.com*; Western Spirit Enrichment Center, Prescott, Arizona. *866/ 663–7747, www.westernspiritranch.com*; Zen Lifestyle Energy Resort, Bali, Indonesia. *0362/93578, www.zenbodyholiday.com*

RESOURCES

Cruise Companies

CruiseOne. A free weekly e-mail message lists cruises that charge little or no single supplement if you want your own cabin. They typically list the deals two to three months before sailing. 630/762–6685; *www.yourowncabin.com*

Cruise West. Small cruises (58–110 passengers total) that will occasionally waive the single supplement. *888/851—8133; www.cruisewest.com*

Intrav European Riverboat Cruises. Small luxury cruises. Single supplement eliminated on certain cruises, certain times of the year. Packages coordinate all details, including airfare from New York. *800/456–8100; www.intrav.com*

Norwegian Coastal Voyage. Take in Norway's coast and the Northern Lights. Discounted for senior citizens and solo travelers during slightly off-peak season (mid-September to mid-April). *800/323–7436; www.coastalvoyage.com*

RiverBarge Excursions Lines, Inc. The only hotel barge traveling America's inland waterways. Single supplement sometimes can be reduced or waived. *888/462–2743; www.riverbarge.com*

5

Soloing with Others

It seems contradictory, but it's not: If you want a solo traveler's freedom without spending too much time on your own, you can have it both ways, traveling alone—with others. Historically, this has meant tooling around in an air-conditioned motor coach. Increasingly, it has come to mean hooking up with a bunch of like-minded folks to engage in a common activity such as cooking, tackling the outdoors, or building houses.

But soloing with others can also mean being with just *one* other, as part of an independent duo. I once traveled to Stockholm with a friend I dubbed "The Vampire"—I only saw her when it was dark. She liked to sleep late and take her time; I was out the door before she got up. We seemed to have the same time-clock around dinner time, when we both enjoyed smorgasbords and a walk in the Old Town. We saved money by sharing a room, and kept our cool by ignoring each other most days and late nights. Our independent duo-ship worked well enough, and no, she never bit my neck.

Mates, spouses, friends, family, even near-strangers can be the other half of your independent duo, and even if you're madly in love, you don't have to be joined at the hip (see more on this sensible concept in Chapter 16, Breaking Away). You will need a clear understanding of what you mean by "independence." Do you want to spend days apart and just come together for certain activities? Do you prefer your own rooms all, or some of the time? Do you want to get away only in the afternoons, or meet only in the evenings?

An independent duo can mix and match—be together or apart, depending on interests. How much free time you have is up to you, and how you work out the coupling, but be sure that you both agree in the planning stage, and are honest about all aspects of the trip.

Independent duos reap a big payoff: shared driving; help with organization, decisions, and chores; and big savings if you decide to room together. But it works to the max when you're both flexible. On a trip to France, my friend Merle and I opted for less pricey rooms on some nights, just so we could each have our own room and some precious privacy, a trade-off that we both agreed on ahead of time.

Besides friends and family, I've traveled successfully as part of an independent duo with my doctor's receptionist, my ex-husband's cousin, my renter, and my realtor. But the two times I traveled with men friends were disastrous. Women be warned: No matter how clearly you agree on friendship only, you may encounter macho reluctance once you get there.

Threesomes

I love them. They provide variety and stimulation. No, Fodor's has not gotten into the sex and relationship niche—we're talking travel only, when three is definitely not a crowd. You can always travel with a couple of friends, but I prefer traveling with a *couple* who are my friends, which offers both the benefits of soloing, and companionship. When you're the odd-one-out of an odd number, it doesn't feel odd at all. Like roses in a vase, three seems to work when you want to solo with others, and a twosome and you works best.

I used to travel as a couple with my friends Judy and Stan, along with my husband; and later, when I traveled with them on my own to New York, France, and Greece it was a different dynamic, but still delightful. They shared a big room and I stayed in a smaller one. When I breakfasted on my own, they didn't care; when they wanted to shop together, I happily headed on a ramble. We were able to communicate honestly, converse enthusiastically, share driving, and add to each others' enjoyment. Most importantly, I paid my entire share of the expenses without exception—a must for duos and threesomes.

IS SOLOING WITH OTHERS FOR YOU?

Religious pilgrimages in the Middle Ages may have been the first group tours, but modern ones date to 1841 when Englishman Thomas Cook transported teetotalers by carriage and train to a temperance convention. Sounds like loads of fun, doesn't it?

The term "Cook's Tour" evolved to mean rushing around to many places with others—the "If it's Tuesday it must be Belgium" syndrome. For years, much of group travel was this sort of thing—"11-countries-in-17-days" rush jobs, with one-hour visits to the Eiffel tower, dinners at tourist traps, and a bunch of strangers on a bus annoying each other mightily after a few days. For soloists, this was just about all you could find if you wanted to tour with others.

Things have changed. Rush tours are out there, but today a "Cook's Tour" just as likely will refer to compatible travelers whipping up foams and roasts in two-week classes led by master chefs in a villa in Tuscany or an inn in Anguilla. Hundreds of group-tour options offer soloists a chance to come together with others to learn and play, sightsee, and relax.

But is traveling with a group really an option for a truly independent traveler? More to the point, is it for you?

Benefits of Soloing with Others
COST-EFFECTIVENESS
Team up, or take a tour, and you can find up-front, volume discounts and shared rooms. Alone, you're apt to feel the monetary

continued on p. 78

Level Best

I can't swim. I don't want to do it," Jane kept saying.
"You don't have to swim," I assured her. "You just paddle."

We were on the shore of a meandering river in Costa Rica, among banana plantations between the Atlantic and Pacific coasts, about to partake in the "white-water rafting afternoon activity" on a warp-speed, five-day press trip.

We had come here from the capital, San Jose, on a colorful little train, which wrapped around cloud forests and valleys, and chugged along like a ride at Disney World.

I had rafted several times, in West Virginia and Alaska, and the experience was the kind of soft adventure that I could handle—skydiving is not for me. The river contained Level Two and Three rapids, a bit tame; I prefer the adrenaline rush of a Four, especially when guides are doing most of the work. But this rafting break would be a chance to relax the pace. Besides, the cold spray of water feels good on a hot day, the bouncing raft carries you past colored canyons and ribbons of shoreline, teamwork is pleasing, and the hint of danger a shivery thrill.

Our group divided into three rafts, each piloted by a guide from a private company. Ours was Miguel, lean and brown with a mop of hair. He had recently piloted a well-known congressman along this very route, who at taxpayer-expense was probably studying . . . rafting. If Miguel was selected to guide our noble legislator, I figured he was worthy of piloting me.

Our raft held six, with Jane hunched in the middle of the yellow rubber vessel, clearly along for the ride without any intention of paddling. I had convinced her that she would enjoy the experience, and that her lifejacket precluded her need to swim.

"This better be worth it," she glared.

"Trust me."

Miguel gave instructions, and we floated along for several minutes. Miguel did most of the paddling; the rest of us went through the motions. I was scanning the trees, looking for iridescent birds with long tails. We were jolted when the first boiling rapids came upon us unexpectedly, but we slid along and around the smooth rocks in a small circle, navigated perfectly.

"That wasn't so bad," said Jane, who unsquinched her eyes only after we passed again to calm water.

The river was tame most of the way, and we chatted about the charming restaurant hosting us that evening. Frothy rapids appeared with regularity, offering manageable thrills. "I like it. You were right," Jane smiled.

Suddenly we heard a noise, and when I turned toward it, I saw a wall of water, roaring toward us. Whoa! A dam opening? I could immediately feel the water rising under the raft, and we started losing our direction.

"Listen to me!" Miguel shouted. "Do what I say, or you'll drown!"

"Stroke left!" I dug into the water. "Right!" The other side dug. We were beginning to spin, as the water level rose and speeded us along.

"Left. Right. Left. Backpaddle!" Miguel was shouting and we were leaning back and forth to his directions so that out oars flashed and scooped, flashed and scooped.

Suddenly, in the raft ahead of us, three people popped into the swirling water, which was now lapping in waves around hidden rocks. We spun around and maneuvered to try to fish out the floating people, some of whom were going under. Before we had gotten into the rafts, we were warned to point our feet downriver if we fell out. But the volume of water made it impossible for anyone to point anywhere. They were spinning.

It took several minutes to get one of the victims into our raft. I had heard the term "drowned rat," many times, but that's what I thought as I observed him. He didn't look anyone in the eye. He just sat, dripping and shivering.

The other raft eventually picked up the other two dislodged writers, and we managed, gratefully, to paddle to shore. We never found out why the water had risen, a first according to Miguel. We waited for a bus silently, and finally when it came, I spontaneously gave him all my Beatles tapes. I had hoped to listen to them along the river. He played them on our ride back to San Jose, and we sang along to "Yellow Submarine," except for the still-stunned people who couldn't get over how close they had come to drowning.

Oh, and then there was Jane, the woman whom I had cajoled to come along. She said it all in two sentences: "Level Two rapids? I won't be finding out what Level Five is!" ❧

pinch of single supplements, full-fare cab rides, tips for help, and portions you can't finish.

EASE

The uplifting energy and support of teamwork are there for you, but you don't need a partner. Luggage is picked up and delivered, reservations are made, transportation is handled, and arrangements are others' worries. Tour leaders—start to finish—can cover every contingency, making choice reservations sometimes years ahead, with know-how in minutia that might drive you crazy.

NICHES

Groups can target specific interests, and with Internet capacity you can find a perfect fit with like-minded travelers. You can safari to Kenya, walk or bike worldwide among solo travelers, or ride horseback through Europe or Costa Rica, all with low single supplements. Alumni groups, museum groups, religious groups, and hobby groups are also available—just select your fit.

Benefits of Pure Solo Travel

INTERACTION

Alone you don't just observe the scene; you become a part of it. Schmooze with the bistro owner or chat with the family sitting next to you at lunch. You can make friends, join in, and share culture. It's also easier to find romance.

CHOICE

Do what you want, and not what you don't. Stare at a grooming gorilla for an hour without fear of missing the tour bus. Skip the folk-dance show and the mandatory shopping stops. Cram your trip with personal delights, or do zilch. Timing, budgets, and goals are yours to decide—and the freedom is a definite plus.

SELF-CONFIDENCE

After navigating and driving around the Austrian lakes or changing money and ordering a meal on your own in Hungarian, going alone to your local Cineplex seems pretty tame. Without even realizing it, you gain confidence that never leaves—and that's a biggie.

LEA'S PICKS FOR AFFINITY TRIPS

A "tour" may mean you just have to sign up for a group rate, and then you're free to just fly away with a "group" and share the same hotels, but otherwise never meet for traveling around or meals, unless you prefer. It could be an "airfare only" deal, where you can be totally independent and you'll never even know who the other group members are. Also, "air and land" packages, can provide all the bookings with one call, for utmost convenience, yet you never have to hang out with anyone else.

Fastest growing are affinity tours—doing what you enjoy with others who enjoy it, too. You name it, and there's a group doing it, from cheese-making in Wisconsin to clog dancing in Nova Scotia. Below are my picks for experiences that allow you to solo with others while still enjoying your independence on the road.

Cooking Vacations

Hotel & Inn at Coyote Mountain. Get a taste of luxury and tropical creole cooking in Costa Rica. *506/383-0544; www. cerrocoyote.com*

Trout Point Lodge of Nova Scotia. Enjoy a Canada inn and a cooking program at once. *902/749-7629; www.troutpoint.com*

The International Kitchen. Resource for cooking school trips throughout France and Italy. *800/945-8606; www. theinternationalkitchen.com*

Cycling

Adventure Cycling Association. Treks in North America and Europe. Schedules are flexible, trips vary in length and difficulty, and vans filled with food and equipment bring up the rear. Participants are paired for tent sleeping—other nights are spent under stars. Soloists can enjoy solitude. *800/755-2453; www.adventurecycling.org*

Dancing in the Dark

Dancing is certainly an in-your-face-and-arms way to meet someone. And you never know where it may lead.

In an Eastern African country of great beauty and even greater poverty, I was one of five visiting journalists on a 17-day trip. We experienced safaris, dusty cities, and elaborate cultural centers, fish farms and mountain lodges, beach resorts and villages. Trailed by reporters, we became part of the story we were covering.

At the end of the trip, feted at a government reception, we listened politely to the tourism ministers' speeches, and then, unexpectedly they turned the microphones over to us, and asked for suggestions on how to improve tourism.

I suggested, in the gentlest way I could, that without a better infrastructure American tourists wouldn't want to visit. For instance, there were no road signs on the highways. Tourists couldn't drive anywhere, because they would have no idea of where they were going.

"I don't see any signage, even on major roads," I said. "You need to have signs at appropriate intersections."

A beautiful minister in a brilliant turquoise-and-tan draped kanga and an intricately wrapped headdress took back the mike. "We did have signs. People used them to build houses."

Silence.

After that, I kept my mouth shut. I felt like dung.

A folkloric show followed the discussion, and performers chanted and rolled and swayed, shuffling their feet in quick steps to frantic drumbeats. Song after song, dance after dance, dozens of the costumed locals honored us as we drank red wine and ate little meatballs created from undisclosed animals.

I clapped and remained focused on the show, the least I could do. Suddenly, a tall, glistening dancer in white pants and bare chest grabbed my hand and pulled me toward him.

I am not one of those people who likes to be on stage. I avert my eyes when volunteers are requested for most things. But after my stupid remark earlier, I couldn't refuse.

I threw off my heels and followed the movements of the other performers, as best I could, much to the delight of the ministers and my fellow press people. Swaying, shuffling, bending, faster and faster. My feet were a blur below me, and I silently gave thanks to my aerobics instructor, Lana. The drums beat louder, and I could smell the sweat around me, or was it my own?

The dancing soon went beyond even my adrenaline-and-guilt-laced capability, and I was exhausted. The bare-chested man who pulled me up suddenly sat me down in the center of the dancers, and twirled around me. His hands darted up and down, and his eyes focused on mine.

He smiled. I smiled back. He circled me and made more hand movements, reaching toward me. I mimicked his, and the ministers laughed and clapped, and then, finally, the drums ceased, and he brought me to my feet and led me back to the side, and bowed to me.

"What does that last dance mean," I breathlessly asked the minister in the headdress. "You all were laughing so hard."

She answered with a smile. "Your new name is Ngunda. You two are now married."

I haven't seen my new husband since that trip. He doesn't write. He doesn't call. Men. ❧

Euro-Bike Tours. Company with 30 years of bike and walking touring experience. *800/321–6060; www.eurobike.com*

Irish Cycling Safaris. Tour Ireland and other parts of Europe. *01/260–0749; www.cyclingsafaris.com*

WomenTours. Many bike tours worldwide for women only. *800/ 247–1444; www.womantours.com*

Soft Adventure & Safaris

Centennial Canoe Outfitters. Canoe trips for singles. *877/353– 1850; www.centennialcanoe.com*

Costa Rica Soft Adventure Multisport Vacations. Biking, hiking, rafting, and other activities and tours for soloists in Costa Rica. *919/755–9292; www.mariahcostarica.com*

Ulusaba Private Game Reserve. Sir Richard Branson, of "Virgin" fame, offers game-viewing safaris through acres of wild bush in South Africa. Staff is attentive and solo friendly. *800/ 225-4255; www.ulusaba.com*

Walking Tours

Backroads. Specialized walking, biking, and camping trips for solo travelers; with notice will pair you with a roommate. *800/ 482-2848; www.backroads.com*

Footloose. Walking tours in New England, Western United States, and Canada. *800/221-0596; www.footloose.com*

Spiritual Development

Chopra Center for Well Being. This ayurvedic center at the La Costa Resort and Spa in Carlsbad, California, pampers soloists with cleansing, healing, and rejuvenating bodywork; however, the real focus is education—lifestyle awareness, natural health practices, consciousness, and spirituality. *888/424-6772; www. chopra.com*

Green Mountain at Fox Run. Not a deprivation program or a temporary solution, this program imparts lifestyle and perception changes. Dormlike facilities are on 26 Vermont acres. *800/ 448-8106; www.fitwoman.com*

Omega Institute for Holistic Studies. Retreats for personal growth and spiritual development, with campuses in New York's Hudson Valley and Texas; workshops in the Caribbean and Costa Rica; and varying travel programs. Basic accommodations, simple vegetarian communal meals, coed massages and bodywork available. Solo guests are typical. *800/944-1001; www.eomega.org*

Volunteer Vacations

Archaeological Fieldwork Opportunities Bulletin. Good general resource for finding digs worldwide. *617/353-9361; www. archaeological.org*

Explorations in Travel. Trips for women over 40, plus volunteering opportunities for those looking for an extended stay. *802/257-0152; www.exploretravel.com*

Habitat for Humanity. Builds homes for the impoverished in the United States and in 100 other countries. A great, enriching opportunity for soloists. *229/924–6935; www.habitat.org*

La Sabranenque. Volunteer opportunities in southern France and northern Italy restoring medieval villages in historic areas. *716/836–8698; www.sabranenque.com*

Passport in Time. USDA Forest Service volunteer program. Project listings by state. *800/281–9176; www.passportintime.com*

6

Traveling with Pets

If going it alone still seems a bit raw, pack a rawhide bone, because your four-legged family member may be your ticket to solo freedom. Think about it: Fido can run by your side as you scour the English countryside for antiques, or Kitty can curl on your lap by a hearth in a French chateau. And if the notion of transporting your furry loved one provokes anxiety (for both of you), read on: traveling with pets is a booming trend, and the travel industry is responding.

A Starwood-sponsored survey of 400 dog owners revealed that 43 percent said their dog seemed "sad" when left behind. Half said they think about their pets "often" when traveling; 26 percent admit they actually talk to them when they call home! (Yes, we're pet-crazed. According to the American Animal Hospital Association, 84 percent of owners refer to themselves as their pets' "mom" or "dad," and 43 percent give their pets *wrapped* presents for special occasions.)

Increasingly, stores and Web sites offer travel goods for pets, from sleep masks to flasks. And there's no longer a need to leave Fido in the motel while you shop. Even large-size dogs are being welcomed by smart retailers, who realize many of us wouldn't tolerate tossing out our pooch any more than our kids. Some Pottery Barns allow dogs to lounge around. Saks Fifth Avenue keeps dog biscuits at the register. At the Bal Harbour Shops in Miami Beach, dogs drink at Dolce & Gabbana water bowls. And Stony Point Fashion Park in Richmond, Virginia, has a doggy comfort station, with plastic bags for waste.

Accommodations and facilities are growing, so, not surprisingly, animals are going along for the ride in record numbers. The Travel Industry Association (TIA) reports that 14 percent of Americans travel with their pets (that's 36 million households). And it seems like just the tip of the tale.

Is Fido Really a Travel Companion?

Solo travelers who bring a pet along are still truly on their own, taking full responsibility for choices, and enjoying a superlative travel mate as well. Win-Win. Woof Woof.

Pets are great when you want to meet someone, and useful threats when you don't. Extra costs are minimal—same room, a bit extra for transport maybe, but lots of bang for the buck. (Or the doe. Sorry. Pets and puns just go together, doggone it!) Traveling together, you can be doing your thing, yet unconditional love awaits, at a touch. You can walk and check out the scenery, share private moments, and relieve your travel stress with snuggles. Animal travel mates may snore, but they don't tie up the bathroom. Pet partners won't make you late, don't argue about where to eat, grab the covers, or insist on watching the adult-movie channel. They kiss you when you return, and love you in the morning, all over again. No nagging, no complaining. Perfection. Okay, so they don't modulate how they pass gas and don't have the best breath, but let's face it, neither do many two-legged companions.

If you're considering traveling with a pet, and don't yet have one: think small, think one, think calm. And for the best candidate overall, think dog.

Size matters. You may long for a Great Dane, but even if you're going to Denmark, a shitzu would be preferable. On the road, less pet is more fun and less effort. There's not much you can do if you already have a St. Bernard, except maybe tailor your travel to minimize the size issue, such as sticking to an RV road trip where you're doing the driving and Fritz can roam as you go.

The smaller the pet, the easier to lift, crate, carry, and bring with you. Small pets can travel in a carrier on public transportation. They leave smaller messes, require less lugging, and are less obtrusive. And they're less expensive to transport. You can even walk with your pet in a carrier-back or in a baby-snuggly.

One is company enough. More than one pet compounds problems. Expenses, clean-up complications, and having only two hands are only part of it. Many lodgings, if they permit pets at all, won't allow more than one—can you blame them? And pets don't really need fellow companions—they need care and attention from you, and if you have to split that attention while you travel, all will suffer. On the road, two's company, three's a potential mess.

Know your puppy personalities. Golden Retrievers are gentle and amiable companions, but too large to lug along on most trips. A chihuahua is tiny, but loud and feisty. (My first dog as a kid, Mijaca, was one of those yappy, trembly breeds; I was always afraid I would squash her in the dark.) If you can find a breed that combines small size and calm disposition, you're in good shape. Ask your vet, and go online to learn about the different breeds. When you're ready, you may want to visit your local animal shelter, but be aware that you can't always tell how a shelter animal will turn out, so for travel purposes, consider choosing an adult animal or a purebred. For online animal shelters and pet safety info, consult Adopt-a-Pet (www.adoptapet.com).

Prepare for pitfalls. Let's consider the downside of traveling with a pet. Cats may be less needy than dogs, but are more territorial, and not as happy trading spaces. My cat Sweetie sleeps through air travel in her carry-on case, and is content when I bring her to a familiar condo. But during her one-and-only stay in a hotel room she continuously checked out every nook and cranny, hid behind the drapes and curled in the bidet, which was unsettling at two in the morning when she jumped up unexpectedly. And cats naturally scratch things, which can get expensive.

Dogs may be better adapters to new space, but they can be high-maintenance, and depending on temperament, may be in-your-face—and every other place. They sometimes bark, slobber, knock things over, sniff inappropriately, and leave deposits. You have to walk them, or set up someone to do it, or cross your fingers with paper on a strange floor.

AAA says that 78 percent of traveling animals are dogs; 15 percent, cats; 2 percent, birds; and 5 percent, "others," including guppies, turtles, iguanas, and assorted critters from ferrets to rats. Is it worth the effort to carry around swishy little Nemo in a water-filled plastic bag? Err on the side of a pet-sitter unless you can justify the rewards of co-traveling with an offbeat pet.

Transporting Pets

Staying as put as possible is best for pets, in surroundings that can become familiar, with space to exercise, and places to eliminate comfortably. Good options are a house, a camping vehicle, a resort, one hotel room for an extended stay, or a cruise.

But is a hunker-down trip what you want? It's your trip after all, and although you'll have to adapt, you shouldn't have to change it too much for a pet. Weigh pros and cons before you leave, and keep your own priorities in mind.

Moving around also means a greater chance for accidents of all types, and for stress, but you don't always have a choice. When you're transporting your pet, you're likely looking at either air or car travel, which I take up in more detail below. Amtrak currently has no provisions for carrying pets, and commuter rails either don't permit pets at all or will require pets to remain in their carriers. Interstate bus lines—and ironically, Greyhound—won't permit dogs or other pets on board, but will allow assist dogs to accompany travelers with disabilities at no extra charge.

Each cruise ship has its own rules and requirements—check them well in advance to allow for compliance time to ensure your ship doesn't sail without Fido.

Many cruise lines do offer floating kennels—special, comfortable accommodations for your pet. The glamorous *Queen Mary 2* had to move their kennel from its original location near a kitchen: dogs were howling all day and night, smelling the haute cuisine.

To ensure your pet's overall comfort and safety while traveling, follow these basic guidelines:

☞ Choose a sturdy carrier or carry-on with a leak-proof bottom, a positive lock, and good cross-ventilation, roomy enough for your animal to stand, turn, and lie down. It should be properly marked, and have handles for lifting. If you're flying, know your airline's guidelines for approving carriers.

☞ Bring your pet's favorite foods and vitamins, especially if they're hard to find. Why should they have to eat leftover bruschetta or tiramisu? And if you're not sure of the water, keep Fido in mind. Pets can get *turista,* too.

☞ Pack familiar toys and bedding, particularly a favorite blanket—anything that will ease your pet's separation from its home base.

☞ Hug your pet often, and use familiar actions and terms—keep things close to normal.

☞ Keep an extra leash and collar with name and info affixed, just in case. Make sure your pet has intact identification; ask your vet about ID microchips (for international travel these may be a requirement), which should include your permanent address and phone number, and the destination address and contact number.

☞ Don't lead a leashed animal onto an escalator. Pick him up.

By Plane

A major airline allegedly shipped a two-ton whale, covered in ointment and sprayed with water, so Fido should be just fine. But know your pet's comfort level before attempting a flight, especially if you plan to have him travel in the cargo section (more on this below).

When my sons Rand and Cary were little we'd visit their grandparents in Miami Beach over the Christmas holidays for a couple of weeks, and we stayed at the house I grew up in. Our little poodle, Apricot, would come along, over-sedated in those days, in his kennel, which was checked baggage. One time, retrieving luggage at JFK airport in New York, the baggage carousel went round and round without Apricot.

"Where's my poodle?" I demanded/beseeched/screeched.

"If he's not here, he wasn't on the plane," argued the airline spokesperson.

"But we put him on the plane in Miami. It was nonstop. He should have come off with us in New York!"

After a couple of hours of desperate searching, we were beginning to think that Apricot was lost somewhere in the Bermuda Triangle. Thankfully, a call came to our home in New York at 3 AM. Apricot, somehow, had been sent to Hawaii! He was at last returned home, stunned and shaken from 24 hours in a crate without food or water. We never flew him again. He had seen enough of tropical paradises, thank you very much.

An optimistic footnote to Apricot's ordeal is that if you're traveling through JFK, the ASPCA AnimalPort—the Western Hemisphere's oldest and largest facility—is dedicated exclusively to animal air travelers. In 2000, "The Boris Bill" increased airline reporting and tracking requirements, tightened accountability, and stiffened fines. That bill was created when Boris's owner arrived on Christmas Eve at LaGuardia in New York from Fort Lauderdale, via a major airline (same one my dog Apricot was on—hmmm). She found only a crushed dog crate, except for a few teeth. Turned out that Boris was being chased around the parking lot by the plane's cargo crew, escaped their clutches, and was found six weeks later in an abandoned building in Queens. Happy ending: Boris survived and was nursed back to health—including dental surgery.

Be a proactive pet owner. Ask to watch your pet being loaded on and off the plane. If you really feel it's warranted, insist that airline personnel check on your pet, and, in extreme situations, take Fido back; trust your instincts! Also:

▷ Checking and cargo are not one and the same. Pets may be "checked" as baggage and you can fetch them from the carousel (as I would have done with beloved Apricot) or shipped via cargo, separately delivered by the cargo owner (you) to the airline cargo facility. Fees for air lifting a pet generally run $50–$75 domestic (in the United States and Canada). Cost for cargo is by weight—the pet crate, food, and all. Each airline sets its own pet pricing. Fees are typically one-way only, so be sure to double check round-trip fares if you and Fido are planning on returning.

▷ If Fido is flying cargo, know that some fumes, such as dry ice, can be lethal. Inquire about what other cargo might be on board. For international flights, four-sided crate ventilation is required. Make sure that the plane has a ventilated cargo hold, that animals will be boarded last, and kept in a temperature-appropriate environment.

▷ If your pet is flying as baggage, and you have to make connecting flights, make the reservations separately, so that you can transfer the animal yourself, which means you'll also have to transfer your own luggage—reprocessing and reboarding. Try to keep pets flying as baggage less than eight hours, as baggage compartments are usually not pressurized—plan your trip so you don't arrive on weekends, holidays, or other busy times.

▷ Review the changeable pet travel guidelines posted online by the Air Transport Association (www.airtransport.org).

PET TRAVEL AGENCIES
A pet travel agency can make your life easier, and Fido's safer. For a fee, they book flights, get pets on the plane, and pick them up, coordinating a safe boarding haven until you retrieve them. Pet transporters offer a worry-free option for overseas trips. And major insurance companies can cover your pet, if it's unusual or exotic. If you're only taking Fido to Slovenia for a few weeks, you probably don't need the expense and major services of an agency that specializes in horse travel or permanent relocation.

Let Them Eat Cake

If you think that France is going to the dogs, you're right on. Almost 9 million canines live in that très chic country, and easily ride public transportation, sometimes govern the sidewalks, and happily dine in restaurants. Mais, oui.

But that's just the beginning. Poodles and other pooches are pampered indeed. At Hermès, dog collars start at $300, and leashes cost $175. At l'École Vétérinaire de Maison Alfort outside Paris, animal medicine students can take a special course in dog psychiatry.

As for hotels, well, humans should be as welcome. VIPs (Very Important Pets) staying at the Trianon in Paris are offered cleansing wipes, doggie shampoo, and a tiny flask of a fruity perfume called "Oh My Dog!"

The even tonier Crillon Hotel, on the Place de la Concorde close to the American Embassy, has a Dog de Crillon program that offers clients a dog tag engraved with the name on one side and the address of the hotel on the other, a sleeping basket with a softball, a bone containing fluorides, a bottle of mineral water and biscuits, a menu that changes daily, and the services of a bilingual veterinarian recommended by the embassy. The hotel chef, Dominique Bouchet, is poised to prepare special meals for dogs with either chicken or beef.

Meanwhile, the Meurice Hotel allows clients to host dog parties in the Belle Étoile suite on the eighth floor. The Four Seasons-George V offers a coverlet embroidered with the dog's name that can be custom-ordered in advance.

But when it comes to dogs, Vincent Smarella, the manager of the Bristol Hotel in Paris, has seen it all. He says one client from Florida arrived with trunks filled with grass sod that she unrolled onto the terrace so that her four dogs would feel at home. Another demanded that her dog's drinking water be served at room temperature in Limoges porcelain with the dog's name on it, and that rugs be laid out on the bathroom floor so the dog wouldn't catch cold. A third required a messenger dispatched to the airport to retrieve veal liver flown in from the dog's butcher in Miami.

Then there was the woman who dressed herself and her dog in matching Chanel outfits.

But before we get too smug, Mr. Smarella said that nothing compared to what he once experienced in a hotel in the United States, where he was required to organize a doggie birthday party every year for 150 guests. "The dog would sit at the dining table with his owners," he recalled.

Asked whether he ever found such requests ridiculous, Mr. Smarella replied with appropriate sang-froid. "I don't judge them."

Competition has ensued to lure dogs and their masters and mistresses. *Animal Fair*, an American lifestyle quarterly for pets and animal lovers, offers annual Dog Bone Awards, for the most canine-friendly digs. Two past winners:

▶ Most Pet-Friendly Hotel, St. Regis, Los Angeles. Dogs sleep in custom-made mahogany bed with down pillows and cushions, and lounge poolside with attendants.

▶ Most Pet-Friendly Resort, Las Ventanas al Paraiso, Los Cabos, Mexico. Dogs enjoy sunlit suppers of Rin Tar Tar (shredded braised beef and steamed rice) on their private patio, or gaze through a personal telescope. Dogs are offered stress-reducing neck and full-body massages. Activities include lounging on a private beach and napping in a dog cabana. And for canines on Atkins, the full-time chef can prepare made-to-order meals.

Is this the end of civilization as we know it, or what? 🐾

By Car

John Steinbeck, author of *The Grapes of Wrath*, wrote a lesser, more personal work—his last: *Travels with Charley*, about his road travels with his poodle. How about you and yours?

☞ Take the animal on short, practice trips before traveling, to acclimate. This will either get him used to the motion, or stress him out completely. If there doesn't seem to be improvement, consider leaving your pet with a sitter.

☞ Don't let Fido jump around the car or hang out the window, ears akimbo. It may seem cruel, but these actions can endanger lives. Cats are natural jumpers who might suddenly pounce at a passing bird or even a fly, maybe by the gas pedal. Keep pets in comfy carriers.

☞ Try not to leave a pet alone in a parked car. On hot days, temperatures can rise to 120 degrees in a few minutes; on cold days, cars can become Sub-Zeros on wheels. If you must leave for a few minutes, roll down the windows just a bit, and keep a blanket for the pet to burrow in if it's cold. Look for a shady spot to park if it's hot. Also, leave water in the car. Pet stores have special travel canteens, perfect for these situations.

☞ Keep your pet with you in the "cab," not in a towed trailer or camper or in the back of a pickup truck.

☞ Carry an up-to-date health and rabies vaccination certificate, especially if you plan to cross state lines.

☞ For your cat, bring a full litter pan, carried in a plastic bag.

Pet-Friendly Accommodations

According to the TIA, 40 percent of Americans have shared their rooms with pets. (Sixteen percent admit to smuggling their pet into a hotel or motel room!)

Increasing numbers of lodgings maintain special rooms, or separate kennels on-site, and hooray—a few of the world's ritziest places offer pet pampering. Four Seasons, Starwood, Hilton, Loews, Marriott, Holiday Inn, Sheraton, and Ramada are among the chains that have begun to adopt pet-friendly postures. And policies at other properties have been changing rapidly as more hoteliers realize the benefit of welcoming travelers with pet companions. But even if you find your accommodations on a "pet accepting" list, call ahead—for size limitations, extra-charge requirements, or other changes.

Dinner with Fido

Pets and picnics work best. Buy your food at a local store, and eat alfresco, with Fido and Kitty leashed, or in a carrier. When you want to eat together a bit more formally, stick to places with outdoor tables. Otherwise, room service, rooms with kitchens, or doggy bags in your room are options.

Few restaurants in the United States allow pets inside, but overseas, animal prohibitions are more lax. Check locally. Face it: you may have to leave Fido in the room, and break away when you eat. But you'll have a loving reunion.

Of course you'll bring favorite foods, or buy similar products, and food and water should always be available.

Adventure Travel & More

You might prefer a solitary jaunt with Fido in a five-star hotel, but a growing number of adventure outfitters are catering to pets, offering weekend trips and longer, where animals are part of your experience—hiking, canoeing, camping, swimming, rafting, quadricycling (pedal-powered buggies with baskets), and even skijoring (where dogs pull their owners on cross-country skis). Campfires, barbecues, white-linen dinners, in-room massages, happy hours with dog treats and wine and cheese, and pet psychics are just a few of the options.

The American Animal Hospital Association suggests dogs get a checkup before you sign them up, and train to get in shape, if needed. Also, physiology and personality should fit adventure demands; larger dogs might do better than little ones. Think about it: a dachshund on a trek would be daffy, and a Yorkie in snow might wind up a Yorkie Popsicle.

Pet travel companies may conduct screening processes and send out questionnaires, and most will dismiss unruly animals (or owners). And pet outfitters now clamor to offer doggy gear, including special sleeping bags, life vests, booties, backpacks and "Powerbones" with high carbs and quality fats. Obviously, single people can easily meet this way, and enjoy the outdoors, too—a nice, new bonus, courtesy of man and woman's best friend, and newest travel companion in the wild.

RESOURCES

International Requirements

If Fido wants to travel with you into another country, he will need an international health certificate issued within 10 days of the trip, completed by an APHIS accredited veterinarian. You can contact them to locate the veterinary services office in your state, to determine whether your vet is accredited, and to obtain (downloadable) brochures: *Traveling with Your Pet,* and *Taking Your Pet to a Foreign Country.* In addition to the APHIS certificate, you may need to meet specific requirements to avoid quarantine. Allow enough lead time, at least six months. *Animal and Plant Inspection Service (APHIS) 800/545–8732 or 301/734–8364, 301/734–5097 for birds; www.aphis.gov*

Rules & Regulations

Hawaii and U.S. territories have quarantine requirements for arriving pets. For territories, contact the embassy, government agency, or consulate at least four weeks in advance.

From the U.S. Customs Service, download the brochures *Licensing and Health Requirements: Pets & Wildlife,* and *Traveling with Your Pet. U.S. Customs Service, 202/354–1000; www.customs.gov*

Also contact the country's embassy or consulate for information about pet travel requirements. *U.S. Department of State; www.state.gov*

chapter 7

Packing for One

Henry David Thoreau might have been thinking of this chapter when he wrote in the early 19th century, "Beware of all enterprises that require new clothes," and, "Our life is frittered away by detail . . . simplify, simplify." We'll elaborate on Henry's advice.

Packing when you're on your own has its benefits. You don't have to worry about changing outfits—you can wear the same polka-dot, drip-dry dress every day, if you want, and no one will comment (as I did on an early European trip, and have never worn anything with little navy circles on it again!).

You can pack for comfort rather than style, if that's your choice. No one is looking over your shoulder if you throw your dirty sweatshirt in with your clean jeans, or forget to fold or roll. I once traveled for months never unpacking, living right out of my suitcase.

But packing for solo travel requires attention. You can't share toiletries and luggage space, so you'll have to keep items to a minimum. And you'll need to organize especially well so that you don't forget the important things. If you're caught without your pills, and a prescription to refill them, there'll be no one to help you get to the pharmacist, or calm your nerves.

You'll probably be the only one lugging your load, so you don't want to wind up like a pack mule. Cut half of what you think you need, and divide that by half, if possible. Or, to invoke the words of fellow travel writer Susan Heller, "When preparing to travel, lay out all your clothes and all your money. Then take half the clothes and twice the money."

While I admire people who actually tie those internal suitcase-belts over their packed clothes, I am not one of them. It is a fight, and a hard-won one, to stay organized, to pack sensibly, to not lose things, and to keep my cool on the road, rolling my luggage behind me. I really, really have to work at it.

So I do. I rarely have people stopping to admire my travel couture, but they don't point and laugh, either. I manage to have a few less wrinkles in my clothes than a prune, and I haven't lost more than an earring or two—well, there was that cashmere sweater in Scotland. And the time I forgot to check in the bathroom in Belize and left my makeup bag (worse than my pills!). And assorted glasses, umbrellas, keys that I'll never see again . . . But I'm getting better.

And believe me, if I can manage, you can, too.

Reading about packing isn't the most exciting thing about solo travel, and can get a bit confusing, so I've created some step-by-step formulas and suggestions.

Before You Touch a Thing

While you're perusing your closets and drawers, no doubt deciding that you profoundly dislike everything in them, consider the following.

Weather, climate, and season. Shoulder season, when the weather swings wildly, is the hardest time to pack because you need more clothes. All-weather fabrics and layers help. Clothing may be more informal in summer, and take up less room, but consider warm, thin fabrics for winter, too. Polypropylene is a light, warm fabric (even when wet), and dries quickly. Gore-Tex is also good.

Activities. Walking, biking, swimming? Golf or tennis? Picking up cute Hungarians in Budapest? You'll need to dress the part, including the right shoes, cover-ups, and hats.

Formality. Will you be attending fancy affairs, keeping casual, or somewhere in-between? Business travel calls for a whole other attitude and dress code from leisure traveling. Do you own two suits whose jackets or bottoms can be matched with each other, or with other single pieces? Consider sending these to the dry cleaner first. In any case, strive for simplicity and neatness.

Local customs. While no one thinks you should rush out and buy a burka or a sari, in some countries, long hemlines, high collars, long sleeves, and covered heads are required. If in doubt, pack conservatively. Long skirts or pants are safe, and big scarves can cover arms, heads, and legs.

Type of transportation. If you're traveling by ship or staying in one place, you'll be unpacking only once (See Chapter 4, One-Stop Soloing) and can afford the space and weight of plenty of clothes. But if you're hopping trains or catching planes, you want to pack concisely. Don't take for granted that you'll find a skycap or help with your bags. Bring dollars or local currency to rent a luggage cart, just in case.

Car travel offers interesting alternatives. Many motorists discover the hard way that using their car trunk as a repository for a large, unpack-only-once suitcase is an impractical, royal pain, especially if they're forced to drag it in and out of hotel rooms. A bunch of smaller bags works best, which is also true if you're driving with others. One late-spring/summer I spent a month driving around Canada reviewing hotels. I used my car trunk, lined with plastic bags, as a closet, placing wrinkle-proof clothes and toiletries I needed into an overnight case, which I brought into the hotel each night. Dirty clothes were kept in a big bag in the trunk, and about once a week I'd head for a Laundromat.

A Word About Lists

Maintain a standard packing list from trip to trip so you don't waste time reinventing it. I keep one on my computer, changing it to "Save As," and then renaming and customizing it to fit where I'm going. Refine your list a few days ahead of travel day; if you wait until the last minute, I guarantee you'll forget the little things that may matter the most, such as the belt that literally ties your outfit together, or your address book.

MINIMAL CARRY-ON WARDROBE LIST

This generic carry-on size wardrobe can be used for a weekend stay or for extended stays: I've used it for both. Choose fabrics that can be washed out the night before, and will be dry and ready to wear in the morning, even if you hang them indoors. Also bring along a tiny blow-dryer to help dry out clothes.

- 3 panties
- 2 bras
- 1–2 pantyhose
- 1 sleeveless top
- 1 pair jeans
- 1 pants outfit
- 1 skirt and matching top
- 2 long and short-sleeved tops
- 1 sweater or pashmina
- Several scarves
- 2 pairs lightweight socks
- 1 tote bag (wear while traveling)
- 1 dressy bag
- 1 pair comfortable dress shoes
- 1 pair athletic shoes (wear while traveling)

☞ 1 pair sandals (use as slippers)

☞ 1 belt

☞ 1 swimsuit

☞ 1 pareo (use as robe, belt, cover-up)

☞ Hat

☞ All-weather jacket (wear while traveling)

Select & Gather

Packing can be pleasurable if you do it right. I put on some favorite music (Enya-style or light classical calms me, the type you hear while you get a massage). I clear the bed, and dedicate several hours—and if I don't use all the allotted time I pamper myself with a bubble bath or a soothing nap for being so organized.

Here are some clothing-selection guidelines that have worked well for me.

Fabrics and layers. Knit and silk blends are easy to pack and don't show wrinkles. Silk is especially useful for travel layering—light and warm, easily packable, quick drying. Cashmere is thin and warm, and a wonderful investment. Today's specialty travel fabrics, found in catalogs, have come a long way on the style spectrum over the last several years. They pack easily, remain wrinkle free, are adaptable for day and evening stays, and dry out fast. That said, you can probably get by with your own wardrobe for your first solo-travel venture. Once you return, you can treat yourself to a few catalog buys when you've determined what worked and what didn't. And that said, who am I to tell you not to go shopping?

Rarely are temperatures "just right" or precipitation predictable. Even in hot climates, there's too-cold air-conditioning, and in cold weather, too much indoor heat. And in perfect weather, changes happen, indoor to out, car to lobby, day to evening, windy to still. The best solution: layers. Wear 'em, peel 'em, carry 'em (remember 'em!) and stay comfy. Bulky sweaters, heavy pants, and big jackets aren't worth hauling. And if you're leaving a cold-weather climate for a tropical one, they're not worth wearing, either. Layers will work just as well at frigid home airports both coming and going, and are a lot easier to shed once you reach your destination.

Solid colors. Prints are hard to coordinate. Stick with a basic color (black, navy, tan) for your pants, skirts, shoes and coats. Add accent colors (maybe white or beige, mauve or black) for tops, and a pop of hotter color in scarves and other accessories (red, green, whatever). Medium and dark colors show less dirt than lighter ones, and as a solo traveler you can get away with some extra wear.

Mix and match. Pack separates for choice and variation: tops that go with bottoms, rather than one-piece dresses or jump-suits. Coordinate colors and you'll maximize your travel wardrobe. Sweater sets with matching shells and cover-ups are great for switches. You'll appreciate subtle changes in your wardrobe by mixing and matching, and you can create several outfits from a few pieces of clothing.

Accessories. Scarves, ties, hair scrunchies, belts, and hats take up so little space and create appreciable changes in your look. You can dress up in countless ways using scarves—long or short, silk or cotton, solid or print. Style them around your neck, your head, or your waist. Wrap a big one like a shawl. Stick a small one in your pocket. Cover a bathing suit, or wear one to bed.

Use a hair scrunchie as a bracelet (or a garter, if you get lucky!). Accessories are easy to tuck into shoes, purses, and all the empty spaces in your luggage, so you can be lavish with them. As for jewelry, bring only the fake stuff and go lightly: Thieves are attracted by flash and not all know what's real and what's not.

Old clothes. Pack your oldest, least favorite clothes and leave them behind as you're finished with them—an effective way to eliminate packing, laundry, and clothes you can take or leave.

FROM ADAPTORS TO ZIPLOCS:
THE LITTLE THINGS YOU'LL WANT TO PACK

- Adaptors for electricals
- Antibacterial gel cleanser
- Binoculars (small as possible)
- Business/calling cards
- Camera and camera batteries (in a sealed bag)
- Cell phone (rent an international one if necessary)
- Condoms
- Day pack
- Dental floss (you can use it for thread, or to slice cheese!)
- Digital watch (a cheap one) with an alarm
- Drain stopper, a flat one, so you can wash clothes in the sink
- Duct tape for repairs (wrapped around a pen for easy transport)
- Extra pair of eyeglasses
- First-aid kit (for starters: prescription and antidiarrheal meds, antacids, aspirin, anti-itch cream, bandages)
- Flashlight and batteries
- Frisbee (doubles as a plate or a rain hat)
- Herbal tea bags
- Insect repellent
- Mirror, a small one, to avoid neck strain if you'll be perusing artistic ceilings
- Neck wallet or money belt
- Paperbacks and magazines you can ditch
- Phone activator (you may need a small electrical device to generate the appropriate tones for your phone machine or voice mail; you can get these devices cheaply at electronic stores)

- ▸ Photocopies of important documents, especially your pass-port, driver's license, and lists of important names, addresses, and e-mails. Keep copies in your luggage.
- ▸ Safety pins
- ▸ Sewing kit
- ▸ Stamps
- ▸ Sunglasses
- ▸ Sunscreen
- ▸ Swiss Army knife, the one with all the gadgets. But check it with your luggage, otherwise, don't bother. I attended a Mystery weekend in Cincinnati and won a wobbly rubber dagger because I figured out that the butler did it, or was it the maid? I forgetfully placed it in my handbag. Anyway, you can imagine the airport security check. Hard to explain, but ultimately comical.
- ▸ Tape recorder to record sounds and thoughts
- ▸ Water bottles
- ▸ Ziploc bags, large and small, to separate goods and place damp items

Plus, someone else in a struggling economy might find your worn clothing a treasure.

As you select and gather:

Check off each item on your list. A sensible way to see what you left out, as well as what you're taking. And remember to bring the list with you so you can inventory as you travel.

Lay clothes out. Top to bottom, inside to outside, on a bed or flat surface. This overview helps you choose and coordinate accessories and colors, and keeps you from forgetting elements, such as caps and belts. For me, this "layout" time is part of antic-ipating a trip; by creating outfits, I not only organize, I fantasize where I'll be wearing my outfits.

Make sure items are clean and in good shape. Especially if you tend to be a bit sloppy, check your travel wardrobe at least a week before you pack, and clean your clothes a few days before you start to pack. Few things will dampen your enthusiasm more than laundering and packing on the same night, or arriving at a destination with a hole in your skirt.

Choose Your Luggage

Make do with only one carry on—as small as possible. If that won't work, move up to the next smallest piece of luggage. With so many security precautions, the possibilities of lost luggage, and difficulties getting around are even higher—especially for solo travelers. Less is *so* more. Really try to fit your things in the fewest, smallest pieces.

If you're purchasing new luggage, the following considerations can make a big difference when traveling on your own:

Hard versus soft. Hardness is overrated. Hard-sided luggage is often molded plastic, and can weigh more than 10 pounds. Unless you're hauling glass or fragile goods there's no need for the extra weight. As an old Spanish proverb wisely warns: On a long journey, even a straw weighs heavy.

I did successfully travel one summer in Russia and Eastern Europe with one medium-size, hard-sided case on wheels. It was a great icebreaker: I had to keep asking people to help me lug it up and down stairs and into trains. And it did make a perfect bench when waiting for the train. However, assume that only you will be moving your luggage into and out of the trunk of your car, through the airport, off the luggage carousel, to the train station, to the bus stop, onto the bus, off the bus, back 2 km because you overshot your stop, up three flights of stairs, and onto the dresser. This is energy that could be better spent scaling a cathedral bell tower.

I'd choose soft-sided luggage, light-weight and durable. Framed cases best protect suits and most clothing. Frameless soft-sided luggage, such as duffle bags, garment bags, and backpacks are fine for casual travel and sports equipment.

Material. Luggage coverings such as needlepoint tapestry or velour may be attractive, but it's wiser to focus on practicality. Leather is luxe, but heavy and expensive; best for smaller bags. Canvas may not be glam, but is sturdy, washable, waterproof, and easily repaired if ripped. Vinyl is inexpensive and washable, but harder to repair than canvas. It doesn't scuff. Nylon scuffs, but is super light and tear-resistant. (Look for a fiber weight of 1,000 or more.) Cordura has the look of canvas and the strength of nylon. Polyurethanes are used for tough, hard-sided cases. Got that? Also, many luggage linings are easily ruined if you don't screw caps on tight. Give an extra twist.

Expense. Again, choose durability and functionality over looks (also something to consider when you take on a travel companion). Check the frame, weight, handles, lid, wheels, lining, and interior features, such as tie tapes and partitions. Designer luggage is a pretty invitation to thieves. And savings from buying a more utilitarian bag can be spent on essentials like spa treatments or shoes.

Color. Coordinating luggage is ideal for looks, and a feeling of organization. Dark colors show less dirt, but are most popular, which make your pieces indistinguishable from most others. (If you tie yarn to the handles, use a bright or unusual color—anything but red, which everyone seems to use. Or place a tape on the bag. Or attach big, noticeable colorful tags, with your cellphone number if you're traveling with your phone.)

Wheels. A necessity when you're solo. Main choices are four wheels, or tilted, two-wheel cartwheels; check them out to see which you prefer. Make sure you can stack your small pieces on the wheeled piece of luggage. As for luggage carts, they're not really sensible anymore, as airlines usually won't check them on board. And as for large, screw-on wheels, which are a pain to place on and off—well, screw 'em.

Locks. The new normal means you have to leave your luggage unlocked for security reasons. Pack with that in mind. Loosen up and just assume people will be pawing through your stuff. New universal locks that luggage handlers can open, if needed, are now available. You want the capacity to lock your luggage when you get out of the airport.

How to Pack

Fold, roll, and stuff so that all possible space is used, and wrinkles are minimized. Pack enough in a carry-on to make you comfortable at least for one night and one day in the event of lost luggage, and pack with easy security search in mind. And if you're checking your bag, remember that overpacking can buy you that dreaded HEAVY sticker; an "overweight" surcharge can easily cost a stinging $50.

FOLDING

☞ Fold on a flat surface, before packing.

☞ Fold clothes that wrinkle easily: shirts, pants, jackets, dresses, some sweaters, even jackets if you turn them inside out.

☞ Fold with clean edges and corners, emphasizing the lines of the garment.

☞ Interfold, by letting garments pad each other at fold lines. Long items such as slacks, dresses and skirts are laid out first, alternating horizontally. Shorter items such as sweaters, shirts, and jackets are laid out vertically. Plastic dry cleaning bags and tissue paper keep wrinkles away.

ROLLING & STUFFING

☞ Roll casual clothes, underwear, accessories, and items that don't wrinkle easily.

☞ Tuck rolls into gaps and spaces to avoid wrinkling.

☞ Stuff things into other things: socks or jewelry into shoes; scarves in sleeves; gloves in hats; anything into pockets, as you travel along.

continued on p. 110

Cinderella Cruise
(Or, If the Shoe Fits...)

A couple of decades ago, I cruised—nowhere. The trip wasn't remarkable for its itinerary (there was none), or its scenery (there was none, really), or its luxury, although the ship was Cunard's *Queen Elizabeth 2*, a Grande Dame of the sea, and I was in first-class accommodations.

It was memorable because of what happened in the first hours of the voyage.

To come upon a great ocean liner berthed on Manhattan's West Side is a throwback to pre-jet days when people wore hats and threw streamers as they departed for the faraway realms of Southampton England, and when it wasn't unusual to have a dozen ships in the harbor, stocking up for their trips across the Atlantic. Today, New York's modernized port seems mostly empty except for day trips up the river, the former air carrier *Intrepid*, now a museum, and occasional cruises such as the one I booked.

My cabin, although small, was paneled in dark wood, and had an old-fashioned porthole encircling a view of the Empire State building. I went on deck to watch the skyline, last of all the Twin Towers of the World Trade Center, as the ship pulled slowly out to wherever we weren't going.

At a surprise get-together right after the lifeboat drill, we met the captain, an extremely tall fellow with bootblack hair and a dazzlingly white outfit with gold trim.

"Do you know where this trip to nowhere is going," I asked.

"No idea. Maybe Block Island." Man of few words, he spied my name tag. "You'll be at my table for dinner." He may not have known where we were going, but he knew his dinner companions.

I returned to the cabin to unpack and shower. Tonight I would go all out. I put my coordinated clothes in the closet and my toiletries in the bathroom. But something seemed wrong. Something was missing. My jewelry? No. My lace wrap? No. My nightgown. No. My shoes. My *shoes*!

I looked again in my luggage, but it was empty, as was the bottom of my closet. In my super organization I had packed my shoes in a bag—and I could picture where I had left them. On my bed. At *home*.

On my feet, sneakers. For a formal dinner in a first-class dining room next to the captain? To wear with my navy blue silk dress my faux-diamond pin, and my blue-tinted pantyhose?

I rang in a panic for the room attendant, and she came in a minute.

"This may sound weird, but I need to buy . . . shoes."

"I'm so very sorry, ma'am, but we don't sell shoes on the ship." She paused, and I got hopeful. "Oh wait, I may be wrong. I think we sell flip-flops."

I was not consoled, nor soled, for that matter. In my stroll around the ship I had passed stores purveying resort wear, jewelry, antiques, books, toys, sequined tops. Why not shoes?

My options were badly limited: wearing my grungy sneakers like a mad-woman. Going barefoot. Maybe the rubber flip-flops wouldn't look so bad. I was clearly desperate. Here I was, going nowhere on one of the world's greatest ships ever, and condemned to my room.

"I'll see what I can do, ma'am."

I lay on the narrow bed and fell asleep and when I opened my eyes, the attendant appeared, transformed in my eyes into a fairy godmother. She was holding a bag.

"Will these do?" She placed before me a tangle of size-eight shoes. Sandals, and pumps, and flats, and deck shoes. Black and white and cordovan and bone and taupe. Strappy and high, low-heeled and comfy-looking—and clean.

"How did you find these?" I asked, my mind racing: Lost and Found? Other passengers? The crew? God?

"We have our ways," she said. "You'll have to borrow them, but you can use them all, if you'd like."

I liked! I just figured that at worst, somewhere on that ship would be pairs of average-size, unselfish feet, shorn of some of their shoes, allowing me to walk the decks of this great liner, head high in the light of day, the mystery of night and the spray of the sea.

I chose two pair, happy as Imelda Marcos.

The shoes fit, and nobody seemed to notice a thing. I did find myself staring to find possible donors and then looking down to see what their feet were clad in, and if they stared at mine.

By the end of that unforgettable voyage to nowhere I truly understood the meaning of luxury and service. And I left a tip big enough for the cabin attendant to buy a pair of Ferragamos. ﹆

▶ Use torn panty hose tubes as "snakes": cut the top and feet off the pantyhose, and fill these stretchable, compact tubes from the top-down, with crush-resistant, bulky clothing.

▶ When you arrive, steam things in the shower to remove any wrinkles.

REPACKING

Packing solo also means repacking solo, and you don't want to leave anything behind. You'll presumably just have your own eyes and memory to depend on, and your eyesight and concentration may not be 100 percent—rushing out the door to catch a cab, too much champagne the night before, too little sleep. You know. So check carefully, thoroughly, and systematically before checking out, and keep these tips in mind:

Do it before bed. Repack the night before your departure, as this will reduce your stress levels and forestall last-minute fits over trying to cram things into your bag.

Don't ferret. Don't hide things around the room; it's too easy to forget where you put them. Place them in a room safe or the lodging's safety deposit boxes, or keep them locked in your suitcase.

Open wide. Open all closets, drawers, the bathroom, and the safe before you start to repack. You're less likely to forget that robe on the bathroom hook or your passport in the safe if all doors are open wide.

Isolate dirties. Carry a parachute bag or big plastic bag and use it for clothes that fail the sniff test as you go along. Or if you have a larger piece of luggage with separated sides, keep clean clothes in one half, and dirty in the other. I wouldn't waste a lot of time seeking out a Laundromat on your last day, but one of the nicest gifts you can give yourself on your return home is a bag of clean clothes you can immediately put away.

Do a once-over, twice. Just before leaving, check as if there were two of you. Focus on places where possessions often are forgotten: medicine chests and showers, the part of the bathtub masked by the shower curtain, bedside tables, under the bed, closets (including the top and the floor), all drawers, especially the ones you were positive you never used, the TV cabinet, and that tabletop strewn with menus and useless hotel magazines that are inevitably covering something you meant to take with you. And if you wear nightclothes, thoroughly check the sheets.

Above all, remember the safe or safety deposit box. If possible, empty it the night before you leave. Distraught colleagues tell of leaving their passports, wallets, and valuables in the room safe, and never realizing it until they were miles, or sometimes days away. So far, I've avoided that horror by being diligent.

chapter 8

Getting There, Getting Around

My young babysitter Lynn was flying for the first time, visiting friends in California. Before leaving from New York, I told her everything I could think of, preparing her for her new experience. I explained the details about takeoff, landing, turbulence, strange noises, avoiding the middle seat, and the best times to use the lavatory. She was apprehensive, but excited to be flying on her own.

When Lynn returned I asked how she enjoyed the experience. "Oh, it was fine, I guess," she said. "But I didn't like when the oxygen masks came down. You didn't tell me about that!"

When you're dealing with transportation, expect the worst and hope for the best. Canceled flights, heavy luggage hoisted into train compartments (they don't call it luggage for nothing), missing the boat, passing your freeway exit. Getting from place to place is a special challenge on your own—a kind of walkabout, the aboriginal rite of passage.

Whatever mode you choose, you'll be tested; count on it. You'll have to navigate and drive at the same time, find the right train, and stand in line and do it all. You can. Transportation challenges lead to the rewards of your destination, and the satisfaction of true accomplishment. Remember, when the going gets tough, the tough solo traveler keeps going.

BY CAR

Driving solo gives you flexibility, freedom, wind in your hair—a chance to stop and view the world at a slower pace, and closer up than with other transportation. You can bring as much baggage as fits in your trunk, and travel door-to-door as you please. But you do need confidence to drive on your own, good navigational skills, quick reactions, and the ability to compartmentalize—to drive, eat, think, plan all at once. If you don't enjoy the idea, better to hire a driver, or take a bus.

I enjoy driving along the open road in just about any way. I've nudged a primrose yellow E-type Jaguar 100 mph plus on the autobahn in Germany, where even in the slow lane you're blinked at ferociously by the Mercedes behind you (when you're going an inconceivably slow 80 mph). And I've sputtered in a half-rusted VW Bug along Vermont back roads, with crimson, gold, and orange leaves falling at a faster rate than the car.

My first true road challenge was when I was 22, on the first day of my honeymoon: a two-month drive around Europe, through about a dozen countries, staying at charming inns and small hotels during the dream vacation of my life. I had never manipulated a stick shift—just practiced the moves in my living room, but our nonautomatic drive, British racing green MGB was delivered in the heart of London with the driver's seat on the American (left) side; we were shipping the car home with us after the trip. With its top down, the shiny two-seater looked to my young eyes more like a toy than a car.

New hubby promptly said, "You drive!" Hmm. So there I was, in a tiny convertible facing the London traffic at rush hour—dozens of roundabout intersections with cars circling from every direction, huge black taxis changing lanes—and I had to drive on the left with the steering wheel on the wrong side—and change gears with a stick, for the first time ever. It was ugly, really ugly. I clipped some side-view mirrors but we somehow made it to the hotel. I learned a lot about myself—and my husband—from that drive, and gained the courage to tackle other challenges years later when I was on my own.

Car Talk

Here are ideas to help with solo driving, and avoid the perils of my London initiation, I certainly hope.

Learn stick. If you can work a stick shift you can usually get a far better deal on rentals, and someday you may find yourself with no alternatives. It may take a few days to get it, but like riding a bike, you'll never forget it.

Consider if driving is best. Think about weather, topography, and the cost of gas. If you're in a city, parking hassles and costs will almost always make having a car more trouble than it's worth. Will you be in a self-contained resort where a car is unnecessary? Or will you be traveling between lots of places, where you can drive to a back-street bookstore or an out-of-the-way restaurant with ease?

I spent a few weeks driving back and forth along the curving, plummeting cliffs of the Amalfi Coast in southern Italy, researching a guidebook for Fodor's, and if I saw a trattoria or albergo that looked promising, I'd stop short and back up—a difficult and probably dangerous maneuver. This is a situation where having a driver would have been safer and more efficient, if more expensive.

Be clear about pick up and drop off. If you're getting a rental, calculate drop-off rates and convenience. Are you best served airport to airport? If you're traveling in different countries, can you pick up and drop off without a problem? Check that there are rental-car offices where you'll be.

Check documentation and insurance. You'll need a driver's license to drive anywhere in the world. Also check if an international driver's license may be useful (see Chapter 2, Planning & Saving). It can get confusing. Trying to drive into Slovenia without an international license, I was turned away the first time, and allowed in the next day. Public liability and property-coverage insurance are usually required; AAA can issue insurance policies. Before taking any insurance through your rental-car company, investigate coverage provided by your credit card, as unsuspecting renters often pay twice for the same insurance. If it's your own car, ensure your insurance is up-to-date. Also, bone up on foreign road language and rules, local speed limits, cellphone regulations, horn-honking and seat-belt rules, and road signs that might be in a foreign language.

Plan a driving schedule. Ideally, I like to drive several hours in the morning after a full breakfast, take a lunch break near a pretty view or in an interesting town, and take a walk. Then I drive 'til about mid-afternoon, settle into my lodgings, and enjoy the afternoon and evening doing anything but get in my car. You can make up driving time in the morning, and if you find lodging before dinner, you're more likely find a better room.

I have been so energized at times that I've simply driven much of the day and night. Your energy level will guide you, but if you leave some extra time for relaxation and sightseeing you'll be making the most of your solo situation.

Pack the car. Toilet paper, paper towels, ziplock bags of various sizes, antibacterial hand gel, bottled water, sealed snacks, and a Swiss Army knife should be along for the ride. In the glove compartment, ideally, I stow maps, a flashlight, pen and paper, insurance and car registration, coins, a basic first-aid kit, a tire pressure gauge, an ice scraper, window cleaner, a rag, a spare pair of sunglasses, and a disposable camera. The last is useful for capturing special moments at scenic overlooks and spontaneous pullovers, and snapping photos of damages should you find yourself in an accident.

And before you even think of loading your wheelie bag into the trunk, make sure you have a spare, a jack, jumper cables, safety flares, and spare fuses. For good measure, especially if you're taking your own car, consider a gas can, spare oil, wiper fluid, tire fixative, a lug wrench, a battery terminal cleaner and, for cold-weather destinations, antifreeze, de-icer spray, a snow shovel, and a bag of sand. There may even be some room for you!

Keep your cell phone charged. Note that I assume that you already have a cell phone. You *must* have one if you're traveling solo, and especially if you're driving solo. Have a second battery handy and, if possible, a spare phone. A friend is probably more than willing to lend you hers as a backup. And if you're overseas, get an international cell phone before leaving home. You can rent one from several U.S. companies and can transfer your cell-phone number to that phone.

Understand the car. If you're using your own vehicle, treat it to a thorough tune up before you leave, and regardless of whose car you use, join AAA or another auto-service group. Trust me, they only need to bail you out once to validate the membership fee.

Open the glove compartment and use your fingernail to puncture the shrink wrapping on your car's instruction manual. Then, yes, actually skim the thing. You don't want to feel around for your brights while you can't see the curve of a two-lane road on a moonless night. Keys, buttons—you alone will be responsible for knowing the light switch from the windshield-cleaner switch, and there's nothing more annoying than the back-window wiper that you can't turn off, or not being able to find an FM station. It takes only a few minutes to acquaint yourself before you start.

Check all the parts you can. Measure the air pressure of the tires before you go and periodically throughout your trip, and give other parts and functions a test as well. I remember a harried, harrowing drive down the Pan American Highway in Mexico from San Antonio to Acapulco. (Same little MGB roadster we bought in London.) We were late getting to our hotel one night, speeding on narrow mountain roads, and yikes, rain started pelting, and . . . the wipers didn't work. Not much choice but to creep along in fear: no shoulders, a big drop, and the slowest drive in the history of Mexico. When I drive solo today I can assure you I would test a rental car's wipers before starting out, and would try not to be on mountain roads at night.

Drive in daylight if possible. Many of us claim not to be bothered by night driving, but let's face it, as a solo traveler you don't need the complication (see previous point). All the more reason to know when the sun goes down, so you can wrap up your motoring before dark. And driving into a blinding sunset is no fun, either.

Don't read and drive. Seems obvious, but if you're driving solo in an area with infrequent road signs, you're more likely to scrutinize your map, especially if you're anxious about beating the sun or making it to an appointment. Don't be a dope about this. Stop the car as many times as you must to study the map or ask for directions. Prepare index cards with the broad strokes of your drive written in big letters, hold it with your thumb against the steering wheel, and flick your eyes at it if you must. Also, use those nifty geopositioning navigation gadgets with caution; fiddling with them can be just as distracting as poring over a map, so familiarize yourself with them before hitting the road.

Ask directions often. Seek out people who might best know the area—police, taxi drivers, and postal carriers are excellent choices—and ask three people to be super sure. Alas, well-meaning folks have led me astray, and I find it difficult to tell if they really know what they're talking about. Sometimes a scruffy kid will be more correct than a man in a tie and jacket, and be more willing to tell you if he *doesn't* know. I tend to ask women.

Make preemptive pit stops. Gas up when your tank is still half full; you can't be sure you'll find stations ahead, and on your own it's especially vital not to run out of gas, or even to worry about it. Also, stop before you really need to "go." (More important for women than men—I've never traveled long distances with a man who hasn't relieved himself off road. Is peeing *en plein aire* a badge of manhood, or something?) I use hotel, store, or restaurant restrooms rather than gas stations—if possible: hence your personal supply of toilet paper and antibacterial hand gel.

Stay alert. How do you stay sharp if you're determined to drive for a while? Calls on your cell phone (make sure it's legal hands-free; I just got a $175 ticket for a one-minute, non-hands-free call about my cat Sweetie). Drink strong coffee, chew gum or candy, sing along loudly with the CD of your choice or the radio. Think about buying or renting a vehicle with a satellite radio, which has lots of options, including all-comedy channels. An audio book—one that's lively but doesn't provoke rage or blinding tears—is also a nice option for the multitasking soloist. Try to leave windows open for invigorating, hopefully nonpolluted air, or blast the a/c to forestall drowsiness.

You should also stretch often, maybe on the hour. Rest stops on major highways are fine in daylight; just be cautious if an area isn't highly populated or well lighted. On a highway I'd head for a restaurant, gas station, or commercial area instead. In a town or in the countryside, I take the opportunity to walk and check out the local attractions and chat up people as I go.

Don't linger in parking areas. And when you return to your car, look around you, into your car, at the passenger side floor, and in the back seat. If you're parked next to a van, enter your car from the passenger door. Most kidnappers/thugs attack their victims by pulling them into their vans while they're getting into their cars.

Also take note of the cars parked on the driver's side of your vehicle, and the passenger side. If a male is sitting alone in the seat nearest your car, and you feel suspicious, you may want to walk back to where you were and get a guard or someone else to walk you back out.

Don't pull over for unmarked vehicles. If it's official, the vehicle must respect your right to travel to a "safe place," such as an open, attended gas station.

Don't linger at traffic lights in dark, crime-ridden areas. Look both ways and risk a ticket rather than a smash and grab, or robbery. One night, waiting at a light under an overpass in the Little Haiti section of Miami, a lead pipe smashed the passenger-side window, and a thief grabbed my purse. In it was jewelry my Aunt Hilda had just given me. (I never told her.) The police said I was lucky the thief hadn't decided to knock me in the head, for good measure. I sensed the danger, but because I was behind another car, couldn't go through the red light.

Several suggestions from this unfortunate experience: avoid dangerous areas, especially at night; don't leave valuables on a seat—put them in the glove compartment, or trunk, or better yet, leave them home.

And maybe I've watched too many episodes of the *Sopranos,* but if you're ever thrown into the trunk of a car, kick out one of the tail lights, stick your arm out the hole, and start waving.

BY PLANE

My first flight was definitely not solo. My mother told me that we were on a DC-3 flying down to Miami, and another passenger was none other than Mayor Fiorello LaGuardia of New York City. We had just departed from an airport that would later be renamed for the Mayor. My mother insists that I was a cute baby with copper-colored curls, and he pulled me onto his lap and pinched my rosy cheeks, as politicians do. We hit some turbulence, I puked on his suit, and LaGuardia yelled, "Get that damn baby off me. Now!!" Anyone can throw up *at* LaGuardia, after all, but I treasure the dubious honor of having thrown up *on* him.

I've put in my share of air miles since then, and in fact I'm writing these words on a flight from Ft. Lauderdale to NYC. Despite the literal ups and downs, I've had few bad incidents. My worst, perhaps, was on a flight in Patagonia, in southern Argentina, where the winds whipped the plane around like a roller coaster and I wasn't sure which way was up; I was lucky to keep my lunch.

Near misses are like fish stories in the travel world. Lightning once struck my plane (it does that pretty often, I'm told), and I did fly on TWA 800 a month before it went down in 1997. I was on a flight from Europe to New York that had to make an emergency stop in Nova Scotia, and then aborted the first take off, and we never found out why. My knuckles remained white for weeks.

Then there was a fire that broke out in the lavatory on a trip to Cleveland, and the jet was met by yellow trucks and a foamed runway. Everyone was calm when we smelled the smoke and there was only a smattering of clapping as we landed. Mine.

Blips aside, I've learned to love flying and I still choose to sit by the window to stare at the sun bouncing off the clouds and the twinkling lights above and below me. Early in my career, Charles Fraser, the genius behind Hilton Head Island and one of the first ecology-minded developers, read a magazine article I had written and invited me down to see his property. I was thrilled. On that trip I especially enjoyed taking the controls—for a few seconds—in his three-seater flying to St. Thomas in the Virgin Islands, and being picked up and flown practically door-to-door at Palmas del Mar, when it opened in Puerto Rico.

Funny things happen, too, while flying. When the door to the cockpit flew open over Angel Falls, in Venezuela, I had the weird view of both pilots looking at a map, and scratching their heads, as if they had no idea of what to do. Once when I was on a particularly tiny plane that labored particularly hard and long to finally lift off the runway, one frustrated passenger yelled out, "I didn't realize we were on a train!" A friend tells me he boarded a plane to Las Vegas filled with men on their way to a barbershop-quartet convention, who sang tight harmony during the entire flight. And on a flight to Israel, practically all the men got up to pray—on one side of the plane. You just never know.

Plane Talk

Go for discounts. As a soloist you have more flexibility with your booking. Consult your travel agent or log onto a bargain fare Web site for your initial research. Be flexible on dates and routes, and remember that if you travel on Tuesday, Wednesday,

The Virgin Flight of Virgin Air

Celebrations and inaugurals are a giddy part of the travel world, and so, a travel writer's world. You get invited for public-relations reasons, not because you're smart or beautiful. I cut the ribbon at the golf course at the Four Seasons in Nevis in the Caribbean—somebody had to, for a photo and article in the papers. I was one of dozens invited on the inaugural cruise of the *Millennium*, a Celebrity Cruise ship (out of Southampton, England where the *Titanic* left on its fateful inaugural), and fanfare and press attention about the ship lasted for weeks. At the 20th anniversary of Walt Disney World, the park was closed early to the public so that 3,000 journalists could frolic on rides, sip champagne, and nibble delicacies with costumed characters fawning over us on Main Street. It's the way things work.

My favorite event was the virgin flight of Virgin Air, more than 20 years ago. A bunch of us were invited to fly from Gatwick in London to Newark to report on the first flight of the airlines' mighty fleet: one used jet. To get to London, I flew on Saudi Air, where drinking was banned, and an elegant man who had brought along a tiny bottle of rum to add to his coke was promptly chastised by the flight attendant, and the bottle confiscated. (Quite different from our Virgin flight back, where liquor and other substances flowed like mighty streams.)

We Americans had a couple of days before the inaugural flight—circulating with the British tabloid reporters, who understood that the whole thing was a party. A pushy MTV crew came along with the invited press, including a well-known, ditsy blond veejay who ran around the city in shorts and a halter top. Her comment on seeing Big Ben: "Oh look, there's Big Bob!"

Richard Branson, the young founder of the new airline, had already amassed fortune and success as the head of Virgin Records, and he was a genial and generous host. For a press conference, we were bussed to his country estate, an ancient stone complex with a record studio as well as endless rooms. We journalists were a combo of awed Americans and increasingly sloshed Brits, as trays of nibbles and drinks were at our every turn. We had the place to ourselves: our host had not arrived at his own event.

We milled around the mansion and rolling greensward, glasses in hand, for about an hour, wondering if Branson would ever show, when suddenly a car came down the endless gravel driveway, and a bearded, scruffy guy in jeans hopped out of the passenger seat, apologizing profusely. Our host had hitchhiked to his own conference, and the stunned driver who now realized who he had picked up was invited to join in.

At the airport before the Virgin takeoff, bands were playing, the sound of Boy George filled the air, and the spirit was rock and roll. But the flight was delayed. Rumor was that there were serious engine problems. Branson was onboard in a captain's uniform—his mum and dad were onboard too, so I figured despite the pressure to take off, he wouldn't risk his parents' lives. After a couple of hours of angst and music and drinks, the engines sputtered on, and we winged aloft to Newark Airport.

Years later, I read that on that first flight of the rehabbed jet, one engine had, indeed, conked out over the Atlantic. But we were all out of it, and never even knew. ❧

or Saturday, prices are often lower. Carriers such as Southwest and JetBlue offer deeply discounted fares throughout the year (see Chapter 2).

Dole out your miles. As mentioned in Chapter 2, it's silly to squander your frequent-flyer miles on destinations with super-cheap fares, but if you've piled up a ton of miles and are looking for a gratifying off-the-top savings, go ahead and chip away at your stash. One trick that makes use of both strategies is buying a coach ticket and using frequent-flyer miles for an upgrade; you'll be earning even more miles by buying the ticket.

Spring for the airline lounge. Airlines have spruced up their airline clubs and lounges, competing for luxury-class customers, and for a fee (in some cases, small) you can enjoy them even if you don't fly first or business. Even using frequent-flyer miles might get you into some of them. The lounge permits you to relax, interact, dine, and in a few cases, even shower and sleep in a bed. And you meet interesting people. I remember sitting in one lounge across from a man in a clown outfit, who was reading the *New York Times* and sipping a glass of wine amid the uptight suits. What fun.

Some specifics: Flagship clubs are at the specific airlines' busiest airports: Delta's in Atlanta, Continental in Newark. A couple of examples in the New York area: Virgin Clubhouse at Kennedy offers lighting that changes hues, stocked refrigerators, showers, wireless Internet, an alcove with a bed, and Ipod digital music players. American Airlines Admiral's Club at Kennedy has a children's room and a cyber café.

See firstclassflier.com for more info on all clubs. And prioritypass.com sells memberships that grant access to more than 450 airline lounges.

Get comfortable in flight. Place a soft carry-on, backpack, or inflatable foot rest (available at travel stores) at your feet. Wear loose clothing. Drink plenty of fluids, but avoid too much alcohol. Pack items available in first or business class: ear plugs, an eye mask, an extra pair of socks, and a small shoe horn. Pack a portable toothbrush and minipaste in your carry-on, nasal passage moisturizer, and a light sweater. Remove your shoes after boarding and add the extra pair of socks (your feet will swell during the flight and you might need the shoe horn to replace your shoes; I've had problems, so I usually wear slides for long flights). Bring music and your own headset. And don't forget some snack food and water—you'll rarely be served on short flights, and if you are, the food might either be pricey or inedible.

Carry on valuables. Bring your computer, cell phone, essential papers, identifiers, and financials. Do *not* carry-on anything that will be confiscated. I often forget this, and have surrendered enough Swiss-Army knives and nail-clippers to stock a cutlery shop.

Have info handy. Among your papers, include names, telephone numbers, addresses, and contact information, useful when meeting unfamiliar people at an airport. If your flight is delayed and no one is waiting, this information will minimize stress. Know precisely where your pick up is going to meet you on arrival.

Losing Luggage

If you fly without changing planes, chances are miniscule that you'll lose your luggage, but let's say the worst happens. If your wayward luggage is labeled properly, you should be fine. You'll usually see an airline agent or two around the luggage carousel, and if they can't help you themselves they'll direct you to a customer-service area where the agents are typically polite and professional about tracing your bag.

I've traveled hundreds of thousands of miles, and I've lost my luggage a total of two times, and in each instance my bag was retrieved (if that doesn't do anything for your *schadenfreude*, see the tale about my dog Apricot in Chapter 6, Traveling with Pets).

With my first bag mishap, I was on a flight from New York to Cleveland to run a writing workshop. I had to change planes—something I avoid if possible. (Not leaving enough time between connections is a truly risky situation with luggage.) Anyway, I showed up for the workshop without my corporate wardrobe, notes, books, or workbooks. I could have worried about what everyone would think, and about the fact that I had no materials. Instead, I plowed ahead. When I greeted my clients in my jeans and tee and a smile, and no materials, I said "Guess what happened?"

"You lost your luggage!"

That broke the ice. The seminar succeeded without my materials (in fact, I created some new ideas, which I incorporated into later seminars). My luggage was found later that day, and a worst-case scenario wound up being not that bad. I learned that I could manage, and that I should strive harder to take nonstop flights.

My other luggage loss was more daunting, as I was flying alone from Malaysia to Indonesia. When I arrived in Jakarta, my luggage did not come off the plane. I kept my cool, and figured it was sent on to Bali by mistake, as that was my next stop. With that premise, I went to an agent, traced the piece, and my goods returned to Jakarta in a few hours. All accomplished with language barriers, and on my own.

BY TRAIN

As travel writer Paul Theroux writes in *The Great Railway Bazaar*, "anything is possible on a train." Indeed, great mysteries are set on the Orient Express or on trains clacking across the continent in a Hitchcock thriller. But at the same time, train travel is literally down-to-earth—fast, cheap, and safe.

And fun. Mediocre meals taste better in a dining car—even at a snackbar—as you gaze at the countryside speeding by. You can play cards and drink merlot in the club car with fellow travelers, and sleep soundly in your own cozy cubical or couchette as the miles and borders pass. Long-distance trains are loaded with the possibilities of the unknown—plus they transport you to areas where flights or drives are less convenient. New, high-tech trains can rival flying time door to door, and allow for wired workstations, comfortable seating, and on-time arrivals. And trains are a great way to meet people.

Of course I've missed a few trains, and have been crowded into others, sans a/c. The worst trip I can remember was in one of those first-class compartments where four of you sit knee to knee, and I sat next to an East German who may have last showered before the Berlin Wall fell. I voluntarily downgraded to second class.

But most train trips, aside from my hundreds of humdrum commuter trips from Westchester County to Grand Central, have been joyful. I remember whooshing past snow-capped Mt. Fuji on the Japanese bullet train; savoring fresh salmon and single-malt whiskey on the Scottish Highlander heading toward Gleneagles; viewing castles at bend after bend along vine-clad hills of the Rhine, in Germany; and soaking up the endlessly flat

Netherlands landscape, crossed with canals and rows of candy-colored tulips.

I trained solo from upstate to Manhattan when I was a contestant on *Jeopardy!*, carrying several outfits in case I appeared in several segments (I only got to wear one). With a friend in college, I trained from North Florida to New Orleans, and a kind conductor let us sneak into a sleeper car. Through big windows I watched a moving panorama of New England in the fall, and I rode Amtrak's Acela from Penn Station to Washington, D.C., to meet a love, exhilarated by both the speed and anticipation.

We can learn a great deal about solo train travel from one incident told to me by my friend Alan, who was traveling across Germany by train. When it stopped at a small station he felt hungry, so he checked the schedule and estimated there was plenty of time to run out to the snack area and buy a fresh, hot wurst. He was just about to pay for the sausage when he heard the sound of wheels squeaking and his train leaving the station. Incredulous, he sprinted back, but got there just as it speeded away—with all of his luggage.

Alan couldn't believe that the train left early, but when he rechecked, he realized he had been looking at the weekday schedule. And it was Sunday. He was despondent, because among the items on the train were his notes for his doctoral dissertation. He immediately notified the station master, who called ahead to the next station. Because Alan acted quickly and resourcefully, an agent at the next station removed his luggage and notes, and Alan took the next train to retrieve them, and continue on his way, about an hour late and a lot wiser. So, never give up—ask for help; transportation agents are prepared for such emergencies. (And—forgive me—eat better, not wurst, on the train.)

My favorite train treks for solo travel include: Canadian Rockies, on VIA; Mexico's Railway in the Sky and Copper Canyon; South Africa's Blue Line; India's Taj express from Delhi to Agra; The Trans-Siberian Express, across the silk route; and

The Benefits of Exact Change

In Bremen, Germany, many years ago, my four-year old son wanted to use the restroom in the train station, so I took him with me into the ladies room. A woman held the stall door open as she left, and my son went in. An attendant saw this and demanded that I pay the equivalent of 10 cents—it was a coin stall. I didn't have the change on me, and she proceeded to lock the stall and then stood in front of it with her hands folded over her ample bosom.

I argued to get my son out immediately but when that seemed impossible, I asked a sympathetic lady to watch him while I ran for help. I cornered the first train agent I found walking by the door—a befuddled-looking man in an official cap, and dragged him into the ladies room where the other women explained that my son was being held hostage for 10 cents. He argued with the commando lady while I extricated my son, and we escaped outside. The agent came out a minute later, his cap askew. Lesson: when traveling, carry change, and ask for help whenever you need it. (I'm sure there are philosophical lessons, too, but this is a book about soloing!) 🐦

the Polar Bear Express, in the Hudson Bay area of Canada, where you can view the migration of the giant white creatures from the warmth of your railcar.

Train Talk

Enjoy the relative spontaneity of rail travel. Trains deal with travelers who make last-minute decisions, so you usually don't need advance reservations, except during holidays or in some busy travel times, and for first-class or sleeper (couchette) service. This allows you maximum flexibility, a special plus when you're soloing and you decide to change your mind.

Check if a city has more than one station. That may seem obvious, but many cities have several stations. Be clear about the one you want when you get your ticket, and if in doubt, ride into the central station.

Remember the 24-hour clock. Trains (and boats) use it throughout the world. When the number is larger than 12, subtract 12 to get the normal time (1800 is 6 PM).

Get definitive schedules by calling the train line. The Thomas Cook International Timetable is published monthly, with guides to principle rail services worldwide, and many major stations have their schedules posted online. But try to follow up by phone and again in person when you get to the station to confirm all times and connections.

Travel light. If you're going by rail, you'll be lugging your bag a little faster and probably a bit longer, and if it's lumped together with other luggage in the rail car you may have to wait a bit—not great when you're catching a connecting train. Simplify with a backpack alone, if possible.

Leave enough time. You'll be busy on your own, so don't add to the pressure by having to run to make a train. Bring a book and leave about an hour to spare, if possible. You can always watch the farewells of other travelers, minidramas going on all the time around you, like in the old movies.

Be sure to get on—and back on—the correct car. You can easily figure out the code: the top part of the train car is usually the name of the train; the next part, the city of origin; then the important stops (not all—there could be 50!), and the last line is the termination city. A yellow band under the roof of the car denotes first class.

Travel overnight to save on hotels. Just remember, you'll be losing scenery through the night, which would be a shame through the Alps or the Rockies, so you want to time it right. And realize that in many trains you'll be sharing sleeping space with strangers—either in a coach car or in a sleeper, divided only by flimsy partitions. (Think Jack Lemmon and Marilyn Monroe in *Some Like it Hot*, but your sleep mate may look more like Quasimodo, and snore as well.) You pay hotel rates for your own compartment.

Safeguard your stuff. Trains and train stations are notorious hangouts for thieves. Thwart them by being careful. Use twists to tie together the zippers on your daypack; a thief will be challenged to undo them. Buy a padlock and short bicycle cable. Lock your backpack and daypack to your train seat (and your bedpost when applicable). And stand in the train car with your back against the "nonopening" door. This way you can see every passenger, none can get your pack, and you're close to the exit door when you get to your destination. Don't stroll the aisle without your valuables unless you've entrusted their care to a seatmate.

BY BUS

A long-distance bus may not be your transportation of choice, but it might be the only way for you to get somewhere if you aren't driving. And it just may be the most economical way of getting around. Yes, downsides are notable. You may not sleep much, as seats are narrow and passengers can be noisier than a car alarm. Usually there's one-class seating, and you're allowed only a couple of bags under a maximum weight. Bus stations are usually in the center of older areas of town, and this can be both positive and negative—depending on the town and when you arrive; taxis are often there to take you farther.

Bus Talk

Find your station. Most larger cities have at least one bus station, or at least a depot at a motel or diner where buses stop. Check yellow pages and the Web for station locations. Overseas, tourist offices, airports, and train stations often have station information. EuropaBus, an extensive network of motorcoach routes, operates in cooperation with each country's railroad system.

　　Also:

☞ Inquire about discounts or package deals when purchasing your ticket; rarely will these be volunteered.

☞ If in doubt, verify luggage weight restrictions.

☞ Check on pet policies. Most buses won't allow four-legged companions.

☞ Get there early, as you would with any transportation. Don't count on the bus company adding an extra section if there are crowds.

☞ Large buses will have restrooms; smaller ones might not, but will make frequent rest stops. Prepare.

☞ For comfort while traveling: read, listen to music, bring snacks, and most important—pack earplugs.

Bus Tours

With jet travel becoming standard in the 1960s, Americans started traveling throughout the world, and one- or two-week bus-tour overviews through several European countries became the standard way to go. I've taken a few such tours and find them excellent alternatives for solo travelers who accept their limitations, but seek the comfort and convenience of group travel. Some tours allow for plentiful free time, and the components of the trip range from budget to luxury. And yes, this is a wonderful way to meet people.

While the multicountry bus tour has become only one of many options, guided bus day tours remain singularly special. Countless times I've enjoyed a first-day overview of a city or region by bus. For me and many other seasoned travelers, a full- or half-day tour is a great way to get a taste of important sites. Half- and full-day tours, as well as evening and night tours, are fairly standard, but theme tours can be truly original. You can go on antiquing trips from New York City to the Catskills, or see homes of the stars in Los Angeles. My favorite nighttime bus tour was "A Movie Tour of Rome," where we visited about a dozen movie locations such as the Trevi Fountain, where *Three Coins in the Fountain* was filmed—you see the real place while scenes of the movie location are playing on a monitor in the bus at the same time. Really clever, and a great way to spend an evening, on your own, with others.

Ferry Nice Dreams

I leaned on the rail, watching the looming, pastel harbor of Procida, the fishing island near Capri where the movie *Il Postino* was filmed. As we docked I dreamed I might rent a room overlooking the water, write a steamy novel and learn Italian from a handsome young fisherman. (I met my second husband soon after that, and moved on to another dream, but I still may do it.)

Ferrying is more than simply floating from one place to another. In rough seas or fog, in glassy waters with dolphins dancing in the wake, or nights with wind whipping and the engine churning, it is the most romantic form of public transportation. It inspires dreams.

In Lake Maggiore I toured from tiny isola to isola, with a soon-to-be-lost love, as if in desperation, and dreamed he was healthy. And yes, I remember the tall Masai warrior in his long dreadlocks and tribal garb on the ferry to Zanzibar, debating with a Muslim, and dreamed of peace.

Through the years, back and forth, dock to dock, walking or driving off; Dover to Calais—mal de mer in a hydrofoil; from Finland to Estonia, Argentina to Uruguay, St. John, New Brunswick, to Grand Manan Island, and Hyannis to Nantucket. Across the Hudson River between New Jersey and New York, and to Block Island, from Connecticut. Many crossings, soon completed.

Maneuvering through the evergreen San Juan Islands off Washington State, which appeared like mammoth turtles in the gray mist, and veddy British Victoria island from glamorous Vancouver. Across the Chilean lakes, framed by perfect volcanic cones; St. Kitts to Nevis in iridescent Caribbean water; in San Francisco, past that fog-wreathed Rock: Alcatraz.

Flashes of memory from tiny voyages. The clinging villages of Cinque Terre along Italy's Ligurian Coast. Drizzley Liverpool, on a "ferry 'cross the Mersey." The archipelago stretching from pine-covered Finland to Sweden, and coming upon the chocolate-cake darkness of Santorini's caldera, And the mundane, crowded vaporetti of Venice, ferrying crowds of tourists and locals throughout that most poignant city, so awesome at plummy dusk.

Miss a ferry by a minute and you're stuck on shore 'til the next comes along, which may be awhile. My first husband and I were camping along the Norwegian fjords in a Volkwagen pop-top camper, when our sons were two and four, enjoying the right to pull up and camp just about anywhere, as long as we were respectful of the land. (Comes, I think, from lots of land and few people; imagine that privilege in California.)

One sunny day, as hubby drove our camper off the ferry, I stopped on the stairs to tie my son's shoe and before I knew it, the gangplank was up, the ferry pulled away, and hubby was swinging his arms frantically from the receding dock, becoming frighteningly smaller and smaller. Despite my anguished cries, the ferry would not return us to him. No diapers, no money, no ID, and no idea where we were going—with two toddlers in tow! These were days before cell phones. I felt lost and despairing.

Within minutes I discovered that at day's end we would return to that same dock. The captain provided ice cream and makeshift diapers for the kids, and I relaxed a bit. But now I feared that hubby didn't know we'd return, and hadn't stayed put. I figured we'd never find him, that we'd keep missing each other like in a bad movie. I would be dumped at the little ferry dock and have to beg for money to call the American Embassy in Oslo, and they would be closed, I would become a bag lady with two waifs . . . a woman without a country.

I never felt so relieved as at that twilight when I saw a pacing figure looming larger as we headed toward the dock we had left that morning. We embraced as if we had been torn asunder by war. He had filled the camper sink with cherries picked from local trees, which we gobbled down, giggling with joy, our shirts stained in juice, our family reunited. That ferry nightmare over. ✒

GETTING AROUND

Public transportation can be fun, efficient, and cheap—as well as challenging, especially in summer when crowded buses and subways may not be air-conditioned. But public transport is one sure way to experience reality—confusion, dirt, and all. City buses, subways, jitneys, trams, cable cars—if you can figure them out, you'll feel good about yourself, and get wherever you need to go like the locals. Just find out what and where you have to pay, and have the change or token ready. Sometimes there's honor-system ticketing. Ask questions if there's an info kiosk, or find a local who speaks English. Study maps and routes, and learn the signage.

Taxis

Taxis are not the most inexpensive means of transport, and not often the fastest. But they are probably the simplest.

If the taxi driver is not using a meter, and if the fare sounds too high, either pass or try and bargain a bit, but agree ahead of time on the fare. It's best to check with a concierge, if possible, to get an idea of a fair fare: They are often doubled or tripled for tourists, especially in major cities. Remember, if you're on your own, no one will witness your pricing agreement, so write it down, and show the driver the amount agreed on. You can tip a bit more at the end, if you choose. As a solo taxi rider, you're probably paying the same rate as a group of four—still, if you want door-to-door service, a taxi will get you there safely.

If you know that you'll be needing a taxi after dark, get the number of a taxi service and call or have someone call a few minutes before you'll need it. And bring your lodging's address and phone with you.

Bicycles, Scooters, Motorcycles

Biking and cycling is as much an activity as a mode of transportation, and many tours are set up for bikers (see Chapter 5, Soloing with Others). Renting a bike might be the perfect way to get around on a sunny day, especially in the countryside or within a resort, and many cities also have bike paths. Faster than walking, healthy, usually inexpensive and fun—biking is one of those activities that seems even better when you're far from home. If you're alone, just be sure you carry water, know your route, and take it easy when you tire.

You can ship a bike in a hard-shell case or cardboard box— airlines provide huge bicycle boxes, or get one at a bicycle shop. Trains often have designated spaces for bikes.

Scooters and motorcycles can be rented by the day in many resort areas and cities. You (usually) get a helmet and some advice, if you ask, but these machines are dangerous if you aren't careful—I've had several friends break limbs. I've ridden on the back of scooters in Greece, Bermuda, and Block Island but I felt as vulnerable as I did exhilarated, so I never scootered solo.

Ferries

I love ferries, be they slow boats, car accessible or foot only, hydrofoils, commuter boats, or overnighters. Ferries are not only economical public transport, but they can be veritable minicruises. The Greek Islands, the Norwegian fjords and the Alaska coast are perfect places to use public transport with overnight facilities in lieu of cruise ships. You can stop and go and stay as long as you want at any port, and the character of the port will not change the way it would when a larger vessel pulls into the harbor and the crowds descend.

On Foot

For the least expensive, healthiest, slowest, and often most interesting mode of transportation, put on comfortable shoes, throw on appropriate layers, smear on sunscreen, bring some water, and walk. Start early so you don't wind up in the dark, and have an idea of where you're ending up. But don't be afraid to get lost or change your mind if you see something special—one of the great joys of walking is the serendipity.

I love to walk alone, forgetting time and distance when I'm in a densely layered city or on a country road. I look up at the tops of the trees and the clouds and the facades and down at the ants in a row and the pavement design and the zinnias in wooden tubs. I study people and the way they walk, watch cars whizzing by and, of course, scrutinize window displays. (I'm not as crazy about walking around suburbs—although even the wash hanging from windows can be picturesque).

One of the loveliest overseas traditions is the early evening walk—*paseo* in Spain, *passeggiata* in Italy, *peripato* in Greece— even the names tingle with pleasure. This walk is the equivalent of "cruising" in cars, but so much nicer. People stroll, usually in one direction, stopping for ice cream or to say hello to friends, or to flirt and kiss. And it's healthy!

For a solo traveler this evening stroll may be a bit daunting, as everyone will seem to be laughing together or hand in hand, but I have learned to enjoy the romance in the air and share the pleasure, knowing that I have experienced it, and will again.

When you're traveling, try for at least one good walk a day, whether you have a destination in mind or not. Towns and cities and many historical districts throughout the world now have areas that ban cars, and these are the best places of all to walk. I remember strolling in Bruges at dawn, with swans tinted pink in the golden waterways, and in Buenos Aires, where ornate tearooms beckoned me to stop in for a sip. And in the evening, Argentine tango bars are smoky and sultry—walk by the doorways and all kinds of thoughts come into your head. It takes some guts to walk in alone, but I did, and enjoyed every minute.

RESOURCES

By Air

Because it's there. Don't care to trek to Everest on your own? Mountain flights offer a panoramic encounter with the highest peaks on earth. The plane departs from Kathmandu and flies alongside the Himalayas for eye-level views of the snowy peaks, and then brings you back in one hour. Cruising close to the awesome massifs of rocks and ice is mind-boggling. As the aircraft takes off and heads toward the east, you see Gosainthan, also called Shisha Pangma, As the plane glides along, the mountains come closer, and then Everest is before you. These spectacular mountain flights are offered by a number of airlines, and can be booked when you get to the area.

Exotic Journeys, Inc. Runs an Everest base-camp trek. *800/ 554–6342; www.exoticjourneys.com*

NEC Travels and Tours. Coordinates several Nepal tours. *01/ 416758; www.nectravels.com*

By Train
Orient-Express Peru. The *Hiram Bingham* luxury train (a partnership between Orient-Express and PeruRail) travels between Cuzco and Machu Picchu. *084/238722; www.perurail.com*

Rail Europe. Eurail passes, tickets, and deals. *877/257–2887; www.raileurope.com*

By Bus
Perillo Tours. Guided bus tour packages, including a popular two-week Northern Italy trip. *800/431–1515; www.perillotours. com*

World Discovery Tours. Sightseeing buses cover many destinations. *800/788–7885; www.tauck.com*

9

Successful Solo Lodging

Some people are adept at quantum physics. I know hotels. I've seen more hotel rooms than a New York City call girl on speed-dial. For years I've poked around lodgings throughout the world for both travel agent and consumer guidebooks, and one thing I've learned is that you never know what you'll find. Checking out a hotel room in St. Thomas, I walked in on a guy sitting at a desk, naked. He invited me to stay but I declined. In Bermuda, I opened the door and found a couple asleep in bed. I don't know who of the three of us was most surprised. I do get management approval, knock, and say "Housekeeping," but not everyone listens.

Critiquing as I go, I've stayed in everything from a cubicle in a former brothel to Presidential suites bigger than my condo. Along the way I've figured out that especially when you're on your own, where you stay makes a difference, but a room doesn't have to be expensive. And you don't have to be a physicist to pick the right one.

For my money, you get better cultural exposure and a truer sense of place if you stay in locally owned establishments, quirks and all. Many of my favorite rooms have been more weird than lavish: In Prague, my charming room had two faucets that said "cold" so I memorized which one was really hot. In Luxembourg, my room had no closet or wardrobe, but a great ceramic fireplace. (I kept my clothes in my luggage and lighted a nice fire, and didn't miss the closet.) Then there was the tiny airport cubicle in a Brazilian airport—dark, a single bed, tiny like a bear's lair. Nothing to do there but sleep. I enjoyed the futon on the floor of the ryokan in Kyoto, in a room with sliding screens and a deep soaking tub, from where I watched the April snow. A former maharajah's palace was a grand shelter on a rainy night in Jaipur. In a coconut plantation in the Philippines, I woke up to coconut milk and coconut pancakes on a balcony in a palm-fringed lagoon.

That said, quirky isn't my thing all the time and it likely isn't yours. Sometimes I seek a cozy B&B that replicates some of the comforts of home; sometimes, a cookie-cutter chain room with space to arrange familiar clutter. In the end, think carefully about how prominently you want your lodging to figure into your solo experience.

Before You Book

Your needs and desires may change, sometimes day to day within a destination. If you're spending lots of time in the room, or you're on business where you'll be working with and hosting others, a large space with a plasma TV may work best. If you're in the Canadian Rockies, or near Lake Geneva, or the Dome of the Rock in Jerusalem, a room with a view might matter more than one that accommodates your laptop's Internet connectivity. When the weather's great, a balcony is wonderful, as is a nearby waterfront location where you may want to stroll. When you need even a little extra maintenance, a hotel with a concierge will usually cater to solo travelers. If you're hardly in your room, you just may prefer to save money for other things.

BUDGET

How much can you afford to spend on accommodations? If your budget is tight, you have to make hard choices, such as between a longer trip or better lodgings, great food or great rooms, or even where in the world you go. If you can spend about $100 a night, you can manage just about anywhere without too much sacrifice. Obviously money goes farther in Podunk than Paris, but even in most big cities you can work within that range, if you're careful. Think creatively about how you budget. If you allocate $100 a night, you don't have to spend that every night: Think about spending $50 for three nights at an inexpensive lodging, then, when it's worth it to you, splurge on a deluxe room with a balcony.

LOCATION

If you're visiting the Grand Bazaar in Istanbul, where you'll be purchasing a brass tray and rug, you'll probably wind up buying bigger and better and brassier, and avoid a backache, if you seek accommodations within a few minutes' walk.

Think about where you want to spend most of your time, especially after dark, and consider choosing a hotel nearby. Finding transportation door to door after that grand dinner or concert can be dicey. Walking alone at night is rarely advisable, and you don't want to be wasting time commuting or waiting for transport when a closer lodging will allow a quick walk or ride, and more time for fun.

When You Book

Book far in advance, especially if you'll be near a destination during holiday and festival times. Do you really want to retreat to the 'burbs after the Toronto film festival? Or board a subway for the outer boroughs after a day of taking on Manhattan?

After disembarking from a ferry on the small Greek island of Limnos, I soon realized that I had arrived a week before the hotels opened—and the few alternative lodgings were filled. I didn't panic. I called several hotels, just in case, told them my plight, and one volunteered to let me stay, even though it was in the midst of a deep cleaning, and not officially open. The manager gave me some linens, I chose a room with a dazzling view of the sea, and I had the entire place to myself, kind of like in *The Shining*, but not at all scary. I could run up and down the halls topless singing "The Star Spangled Banner" and no one would care. (You'll have to guess if I did.) I went into the kitchen and found a spoon and bowl and had some yogurt and honey for breakfast, sitting in the enormous dining room by myself. It was a memorable solo experience—and the closest I've come to spending a night on a bench. Lesson: never give up. A few more booking tips:

Safety first. Select a hotel with room-entry only through a main lobby, rather than separate entrances for each room (Marriott Courtyards, Hampton Inns, and Days Inn are among lodgings designed with security in mind.). Avoid ground-level rooms. Even if they're only accessible through the lobby, their windows expose you more readily to thieves and noisy passersby. Ask for a room in a well-lighted area. Book rooms with smoke alarms and fire escapes; if not, be extra vigilant: Don't accept a room at the end of a long, isolated hall with no exit. Choose rooms below the fifth floor for access to fire ladders. (For more on "Lodging Safety," see below.)

Strive for best rates. Avoid paying the rack rate—listed on price sheets—the rate a place would hope for, but savvy solo travelers can almost always beat. Deal with hotels individually rather than through their toll-free number, as front desks have lots of latitude when it comes to negotiating; the higher the room price, the more the potential discount. (For more on saving, see Chapter 2, Planning & Saving.)

If you know you're checking in late, especially at a B&B, advise the front desk so they'll hold the room or leave a key.

Make reservations for at least the first and last nights of your trip. If you're on your own you'll have greater flexibility, so if you're not satisfied with SoHo, you can scoot, and if you adore Malta you can remain as long as the knights did in the Middle Ages. Just cover your arrival and departure, and you'll be free to float. That said, for ultrapopular lodgings like the government-sponsored paradores in Spain and pousadas in Portugal, you may have to book a year ahead.

Check the pet policy. If you're traveling with Fido, ensure that the lodging allows pets. Likewise, if you have no desire to mingle with animals, ask about the pet policy. (For more on this subject, see Chapter 6, Traveling with Pets.)

At the Lodging

Keep bargaining. Bring a business or organization card, and ask for discounted rates if you haven't already gotten a discount. Or, just give the front desk a reason to save face and drop the rate. Last resort: "It's my birthday (divorce, anniversary)."

Try this line for an upgrade. If rooms are available, then an upgrade usually is, too. As a solo traveler, you can impress a front desk with gentle spunk. I've used variations on the following: "I travel the world on my own and see lots of plain rooms. I don't know if it's possible, but if you could upgrade me tonight—space available, of course—it would be such a joy to me, a really special night." Chutzpah, or just being a savvy soloist? A bit of both, perhaps, but I often get the upgrade.

Inspect the room before your bags are placed inside. Solo travelers are often offered the least desirable rooms, even when paying a single supplement. To avoid this, mention politely when you make the reservation, and again when you check in, that you prefer to see the premises first. The tendency will be to give you a room that passes muster. Don't hesitate to reject ones that are not clean or are—or will be—too noisy (street-side, above a club, next to the elevator).

Avoid both obvious and hidden surcharges. Weigh the costs of calling from the room versus using your cell phone or phone card. Use the minibar for emergencies only. Avoid high laundry and dry-cleaning prices (unless as a gift to yourself for going it alone). And that shiny box of assorted chocolates on your desk might not be free, or worth opening. Check your bill carefully, and question charges you don't understand.

Reclaim your passport. If you have to leave your passport when you register, be sure to get it back, ASAP. Keep a photocopy on you and another in your luggage, too.

Holy Ping-Pong!

My niece, Erica, has traveled quite a bit on her own, and offers this choice anecdote, which illustrates how easy it is to meet people when you stay in small, interesting accommodations.

I was staying at a monastery on the Swiss–Italian border. Six monks and a few guests were there. The monks mostly kept to themselves, and the guests enjoyed the tranquillity and mountain scenery. Their monastery, St. Bernard, is about an hour and a half from Monte Bianco (Mont Blanc), and right in the middle of the Alps. The stone building is set in high meadows with purple flowers and cows with bells on. In the distance, on top of the green, are the snow-capped mountains, and all this you can see from the monastery windows.

The place has full board, so the guests sat around the table together (sans monks) for dinner. During one meal, one of the guests mentioned that Pater Rene—the Ping-Pong champ—lived there. When I questioned further they told me he was the oldest monk, as well as a painter and sculptor.

I sort of laughed when they said he was a great Ping-Pong player, as I am really pretty good, and couldn't imagine an old man being able to keep up. But before I knew it, a date was set: that night, around 8, we would all gather in the basement and have a Ping-Pong tournament. And Pater Rene would come.

When we went downstairs I was shocked to find a huge stone room—scary and holy looking—with nothing in sight except for a mint-condition Ping-Pong table right in the center of the room. A few of us started hitting the ball around, and I was clearly the most advanced player there.

But then Pater Rene came down the stairs (it took him awhile, he walks slowly). And everybody stepped back to let me have the first game with him. The sight was hardly formidable—across the table stood an elderly man, no taller than 4 foot 10, wearing a black cloak and a long wooden cross dangling from his neck. The ropes at his waist barely held the cloth on.

"Andiamo," he said.

And so we played. And to my complete shock, as soon as the paddle was in his hands, his whole figure lit up (as if illuminated by God himself).

He was hopping back and forth on the other side of the table, slamming balls back to my side left and right—many too fast for me to even see, let alone hit. He looked like a tiny, fast bird, leaping here and there, the wooden cross at his neck in full swing.

He beat me by 10 points at least, but kept asking for another game. (All this, you have to remember, was spoken in Italian—and keeping score was tough: "dici otto, dici.")

I was the best Ping-Pong player he had met at the monastery he kept telling me, asking again for another game. And then when the other players wanted a chance, he offered to play a doubles match, as long as I would be his partner. We never lost.

We became friends for the rest of my visit, playing Ping-Pong in the stone cellar every night. His frail form could barely make it down the stairs each time, but as soon as he picked up the paddle, he had the spirit in him. By the end, I had learned to beat him about half the time, and he was constantly giving me pointers on my game. When I returned from that trip I was good enough to make the varsity team at my college.

Months later I received an e-mail from one of my fellow guests: Pater Rene had died 3 months after our chance meeting. He was 91. 🐾

Ask for late checkout. If you want to spend more time in the area, request a late checkout as far in advance as you can. Most hotels will offer a couple of hours extra, but then may charge a fee—inquire. At least ask if the front desk might keep your bag in a locked room while you explore for the day.

LODGING SAFETY

Don't let the desk blab your room number. If the hotel staff announces your room, ask for another and explain why. Alert them that you're concerned about security and that you need them to respect that. Have the bellhop accompany you to and from your room if you feel more comfortable.

Avoid stairs. Stairwells may offer exercise, but are an ideal spot for crime. Elevators are generally safer, but don't board one if you're not wild about your car mates, and if you want to back out gracefully, pretend you forgot your key. Otherwise, have your key ready in the elevator so you don't have to fumble at your door. And if someone follows you out and tries to attack, knock on doors and scream for help.

Don't advertise. Don't put the tag on the door that asks for maid service, but do use the Do Not Disturb sign and keep the TV on when you're out.

Reject all pop-ins. Don't let a hotel staffer or anyone else in your room unless you're expecting someone; otherwise, call the front desk and ask the person to wait outside for clearance.

Lock it all. Lock all doors, and windows, even when you're in the room. Lock valuables in a safe. Lock your luggage. If you're issued a spare room key or key card, don't leave it in your room for someone to take. Also consider bringing your own personal alarm, such as a motion sensor that hangs on the inside door-knob and will go off if the outer knob is turned.

Be your own fire warden. Know where the exits are. In case of fire, stay low and cover cracks in doors and windows with wet towels; wait in your room for help if the door is hot, or break a window if needed, and use that fire escape. Know where your key is, and take it with you in case of emergency. And, on a lighter note, if you're really safety conscious, sleep in something you can run out in. (PJs with attached feet won't do.)

WHERE TO STAY

Following are typical lodgings and lodging arrangements you encounter as a solo traveler. I list favorites when I can: look for "Lea's Picks."

Single Rooms

The best deals for solo travelers are rooms designed and priced for one occupant, and you'll find these mainly in foreign countries. However, they're often the smallest, worst-placed rooms available. (In older properties single rooms were often servants' quarters.) The rooms may be carved out of attics, the bathrooms whittled out of closets. I remember the primary colors in a single room in a modern Stockholm hotel, tighter than a ship's cabin, and the narrow bed in a below-ground room with no window, in Belgrade. If you aren't spending much time in your room, it may not matter. And remember, you can use the property's public rooms just as much as those paying for double rooms or suites. Write in the business center, read and meet others in the lobby or sitting room, swim in the pool. You can be a smart soloist if you use the entire place as an extension of your room.

Resorts for Singles & Soloists
More popular toward the end of the last century (the 20th, that is), these informal, adults-only resorts have numerous activities and communal dining. Club Meds, among other single resorts, allow you to sidestep the single supplement if you take on a same-gender roommate.

Concierge Floors in Major Hotels
Concierge (or Business or Executive) floors are havens for solo travelers. Security is often heightened, with a floor concierge and special elevators. The exclusive lounge is a comfortable area for schmoozing, reading newspapers, or grazing (usually with complementary nibbles and/or drinks), and a free continental breakfast may jump-start your morning. Ask if these floors are available when you make reservations at hotels catering to business travelers. Rooms are slightly costlier, but the payback is worth it. Chains with these floors include Doubletree Executive Hotels, Holiday Inn Select, Hyatt, and Radisson.

Hotels with Concierges
In today's service market, concierges duties have expanded; some even double as masseuses. "Ambassadors of the House" at Tamarind Cove in Barbados greet guests at the airport, accompany them to the hotel, and continue to offer personal care. Guests at Australia's Hyatt Regency Coolum can ask their "Resort Host" where to go, what to do, and how to get there. And all

MGM Mirage Properties, including, the Las Vegas Bellagio Resort & Casino, have concierges—usually more than one—and a super-attentive staff.

Solo-Friendly Chains

You know what you're getting when you stay in a chain, and that can be comfortable indeed. Frequently offering good deals for soloists are Fairmont Hotels & Resorts, Four Seasons Hotels, Italy's Jolly Hotels, and Sonesta Worldwide Properties. Among the better budget choices are Country Inns & Suites, Microtel Inns and Suites, and the small Park Inn chain.

Inns

At inns you can dine in, and walk a few steps back to your room. They're typically casual places and other guests tend to be especially friendly. I have detoured many times to overnight at my favorites.

Lea's Picks. The Inn Spa at Poplar Springs, Casanova, Virginia. *www.poplarsrpingsinn.com*; Ram's Head Inn Shelter Island, New York, *www.shelterislandinns.com*

B&Bs

Beds-and-breakfasts are right-on for solo travelers. Among the standard amenities are a private room (and, often, a private bath) full breakfasts at communal tables, drinks in the parlor, the opportunity to trade information and travel stories, a friendly house cat or dog to pet, and pastry and coffee anytime.

When researching my book on B&Bs and inns in New England, I stayed at hundreds of properties, and what made or broke them most times were the owners: sometimes in your face, sometimes not around, always different. You never know when you'll come upon a Basil Fawlty or some other similarly memorable character, and traveling solo, you'll often connect.

One socialite-owner of a stylish B&B in upstate New York provided extravagant touches including a Matisse portrait (of her mother!) on the wall, and lavish, gourmet dinners she prepared with much chopping of fresh herbs, and outrageous stories of her infamous lover—but only for special guests. We became friends, and she invited me to fascinating dinner parties and other events—a bonus of arriving alone.

Lea's Picks. Cliffside Inn, Rhode Island, *www.legendaryinssof newport.com*; John's Gate Bed & Breakfast, Niagara-on-the-Lake, Ontario, Canada, *www.johnsgate.com*; Tasburgh House Hotel, Bath, England, *www.bathtasburgh.co.uk*; Le Clos de la Rose, Saint-Cyr sur Morin, France, *www.rosa-gallica.fr*; B&B Paula in Holland, Haarlem, The Netherlands, *www.enjoy-europe.com/ b&bpaula*

Homestays

To feel really at home, stay *in* a home, the easiest way for solo travelers to meet and live with locals. Others may be sharing the house as well, usually with the family, and often there's a minimum stay, maybe a week or so. This alternative varies from deluxe to less private, less charming, and less regulated than a B&B experience—and less expensive. You may have to share a room or a bath, but if you're willing to spend a bit more, you can often negotiate this. Kitchen privileges are usually included, you'll probably have a key to come and go as you please, and sometimes a private entrance. The family may even guide you around—maybe for a fee.

Obviously, homes and hygiene vary, so check on this aspect, and get referrals before committing. Some travel packages cover air costs and lodging, and could include a couple of meals a day.

My favorite home stay was with the Laird of McDonald. (No, not Ronald McDonald! The lord of the McDonald clan, on the Isle of Skye, in Scotland.) An inn adjoined the mansion, but as I was solo, I lodged with the laird and lady; I stayed in their son's room, amid toy trains on the shelves and boyish-blue decor. The laird was elegant and formal in his plaid kilt (no, I didn't peek— I was his guest, after all); his wife was bottle-blond, talkative, and a cooking teacher. Maybe they hosted guests because of taxes, but whatever the reason, it was a bonnie, bonnie sojourn I'll never forget.

Welcome Traveller (www.welcometraveller.org), operating in 40 countries, is a hospitality/homestay club that matches up travelers and hosts.

Hostels

What's the best lodging choice to meet other solo travelers from around the world? Probably hostels. Sleeping arrangements are often in women's and men's dorms, so you'll be listening to strange snores, but if you don't mind the basics and lack of privacy, hostels are great deals, and not just for young travelers. Separate cubicles or family rooms might be available, and for a bit more you may be able to book these if no families are around.

Usually there's a communal kitchen, and separate showers and toilet facilities for men and women. Most hostels are clean, but check them out first; you can bring your own sleep-sack or linens and towels, or rent them there. Curfews are enforced, so you'll need to be time-conscious. And, sorry to say, safety can be an issue when you're sleeping among strangers, so be extra cautious about leaving money or valuables around. And leave the silk teddies for private rooms.

Rented Rooms/Guesthouse

As you get off the ferries in the Greek islands, people will be holding signs, "Rooms for Rent." What a wonderful, flexible way to travel, ferrying island to island, choosing a room as you dock, and staying as long as you wish. Especially if you have lots of time, this option is cost-efficient, but insist on seeing the rooms before committing. My friend Jen suggests that public areas can be deceiving—don't pay 'til you've seen not only the guestroom but the bathroom, and turn the tap to see if there's enough hot water. Prices are low—maybe half of what you'd pay at a small, basic hotel.

I've found the majority of rented rooms to be cheery and clean, usually with a shared bath. Meals are not provided, unless stated up front, although there may be cooking facilities, as modest as a hot plate. Airport and train-station accommodations desks will often have listings, and signs are often in windows near transportation hubs. Off-season, when larger lodgings may be closed, rented rooms may be the only game in town.

Time-Shares

If you like counting on a comfortable apartment or condo, this is a great way for a solo traveler to make friends and revisit them; enjoy places, and return. And even better, you can probably swap your timeshare for another, somewhere else in the world. These lodgings are kept in good order, with ample space and generic taste, as maintenance is controlled. Just bring the ca-ching to buy your share, and you're in the game.

Home Swapping

Not for the faint-hearted, this deal requires you to give up the sanctity of your home for a short while, while you invade someone else's. I'd use an agency, although you can swap through friends, word-of-mouth, bulletin boards in grocery stores, or on the Web. When you swap informally, you have less control, and if you're not paying a small agency fee, you could wind up with a marble-floored pied-à-terre with no bed. True tale; risky business.

At a minimum, ask for pictures and parameters, address and phone, agree on a deposit (to cover breakage and pilferage), and check for insurance on both ends. Also, try to get a few references, preferably from previous exchanges.

As for your place, remove valuables and breakables, use a cleaning service or devote a long weekend, fix up anything potentially dangerous, and ask a friend to look in while you're gone, to tattle if necessary.

A colleague who swapped a Manhattan apartment for one in Paris left her apartment neat and clean; the one she selected had high ceilings, ornate chandeliers and an iron-railed balcony overlooking the Eiffel Tower. Problem is, you couldn't get to it. Boxes and stacks of old magazines blocked the balcony, piled high as the tower, probably there since the turn of the millennium.

RESOURCES

General Lodging Sites

Connecting: Solo Travel News. Network on the Web. Find B&Bs, hostels, resorts, and discount hotels. Caveat: the network accepts site listings as offered and makes no independent effort to review or verify claims. *www.cstn.org*

SoloTravelPortal.com. Get the skinny on single rooms. An accommodations page is updated frequently. *www. solotravelportal.com*

Small Hotel Chains

Hotel d'Inghilterra. Furnished with antiques, in the heart of Rome's Spanish Steps area. Two-night shopping package available; attentive staff. *Via Bocca di Leone 14, 06/699811; www. hoteldinghilterraroma.it*

Red Carnation. Choose from nine luxury boutique hotels in England, South Africa, Switzerland, and the United States. *877/ 955–1515; www.redcarnationhotels.com*

Relais & Chateaux. Strictly administered, deluxe group of independently owned chateaux, country houses, manors, and quality restaurants worldwide that cater to solo travelers. *800/ 735–2478 or 212/856–0115; www.relaischateaux.fr/site/us*

The Springs Resort and Spa and Andalusian Court. Spanish/ Moorish-style boutique resorts with spas and fitness centers. *619/297–0009; www.thespringsresortandspa.com*

chapter 10

Eating Alone

There's only one thing lonelier than sleeping alone, and that's . . . eating alone." So philosophizes a regular patron at the restaurant featured in *Mostly Martha*, a wry movie about a love-starved star chef.

Yes, indeed, some people will endure anything—even a lifetime of bad sex—just to avoid eating solo.

On the other hand, M. F. K. Fisher, the late, great food and travel writer, gloried in the solo dining experience. In *Long Ago in France*, she writes about a return trip to a city, ". . . I went off, feeling infantile to keep a date I had made with myself. There was nothing really furtive about it, and I could have easily said the truth, that I wanted to dine *alone* in Dijon . . .!"

Some deal with dining alone as a peaceful, sensual treat—a chance to concentrate on the joy of food and reflect on their day. Others would rather run into the restaurant kitchen, stir steaming pots of tripe, serve it to 10-percent tippers, and then scrape it off 100 plates—anything, rather than eat by themselves.

I'll be honest. I don't love eating solo. Sometimes I don't even like it much. But even worse, I don't like the idea of not experiencing *everything* wonderful when I travel, and that includes fine dining, casual grazing, nightlife, and any pleasure that I would enjoy if I were with someone.

I remember one Thanksgiving in the Cameron Highlands of Malaysia. I was by myself in a faux Tudor inn set amid tea-leaf terraced hills. I was on assignment and missing my family. But I reluctantly hauled myself out of my beamed little room into a beamed little dining room, and ordered a chicken drumstick, silently wishing myself a Happy Thanksgiving. The waiter was solicitous, but I was shocked and thrilled when he brought the chicken with a tiny paper American flag he had drawn—stuck in its thigh. He somehow knew. We smiled. That difficult meal alone remains a golden memory of that holiday, and of my travels.

Debunking the Stigma

I know what you're thinking. If you eat alone, you'll be perceived as a lonely-heart, unable to be with someone. Yes, eating is considered a communal pastime, best enjoyed with like-minded indulgers, who can comment, taste, and share. You can feed each other, and nuzzle and play footsie. Dining with others is an appropriate setting to toast and gift and sometimes, even propose.

However, you can also bicker and yell and judge and sit in silence and throw rigatoni in your partner's lap. And even separate, as my first husband and I did, at a table in front of a crackling fireplace in a lovely restaurant on our 20th anniversary.

I would have rather dined alone that time, for sure.

I remember how I felt as a kid when I saw an old man (was he 45? 50?) sitting by himself in a cafeteria in Miami Beach at five in the afternoon—an early bird, as I guess I was, sitting with my grandfather. Pity filled my innocent little heart, and a whole story unfolded in my mind. No one was in the man's life, I imagined. His wife had died, his children had moved away to the other coast, spending what little pension he had left. They never visited him in his hot little efficiency apartment. He was alone, and with every mouthful, closer to a lonely, premature death.

Just because he was eating by himself.

My current not-so-innocent heart now figures that the guy back then was probably fortifying himself for a late date with his snowbird hottie. He was hungry!

But that's one of the problems of eating alone—our own negative perceptions, stoked by our own past experiences and misconceptions. Those of us who eat alone are often the most self-secure, gutsiest, and most successful of anyone. We have significant others and families and careers and more. Remember that. What makes us special is that we can choose to eat with others, or our cat, or on our own, which makes us particularly special.

TRAINING FOR A TABLE FOR ONE

If eating alone in a fine restaurant is the solo traveler equivalent of scaling Mt. Everest, then these more modest "climbs" will help you train, if you will, for your peak table-for-one-experience. Until then—and beyond—these ways of dining are also pleasurable alternatives to dining solo in restaurants—and, I bet you'll find, often preferable to dining with a companion. The options are presented here, roughly, from least to most daring.

Room Service

I always feel a bit special ordering room service. Where else do you have a spiffy server coming to your door, often rolling in and setting a table, politely serving you well-prepared food on heavy china, and then leaving you alone? You can eat standing up, or in the nude with a linen napkin tied around your neck, or prone, eating with your fingers, like a Roman emperor. On your own, nobody will tsk-tsk—and you don't have to clean up. Put the remains outside your door, and magically, they go somewhere else, usually without a call.

So for me, aside from the expense, room service is not a refuge from dining out, but an attractive option. I may eat a main meal out for lunch, and then a light meal in my room— maybe on a balcony overlooking the Colisseum, reflecting on my day in Rome; or on the bed, watching a movie classic like *Casablanca,* or with a mystery in hand. It's sensory multitasking.

One cautionary note: unless you're desperate or have completely missed the room-service window, try not to give in to the cold allure of the minibar. Besides being a caloric melt-down, a bag of chips, some cookies, a candy bar, and a bottle of water cost more than a regular meal in most restaurants.

Takeout/Picnic

A fun and cost-effective alternative to prepared meals is shopping for a picnic. Food shopping is one of the best ways to talk with locals and learn their customs, whether in a supermarket or corner store. Open-air or center-of-town marketplaces on market-days are best of all. The colors, scents, and even feel of abundant foods and assorted goods—and the raucous commerce of folks going about their daily routines make this activity worthwhile, whether you buy anything or not. Hawkers, farmers, and canny shoppers offer a shot of reality in an all-too-often touristy world. And shopping with the locals can lead to a simple, customized meal, on-site or later.

Delightful memories center on buying foodstuffs and putting a meal together. The friendly shopkeeper, the haggling in a stall of pungent, jewel-toned spices. Sharp images these, with all senses engaged. If I'm hungry right then and there, I'll spread out on a bench or on the grass, and eat gloriously, messily, as I observe the world before me. Try to remember to bring some napkins, and a bottle of water at least. If you're fussier than I am, you can pack one of those disposable plastic plates that can be washed, with a sturdy plastic knife and fork.

I've enjoyed spicy tandoori chicken on a beach near Bombay. In a field of scarlet poppies in Provence I picnicked on runny cheese (nobody to offend when you're on your own!), pistachio-studded duck pâté, a crusty baguette, sun-warmed grapes, and Beaujolais from a plastic cup. In Maine, I've sat by a lobster pound, in my car or on a wooden bench by the Atlantic, gorging on the crimson crustacean, dripping in butter. In Copenhagen, by a lake in Tivoli Gardens rosy-cheeked children played tag and smiled at me while I ate open-faced smoked-salmon sandwiches, and I smiled back with my mouth full. In Cyprus on a turreted wall looking out to the turquoise sea, I downed tangy goat cheese and olives; in Amsterdam, it was fresh herring and beer along a canal; in Tunisia, brik pastries in a green oasis of date palms and bubbling springs.

And remember, you can often bring food into your room for a private picnic (check ahead if you're not sure of your lodging's policy). Groceries, delis, or convenience stores with salad bars or takeout are sprinkled throughout most cities. In London, watching the cool autumn rain from a warmish room, I relished fish-and-chips doused in vinegar, washed down with steaming Earl Grey tea. It felt as cozy as home.

In Your Lodging

If you like the idea of going out to eat without the hassle of going *outside* to eat, a lovely compromise is dining in the public area of your own lodging. You'll get the chance to clean up, enjoy a served meal, drink your fill, and then just walk back to your room.

If this appeals, make sure to book a place that offers meals, especially dinner. Major hotels often provide both informal and fancier choices, but for solo travelers who enjoy eating out, a small hotel or inn is perfect for comfortable dining. You may want to choose based on a lodging's reputation for good food rather than for amenities or facilities you may never use, such as the exercise room.

While I was researching a guidebook on country inns in New England, I preferred staying at lodgings known for their food. What a pleasure to relax in your room and have the aromas of buttery onions and carrots and mystery spices teasing you like food porn. And after the meal, I often join fellow lodgers in the parlor or bar area for some good conversation over coffee or cognac. It's really easy to socialize in a small lodging, and not awkward at all to say goodnight and walk a few steps to bed.

Informal or Fast Food

Throughout the world you can feel comfortable at fast-food restaurants, diners, cafés, food courts, supermarkets, coffee shops, delis, brasseries, osterias, wine bars, tavernas, pubs, and cafeterias. Small cafés, bistros, and other local places that serve good simple food will be welcoming, in part because many fellow diners also will be on their own. And if you find a place you like, you can become a regular and enjoy special attention and service.

Informal establishments often have bars where singles can eat and meet. I usually choose these friendly, sometimes boisterous places and return several times—a home base away from home. The wait staff may talk back, recommending specials and sneering over poor choices, but they make you feel welcome in an offbeat, family way.

Sitting in a Parisian café along a busy boulevard, or on a piazza in Italy, it feels natural to be by yourself, as if the table you sit at is yours alone, and indeed, some tiny tables barely yield room for one. You can nurse an aperitif or Coke and snack for hours, and others will be doing the same, people-watching or just ruminating about life . . . or their navels. Great places to read or write. And observe.

Language problem? Carry a phrasebook, if possible, but someone will usually help you, perhaps in broken English. You can always use hand signals, indicate what others are eating, or even go into the kitchen and point to what you need. I've done that a few times, and laughter was a large part of the experience. I still don't know what I ate in Bosnia, meat stew I think, but it tasted good.

As for fast-food chains, worldwide they are usually no-nonsense, well-managed, relatively clean, inexpensive, reputable, easy to find—and predictable, which is both good and bad. I've been asked, "Do you want fries?" from people whose faces are ringers for those on ancient Mayan pyramids. Chains can be comforting when you're on your own. When I tire of smoked pig's feet or pickled seaweed, I can enjoy fried chicken or salad or a burger at moderate prices in a familiar setting. Then I rev up enthusiasm for more colorful places, and local foods.

Communal/Informal/Bar Seating

Japanese restaurants with sushi bars are obvious choices. You can chat with and watch the chefs, and talk to other diners. But many new restaurants—especially in big cities—are offering alternative seating, besides at bars: one or more long tables for people who want to eat and meet. And people seated with you are typically interested in conversing.

A variation for solo diners is a chef's table, often near an open kitchen where you can watch the chef perform. The experience may involve a special, set menu, served at a certain time. You usually need reservations to be part of it. The chef's table is more common in cities with lots of single people and travelers; ask if one is offered when you make your dinner reservations.

A captain's table on a cruise ship is usually occupied by VIPs, returning passengers, guests celebrating special occasions, and passengers who request to be seated there. If you wish to dine in this company, make your request at the time you book your cruise. Otherwise, you'll find that the maître d' usually attempts to seat single cruisers together, and you can request it.

Sharing a Table

Consider choosing a busy dining establishment—on purpose—and tell the waiter you'd be happy to share a table with another single or a couple, or even more. Especially overseas, you'll often find yourself sitting with others.

But not always with much conversation.

I remember a tiny tea table at Fortnum and Mason's elegant food store in London. It was hardly big enough for two, but an elderly couple joined me, averting their eyes as they sat down. We were practically touching knees, but did not converse. Eventually the man's head hit the table, and he started snoring. "He had a tiring day," his wife offered, as she continued sipping her tea. I snorted, barely stifling my giggles.

The easiest way to avoid awkward silences is to be the one to try to start a conversation: smile, say hello, and ask a question right away. After that, silence is just silence, not an issue. Some people just like quiet.

TABLE FOR ONE: BRING IT ON

Okay. You've tried some of the methods above, even enjoyed them. You're pretty sure you're capable of casual dining out without too much of a problem. Now it's time to scale Everest: a table for one at a fine restaurant. Why? Because it's there, and you deserve the finest dining imaginable. And to kick it up one more notch, let's try it on a Saturday night. Even some die-hard soloists won't warm to this idea. But then, they don't all have this book yet, or these tips for not only surviving, but enjoying the big night.

Bring stuff to do. If daydreaming and people-watching don't sustain you throughout your meal then there's no shame in keeping busy. Bring a book you really want to read, with a battery-operated book light in case it's dark. Write in a journal, write postcards, or play word games and look absolutely normal. You could tote an MP3 player and discreetly listen to music. Bobbing your head Stevie Wonder–style or singing along crosses the line, of course. As does talking loudly on a cell phone. As for knitting, that's debatable!

Business props, whether you them or not, can add to your comfort level. A PDA or laptop are commonplace for business travelers, and one solo traveler I know regularly works between courses. I write notes by pen when I want to stay busy; it somehow leads more easily to talking to others, who, sometimes obtrusively, want to know what you're writing. And when I'm in a foreign country, I often pass the time studying the language from my pocket-size phrasebook. If you do this every time you dine, you might even learn the language—a nice alternative to dining with a companion who's not teaching you a thing.

Only stick around for a few courses. If you feel uncomfortable once you're seated, order just a drink or maybe an appetizer, and then see if you want to order more. No one says you have to eat a whole meal. You could enjoy cheese and wine ahead of time in a café, or dessert afterward at an ice-cream shop or bakery. This will allow you to experience a special restaurant for only as long as you're comfortable, and you might even save a few bucks.

How to Get Good Service

One way to achieve some measure of good service is to ask your concierge to make your reservation. He or she can request a good table and special attention, and the restaurant will try to please if they're smart enough to realize the power of volume business. Once while lunching at a famous—and expensive—Paris restaurant, the waiter ignored me. For hours I got snide remarks and glazed looks as I sat with my unopened wine and unbrushed crumbs. Afterwards I complained to the manager, who half-listened and offered me an aperitif. When I reminded him that the reservation was made by the concierge at a famed hotel (I named them both), and I would have to tell him of the experience, the manager brought the waiter over and forced him to apologize. And then the manager comped the meal.

If you don't know where to eat, let the concierge suggest a restaurant and you'll be more likely to get good service. And if you don't have a concierge, walk into a hotel that has one and when he or she is not busy, explain your situation and ask if they might make a reservation for you. This works for me. Offer $5 or $10 or more based on the concierge's effort.

If you're more of a do-it-yourselfer, you've obviously capable of making the reservation yourself, but from the get-go be as daunting as possible. Consider this a game you want to win. Call ahead for a reservation, and make it memorable—speak assertively, use titles, and make your request clear. Something like:

"Hello, this is Dr. Victoria Hunter and I've heard incredible things about your restaurant. I want to reserve your best table, and I'll come early so I can get it. What time do you open?"

This kind of repartee establishes that you're aware of the restaurant's reputation, you're not going to accept a seat by the

continued on p. 164

Tastes Like Chicken?

Frogs' legs, snails, wild boar, tripe, kidney, squid in ink, zebra—when described in a foreign language, and garnished with parsley, we'll dig in. If you've eaten stews around the world you've eaten every part of an animal. Same goes for sausages: lips to tips.

I've consumed foods associated with exterminators. In a café along the Pan American Highway in Mexico, a crouton in my bowl of tomato soup had six legs. (Since then, I eat and drink carefully in Mexico—but still manage to get sick most of the time.)

In a well-known Washington, D.C., restaurant, a cricket was an unwelcome crunchy addition in an otherwise ordinary veal cacciatori. When the apoplectic manager comped the bill, I mock-whispered to my friend, "Got the cricket? Worked again!"

Lobsters look suspiciously like giant water insects, and shrimp, like little ones. In Bangkok, our group of Americans and Thais made faces as we consumed a pile of unpeeled shrimp. We Americans, of course, removed the tops, and ate the bottoms. The Thais did just the opposite.

"How can you eat the eyes and brains?" asked one disgusted American. "How can you eat the filthy waste tube?" asked an equally disgusted Thai. We solved the problem by exchanging the alternately disgusting segments, wasting nothing.

Strange, isn't it, that worms to some are as yummy as eels to others—but many of us can't stomach either. I will not eat sheep's eyes, grubs, ants, dog, or cat. I *have* eaten alligator and iguana, which taste, yes, like chicken. (Would a person used to eating reptile say that chicken tastes like iguana?)

In Chiang Mai, in the northern hills of Thailand, my friend and I trekked through the jungle on dainty-footed elephants; mine was Sarah, and when we disembarked, I was more ravenous than the pachyderm. We ran to the first decent-looking restaurant in our path, which had a snake pit by the entrance, like a lobster tank, and we selected our unlucky boa and cobra from among the wriggling masses. The boa became a burger, filled with what tasted like pebbles; the cobra was tender, but left funny ribs on the plate. (Snake also tastes like chicken, perhaps because reptilian dinosaurs are the precursors of birds.)

In Tokyo, I savored a porcelain bowlful of blush-pink gelatin, which turned out to be jellyfish. My son Rand, a magazine editor, once ate blow-fish, the possibly deadly *fugo*, for a story, but happily did not tell me about it until the critical period was over. (He also did not tell me 'til much later that he researched stories on Mafia wise guys.)

My favorite odd-food memory began with an invitation, along with another writer, as guests of a new, harbor restaurant on the Kowloon side of Hong Kong. I had been solo dining for days, and was delighted to have some company.

We first toured the kitchen, which looked like a mordant petting zoo, with cute, caged, and presumably delicious rabbits, lambs, and such, alas, awaiting selection.

Our prechosen menu was highly unusual, a sign of honor, I'm told. For an appetizer, we enjoyed sashimi of geoduc. The waiter rolled out a table with a clam atop, big as a roulette wheel, and shaved the raw foot before us. Ouch.

Shark fin soup followed; the rest of the shark sacrificed for this sup-posedly aphrodisiacal dish. I wasn't interested in making love right then, and felt terrible about the waste.

The owner, sitting with us, Buddha-like, observed our repast without touching a morsel, and his wife picked at tea and rice. My dinner com-panion, a science writer I dubbed Macho Man, bragged throughout the feast of the many icky foods he had consumed in his travels, including monkey brains and locusts. I didn't care for him, or his showy culinary sophistication.

He downed the first courses with gusto, and I liked him less with each enthusiastic bite. When he learned that dessert was to be sea fungus in milk, he exclaimed it a delicacy he had enjoyed once in China.

The main course was the most unusual of the meal—a sliced meat, mild flavor, but succulent. Macho Man chewed carefully, but couldn't rec-ognize the taste, and finally asked our hosts what we were eating.

The restaurant owner's wife, who had been silent throughout the meal, looked up from her rice, and whispered, "Deer penis."

Well now . . . Macho Man threw down his chopsticks, in a reflex action.

"Finishing that?" I questioned, chewing innocently.

A "Gotcha!" moment. I kept the menu. And yes, it tasted like chicken. ❧

restrooms, and you want to eat when the restaurant opens—the most comfortable time, because you will already have established your territory, and all who enter after you are newcomers. You don't have to face walking into a room full of talking strangers, the toughest part of the whole experience.

If you have some trouble, make up as much as you're comfortable with (a game, remember?), such as, "By the way, I'm writing about this restaurant." And there's a grain of truth in that: blogs, journals, and postcards are certainly at your disposal. Just try to make your pitch as valid and important as possible. And if the writer thing works, carry a pad and pencil when you arrive and place it on the table when you sit down. It's the same thing working journalists do; it makes some servers self-conscious (or at least conscious), which is not entirely undesirable.

When you arrive, introduce yourself as you did when you called in your reservation, though casually—"Dr. Hunter" will do. You may not get "the best" table, but you probably won't be getting the worst. Arguing where you'll be seated, and then getting relegated to a bad table anyway is not desirable. Alas, too many times, you feel less than good about yourself if you're shunted away in a dark corner like a troll.

I recently reserved a table at a glorious upscale restaurant in Miami Beach, a former Spanish-style house a block from Lincoln Road. It was 7 PM, the place had just opened, and not a table was yet occupied. So where was I placed, despite my reservation? You guessed it: the worst table in the room.

"I don't want to sit at this table," I said. "I would like to sit at *that* table." I pointed to a corner table for two with a view of the room and the garden beyond.

"But that's a 'romantic table,'" said the hostess.

"I'm a 'romantic' person," I countered. "And if you'd like a demonstration, I'll be happy to give it to you."

My cheekiness was not effective. So I shifted my approach: "I'd like to speak to the manager, please."

She paused, then looked me up and down. "I'll speak to him for you." And she left.

Now, I was ready to argue, and to tell the hostess that I write about restaurants and it would be a good idea to put me at a table where I would not be next to the busboys' station and write a bad review about the noise. But I didn't have to. The hostess returned, smiling.

"The manager says you can sit at any table you like."

And I sat at the corner table and had a lovely dinner, feeling decidedly untroll-like.

If You Still Feel Like You're on Display

After all this training and easing in you might still feel like all eyes are on you. But in a sense, that's part of what you're trying to embrace. No doubt, eating out at an elegant place is something of a big deal. People make reservations, wear dark jackets, totter around in Jimmy Choos, go through the motions and rituals of a major event. You have to enter, with many pairs of eyes scrutinizing you.

On the other hand, it's all relative. One evening when I was savoring the last remnants of blinis and caviar with my husband at the long-departed Russian Tea Room in Manhattan, the waiter tipped us off that someone famous was due any minute, dining at the table next to us. Hubby could care less, and went off to pick up our concert tickets next door, at Carnegie Hall. But I lingered for a couple of minutes, all eyes.

Sure enough, in walked Miss Monica Lewinsky, by herself, in black, staring ahead at no place in particular with a slight smile set on those notorious lips. Now that was one tough solo entrance, as otherwise sophisticated New Yorkers—including moi—openly stared. Most people in her situation would have avoided dining out in a famous restaurant. They would avoid going out at all. But she seemed to flaunt her infamy—and on her own no less—for a great bowl of borscht.

Even if we never did a notorious thing in our lives, we may feel judgmental eyes on us when we enter a dining area alone. Fine dining is a bit of theater, and solo diners, by our singularity, are the stars. So enjoy the chance to be really special. Fantasize, if you wish. Waiting for lamb chops in Prague, sipping sweet wine, I once imagined being a spy, awaiting my contact. Or act the diva, just a little bit, even if you normally don't like attention. You'll never see these diners again, so have fun and make them figure you're a mysterious, independent person. Dress daringly, depending on where you go. Smile dazzlingly. Wear dark sunglasses and look a tinge dangerous—an easy way to watch people without them knowing it.

When you dine solo you're not just eating. You can observe, listen, make plans, or make eye contact with a friendly face across the room. You have the freedom to imagine. You also have the strange and fascinating power of making other people aware of themselves, and I guarantee, you'll have some of them wishing they could switch places with you.

It can be fun, indeed.

chapter 11

Shopping

N o regrets!" That's my motto. Step into my little world and you'll find material reminders of the bigger world, all over the place. Mirrors of varied shapes and sizes on the wall behind my bed, and embroidered pillows strewn across the headboard. And set around, furniture, tea caddies, masks, frames, paintings, pots and pottery, puppets, books, clothes, a bit of this and that. Years of shopping have rewarded me with precious items, and yes, tacky ones, too. I've grown to cherish most all of them—beyond the material, to the memory.

And so many memories, through the years, of the great deals and the special people . . . the scruffy boy in Morocco who ran after me with a large painted box for $50. "Lady, Lady!" It was bulky and overpriced, so I walked away. He followed me—$45, $35, $30. He hawked as I boarded the bus. "Lady, Lady!" I still didn't want it, but he insisted and shoved it into the bus window with a smile as the engine started: "Lady, for you. Five dollars." It has been a charming part of my decor, since, but it is the boy I remember.

The blond former Soviet soldier in 1995, selling off his uniform, piece by piece. I bought his hat for the full price he asked—$10, and then gave him $5 more. He spoke in Russian and broken German about how he had worn it in his happy service in East Germany, and now he desperately needed the money. I hang it on a hook in my hall, and remember his sad smile.

In a Guatemala City general store where locals shopped, the red, gold, and blue painted wedding chest I found under a heap of cleaning rags and bought for $15; later that day I saw the exact chest in a room display in the city museum.

Walking in Cardiff Wales with my penny-pinching British friend Dorothy to a back-street shop, and discovering a sampler embroidered with birds and Biblical images by "Marianne" in 1813. Priced at $30, Dorothy held out for less, and I got it for $25. It hangs in my hall, and I remember Dorothy, now long-gone. She would be delighted by how much it has appreciated.

The collage of fabrics in a jacket I bargained for in a flea market in Aix-en-Provence. The young woman with thick hair who created it was an artist in cloth—I passed the first time around, couldn't stop thinking about it, and when I returned to the stall, the jacket was sold. So I bought an even nicer one, and never regretted it, though it cost me more.

The colorful, conical hat bought for $1 from a boat at the floating market in Thailand, its pointy shape now punctuating a collection of paintings and carvings, behind my living room sofa. The mirror I found in the back of an antique store in Lima, green and dusty and only $10. Now its hand-beaten copper frame shines in its original glory.

The ancient earthenware vessel my friend bought in an Asian country. When we flew out, he hid it in underwear (which he was wearing!) afraid that custom officials would confiscate it. (He did get envious stares walking through the airport, I noticed.) Anyway, he had chutzpah; I doubt he would have made it through today's security checks.

There are also the duds—the purchases that looked (a lot) better while I was traveling, and that I paid too much for. The glass "amethyst," the fake French antique clock, the endless sketches of cliché town squares and coastlines, the mud-colored batik cloth I have no idea how to wrap around my body.

Some mistakes I've given or thrown away, but I keep a few in the guest-room closet—keepsakes to visit now and then, and maybe rotate into the main rooms, on a whim. Why I bought them, I'm not always sure, but I certainly remember the experiences. Ugly bowl shaped like an octopus, $30. Memory of buying ugly bowl shaped like an octopus: priceless.

Shopping: The Solo Traveler's Friend

Does anyone have to convince you that shopping is a good thing? I didn't think so. Shopping is perfect for soloists: a delightful pastime on your own, offering unlimited interaction with locals, the allure of surprise, possibility and discovery, and a chance to delve deep into an interest and activity.

And if that's not enough, there's:

Material reward. A pampering pleasure: buying a keepsake, perhaps a necessity.

Exercise. Walking, lifting, running to grab the sale item, wriggling as you try on clothing, hunting for price tags, unzipping, rezipping, moving, unhanging and (sometimes) rehanging clothes, hardly realizing you're doing it— this is healthy!

Connections. As Shakespeare's Merchant of Venice said: "I will buy with you, sell with you, talk with you." With fellow shoppers and shopkeepers, artists and artisans, you'll chat, learn, bargain, laugh, and hear and tell stories, and sometimes more.

Lasting memories. Each time you enjoy your purchase you can relive and remember a travel experience: the talkative shopkeeper with the bushy mustache and heavy cologne who gave you a huge discount on the gold pocket watch; the sharp blades of sun and shade knifing through the roof slats of the stall where you bought the brass bells. Places, people, moods, environment, romance—all can be triggered by even the smallest tchotcke. Besides, shopping is fun. You know that. If you can afford it, you don't need an excuse.

SHOPPING TIPS

Your baseline rule for shopping is the "3 P's": Price, Practicality, and Portability. Does your item pass the "P" test? If not, rethink the purchase. Read on.

Budget. You don't need lots of money to shop, but you do need some. Stay within a reasonable, realistic budget, which you should figure out ahead of time. And don't fret, you can have just as much fun shopping for miniature elephants as for major emeralds (well . . . almost).

Write down things you would like to buy. A list gives you an excuse to shop, an idea of where to shop, and saves you from forgetting special items, gifts, and sizes. It also thwarts impulse shopping, unless something is really a "wow."

Comparison price if you're looking for something specific. Don't be caught in the moment with no idea of what an item usually costs. It's hard to bargain effectively that way, and hard to know if you're overpaying. To check out fair prices before you shop, you can visit stores at home, or go online.

Be precise in pricing. Special calculators found in travel stores can help you price in the country's currency. Be sure you know the going exchange rate, which changes daily.

Carry some cash. Often you can get better prices when you don't have to use credit cards. ATMs are now just about everywhere. Make sure you get unmarred, nonripped cash, count your change both giving and taking, and carry your money discreetly and securely.

Buy good things at good places. The higher the item's expense, the less you can afford a major mistake. You don't want to buy a fake and pay more than you should, or depend on your bargaining skills to get a fair price when there's lots of money at stake. Be conservative when you're dealing in big-deal costs, and stick to reputable shops. Museum shops and government shops offer traditional, fairly priced, top-quality goods, and are a good place to start. I have a beloved old ceramic rooster I bought in a

LEA'S & JUDY'S TIPS FOR CLOTHES SHOPPING

My friend Judy dresses to die-for, and has the best eye around for buying beautiful clothing at good prices. She can spot a designer label item on sale from across a department store. Some of our tips:

Start with sales racks, always. Zero in on the biggest discounts first. But don't buy anything just for price. A dress is no bargain if it just hangs in your closet.

Ask if there are any "last-minute sales." It gives the shopkeeper a chance to lower prices and save face.

Consider slightly damaged goods. If the price is reduced because of a tiny spot on the shoulder of a blouse, and you know you would always wear a jacket over the blouse, it may be worth buying. Also, many flaws can be fixed.

Don't limit yourself to your current size. If an item is appealing and a great buy, but not in your size, purchase a bigger size; you can often alter it. Unfortunately it doesn't work the other way around, unless you lose inches. An incentive?

Consider second-hand shops in fancy neighborhoods. These stores offer great potential buys. Places like Palm Beach and New York are filled with last year's designer clothing, marked down heavily.

Strategize at outlets. With sometimes hundreds of stores, crowds, and goods all over the place, outlets can be overwhelming. Write down what you want, and start with that. If you have time left over, browse for other purchases.

Mix expensive items with not-so-expensive ones. Great shoes, an antique pin or a charming belt can draw the eye away from a basic, inexpensive black dress.

Pick up fun, easily packable accessories while on the road. These include scarves, jewelry, T-shirts, caps or hats, watches, shoes, leather goods.

government shop in Madrid many years ago. Its beak is now broken, but it sits proudly on my balcony, facing the sunrise, eternally crowing.

Buy local crafts. Avoid souvenirs mass produced in faraway factories. By supporting local artisans you help perpetuate their traditions, crafts, and culture. And their goods give you a true, forever feel for where you visit. Shops geared to tourists tend to be the worst offenders—stuffed animals, mugs, T-shirts, and such are often produced on the other side of the world.

Shop where locals shop. Ask the locals (especially those who run nice shops) where they would go. Besides shops, look into department stores, hardware stores, food stores, pharmacies, and malls—again, avoiding items you could purchase anywhere else in the world.

Beware of kickbacks. Guides who take you shopping as part of a tour, or on their own, usually get a piece of the action. Don't be pressured to buy. They may say, "It's the best place," or, "You need to buy something here," but I prefer to shop on my own, without a hidden agenda goading me on.

Evaluate space and weight. You are on your own, remember, so you don't want to be lugging a 10-pound pewter platter for two weeks. Don't even look for heavy, bulky items unless you're prepared to ship them, which will take time, effort, and extra money. As a rookie, I once lugged a pair of onyx elephant book-ends for weeks, and they rolled around my suitcase, and smashed a bottle of wine. Goodbye, wardrobe.

Consider shipping, but not always. Don't let shops ship your goods, unless you trust them. You're generally better off mailing purchases yourself, if you're willing to take the time and trouble. Higher quality tourist shops (in stable, tourist-oriented countries) are usually dependable. If you do ship, you'll need the proper wrapping, tape, and string; also, determine postal rates, put the address destination inside and out, and be reasonably accurate about contents. If you're shipping from overseas, obtain a shipping agreement. Make sure that the terms for insurance costs, customs, and duties payment (and anticipated amounts), shipping-fee total, method of shipping, port of entry into the United States, and delivery from the port to your home or office are clear and in writing, together with a detailed itemization of pieces shipped.

Decorate through travel. Wherever you go you can find items, fabrics, even colors you'd never come across anywhere else, often at better prices than at home. Bring swatches, measurements, photos, and list goods that would be useful or attractive in your life. Unique art and artifacts personalize your environment: Look for things that can become other things—pots that can serve as lamp bases, lace that can be framed as art. Lifestyle magazines often feature ideas about decorating through travel; leaf through a few for inspiration.

Think "gifts." Another excuse to shop. And when you're in doubt, the perfect rationale. "I can always give it as a gift." is one of my favorite sayings.

Evaluate need and desire. Do you really, really need the hand-woven Navajo blanket if you live in Florida? Hmm . . . well . . . you can always give it as a gift, or hang it. Desire often trumps need.

HOW TO BARGAIN

When traveling alone you may go for hours without talking, by choice. Giving and taking in the marketplace pushes you into social interactions with locals on their own ground and gets your adrenaline and your voice going.

Some shoppers are naturals, but bargaining is an acquired skill; the more you do it, the better you become, and the more at ease you'll feel. Just realize that you probably won't approach the skills of your opponents. It's like betting against the house in Las Vegas—the odds are against you, but there are times you will win the game, and maybe even hit a jackpot. You don't want to be a naive tourist who accepts the first price, but bargain for the experience and the sport, not to be greedy, and not all the time: Bargaining doesn't—and shouldn't—apply to every type of shopping. In certain cultures, too much bargaining, sometimes any, is frowned upon. Check with your concierge, or a knowledgeable local if you're not sure, and proceed gently and gingerly with your counter-offers.

You can't bargain much on food or perishables—unless the timing is right (the end of the market day), you buy a large amount, or there's a special sale. You don't bargain in department stores or fancy shops; the best you can hope for is a sale or a "discount" for buying more than one item, or being a senior citizen, or being "in the trade," or just that someone is in a generous mood, and finds an excuse, such as a flaw in the item.

Some think of bargaining as a game; I sometimes feel it's a waste of time. My attitude is, "Let's get down to an acceptable price for both of us. I have better things to do." But bargaining is expected if you're shopping at stalls, souks, flea markets, fairs, bazaars, thrift stores, some galleries, and antiques and vintage stores. If you don't haggle neither you nor the seller will be satisfied; you'll feel you paid more than you had to, and the seller will feel she could have charged more. So prepare to negotiate a bit, even if you don't really want to.

Being on your own should help you. Use it to gain connection with the shopkeepers. Smile, converse, get them interested in your independent travels. Then bargain hard.

Lea's & Dovia's Haggling Hints

The best shopper I've ever met is my friend Dovia. I spent several weeks with her in Turkey, and she gained the respect of some of the toughest shopkeepers in the Grand Bazaar. They were scratching their heads when she left: "How did that nice lady buy my rug at that price?"

Here are some bargaining tips from both of us:

☞ The safest and most comfortable way to make a high-end travel purchase is in a shop in a good hotel. Prices may not be bargains, but are generally fair, and the merchandise is guaranteed.

BARTERING

Bartering is a fun way to shop in less-developed areas. In the Peruvian Amazon, we were told to bring T-shirts, pens, makeup, and sunglasses—we traded them for macrame necklaces decorated with seeds and berries, musical instruments, and blow guns.

I did well trading my son's Cub Scout pants with a wolf emblem, but one tribe's favorite item was the woman's girdle from the 1950s, brought by a man (!) in our group. The chief of the tribe had never seen one before. He first stretched it out like a sling shot, but wound up wearing it on his head. He sat in the center of the tent, with the girdle askew, like a rubber beret, and he requested our group run around him in a circle. We were afraid not to—rumor had it that he had shot a blow dart to express his disapproval of an earlier group. Like I said, a fun way to shop!

☞ Be knowledgeable about an item, so that you're comfortable negotiating. Go to fixed-price government stores to get an idea for local handicrafts. Comparison shop before you negotiate. Shops often mark up an item by half.

☞ In your own mind, cap the price. And stick to it.

☞ If you low-ball an item too much, the response will be, "No!" Be respectful, polite, and realistic. Your goal isn't to leave the seller without a profit—just less of one. Take no more than a half to a third off the original price. And settle for a compromise somewhere between the original price and your first response.

☞ Find a flaw. A small chip, a missing button—these often don't spoil an item, but open the door for a discount.

☞ Save face. Allow the seller some possible reason to lower the price—first or last purchase of the day, a birthday (yours or his), or that you both have mothers named Mary. Help him find an excuse.

☞ Be prepared to walk—you can always return and negotiate again. If you really don't want it, or pretend you don't, you'll get it for less.

☞ Don't show your hand. A poker face and a la-dee-dah attitude equal a better deal. Jumping up and down and shouting, "I love this!" is not the way to go.

BARGAINING IN ACTION

Let's put these tips into a few useful bargaining scenarios, based on Dovia's real-life negotiations. Note the nudging, sometimes begrudging interplay of both buyer and seller and the patient, respectful back-and-forth banter.

Scenario #1: You've found a colorful ceramic plate in a street stall, with no markings on the back, priced at $25.
  You: "I can't buy it at that price."
  Seller: "How much are you willing to pay?"
  You: "$10."
  Seller:"I can't sell it at that price."
  You: "Let's split the difference. $18."
(Sometimes that's a deal. Great. But even if he doesn't come down, buy it at $25 if you want it enough. When the amount is small, give in more.)

Scenario #2: You're in a vintage goods shop.
  You: "I collect sterling-silver napkin rings. Do you have any?"
  Seller: "I have some for $60, $70, and $80." (The shopkeeper suspects you are a serious buyer.)
  You: "I like the one for $80, but I can't spend that much. Can you do any better?"
  Seller: "Best I can do is a 10 percent discount. (The price is now $72.)
  You: "I wanted to spend $60."
  Seller: "No!" The end, or, potentially:
  You: "I'll compromise. I'll go up if you go down."
(At this point a sale can probably be made for an amount between the last two prices.)

Scenario #3: You spy a pair of Delft candlesticks (vintage 1980) in an antiques store.

You: "Are you selling any old Delft candlesticks?"

Seller: "Old Delft? Very expensive and very hard to come by."

You: "Really? How much is this pair?"

Seller: "$90. Since you're so interested I can give them to you for $85."

You: "I'd like something with more vintage, or that looks old."

Seller: "That's all I have."

You: "It's not exactly what I was looking for."

Seller: "They're all yours."

You: "I'll buy one candlestick at $45."

Seller: "I can't split them."

You: "I'll give you $50 for one." (You know he won't split them.) "You can make more money if you sell them individually."

Seller: "But I can't split them."

You: "I can appreciate that. But maybe you could do a little better."

(It can go either way. Remember, splitting up a pair, or buying two of something are both ways of getting discounts.)

Scenario #4: You admire the windows of a leather shop. The shopkeeper sees you, and comes out.

Seller: "I have beautiful Italian leather gloves. Silk lined, all colors."

You: "I could always use black. How much?"

Seller: "These would be $125 in the states. $75 here."

You: "Do you have cashmere-lined gloves?"

Seller: "Cashmere are $85 a pair."

You: "I'd pay $75 for cashmere. The silk should be less."

Seller: "10 percent off."

You: "$60."

Seller: "$65."

You: "Deal."

Scenario #5: You're browsing at a flea market.

You: "Sir, excuse me, are these scarves Pucci or copies?"

Seller: "Originals. I bought an overproduction and can sell them cheap. $150 each."

You: "I don't care for this color."

Seller: "I have six other colors."

You: "These two are pretty. I don't care if they're original. They're for gifts. $300 is much more than I can spend."

Seller: "$250."

You: "It's hard for me to know if these are originals or copies. If I buy two, how much will that be? How much better can you do?"

Seller: "OK. $225 for two."

"I'll give you $175 cash or $200 on Visa."

(Always know at what price you want to cap it. And offer cash as a way to cut the price.)

Scenario #6: You're at a street fair.

You: "You really have beautiful shawls." (Praise helps—just not letting them know how much you want it.)

Seller: "Why don't you buy one, lady?"

You: "I really love paisley."

Seller: "I have paisley shawls. $50 and $75."

You: "What's the difference?"

Seller: "Finer wool with fringes is $75."

You: "I'd like it if the $50 had fringes and the $75 didn't."

Seller: "That's the way they make it."

You: "Can you make the $75 more interesting for me, even though I'm not interested in the fringe? Like $50."

Seller: "No. Sorry."

You: "How much?"

Seller: "$75!"

(Be prepared to walk. But do you really care if the shawl has fringes?)

WHERE TO SHOP

Markets from Flea to Farmers to Food

Markets yield a confluence of activity that goes back to the agoras in Greece. The sensual overload and collective energy of the buyers and sellers pulls you in, and gives the solo traveler a meaningful opportunity to pass the time and understand a destination.

A few of my favorites: Covered food markets in Baltimore, Maryland, and Lancaster, Pennsylvania; The Thai Bird market in Bangkok; the night market in Chiang Mai, Thailand; and the glorious Sunday market in Chichicastenango, Guatemala (my second-favorite travel name; first, is silly-sounding Lake Titicaca, in Bolivia).

Any regional market on market day is a favorite place, with umbrellas shading tables laden with foods and spices and clothing and live puppies and bric-a-brac, and buyers squeezing melons, and deliberating on a pair of sandals while children run on the periphery and dogs pull on leashes. Life at full blast.

Some tips on market shopping:

Go early. As in 5 AM, sometimes, when only the dealers are out, for the best selection. I found a charming Adams-period bench at the Bermondsey market in London; I hesitated, and when I returned, a SOLD tag was hanging on the delicate arms.

Go late. Last day, last hour, for best deals. Vendors often would prefer to sell with minimum profit rather than drag their stuff back into the van. I remember waiting 'til the last minute to pounce on a large 19th-century scale at a flea market in New Hampshire. My car trunk was cleared for it, and the lady seemed relieved that I would spare her the trouble of packing it up, once again.

Overview first. Like a buffet, if you pile on early you may miss the best stuff. Do a quick runaround and take some notes of locations and items. Then concentrate on the areas where you can buy the best and most, and you won't waste time.

Be skeptical. Don't assume an "antique" is old. Signed relics can be forgeries, as can certificates of authenticity. For jewelry or other valuables, stick with the fun stuff if you're in doubt about quality.

Be flexible. Your purchase may need repair or refinish, but that is why it's cheaper, and part of the fun. Be prepared to spend some bucks when you get home.

Bring cash for better bargaining power. But bring smallish bills, and be careful, as market areas are magnets for pick-pockets. Don't count on market vendors accepting credit cards.

Dress comfortably, dress down. There's no advantage to looking well-off when you're bargaining or walking around with goods—and comfort is key for successful shopping.

Leave enough time. If you rush, you won't have the luxury to overview the goods. Besides, shopping is the sort of activity where strolling, talking to vendors, and feeling the goods are part of the fun.

Bring expandable carriers. Sometimes you won't get help, and vendors won't have bags. A string bag and/or a parachute bag are excellent. Even if you are prepared, think twice about buying too many large items too early in your trip.

Antiques, Vintage Stores & Art Galleries

What is it about poking around an antiques store or a barn filled with vintage goods, or strolling through an art gallery? The past can hang heavy in every crack of an old chair, and the creativity of an artist's brush strokes can excite your imagination. Often you can talk at length with the experts or the artists themselves. This type of shopping offers a superb experience, even if you don't buy anything. Often antiques stores and art galleries are clustered together. Seek them out as a wonderful pastime.

Fairs

Annual or biennial world-class art and nature fairs are events where you can view and meet the best of the best, and enjoy a learning experience, if not a shopping one. These gatherings are superb places to meet people interested in what you like.

Maastricht, in the Netherlands, hosts the world's greatest annual fine-arts fair in mid March. The hilly town by a river looks more like Belgium than typically flat Holland. Art Basel, now in Miami Beach each winter as well as Basel, Switzerland, in summer displays the world's finest artworks, for sale. The

New York City Armory antiques shows, and the late-winter Philadelphia Flower Show are other famed annual fairs, and among my favorites.

Local, juried art fairs are smaller and less grand showcases for talented craftspeople; typical are the Coconut Grove Art Fair in Florida and the fair in Sausalito, California. State fairs focus on displays more than shopping, but along with farm tools and animals, they offer local crafts and foodstuffs at fair prices.

Auctions

New York, London, Paris, and many major cities have famed auction houses such as Sotheby's and Christie's, which deal in sophisticated tastes and high-end goods. You can learn a great deal by looking over the pieces, and sitting in on the bidding.

But small, rural auctions can be more fun, and you can sometimes find a real bargain. In New Castle, Delaware, I was attending a country antiques auction, when suddenly a small Tiffany stained-glass window was put up for surprise bid. It was a steal, because Tiffany collectors weren't there to bid up the price—but still, unfortunately, over my budget. I think about that glass many times, and wish I had scraped together the money.

One piece of advice: don't ever bid if you don't want something. At an auction in Hampstead, England, I assumed there would be bidders after me, so I raised my hand early in the bidding, just for fun, and wound up with a chandelier. I never hung it, as the glass shattered on the way to the car.

The best advice at auctions: keep still.

Garage Sales & Yard Sales

Some of the best deals anywhere are at garage or yard sales, where locals sell off personal goods, often for only a fraction of what they're worth. Sometimes they're run by professionals who have an idea of fair pricing, but often the owners themselves underprice, just to get rid of the stuff. Come early for best variety, late for best bargains.

One item I wistfully remember from a long-ago garage sale is an Elvis Presley album he recorded for Sun Records. It was

continued on p. 184

There *is* an H?

My first visit to Brazil was on a press trip in the mid-1980s, and it was crammed with extremes. We visited clubs where year-long preparations were proceeding on costumes for Carnival, amid piles of sequins and feathers and lots of smiles and strutting, and watched thonged beachgoers preen along undulating, mosaic-tiled sidewalks hugging the shore. We attended a Santeria service in a hot, cramped church, the worshippers dressed all in white. We stood in the back, instructed not to make a noise while a live chicken was sacrificed on the altar. I could smell the blood, and I empathized with the chicken, but wisely stifled a squawk.

To shake away the memory, I sambaed at a Rio dive 'til early morning. The music rolled in waves, and we swayed our hips in a kind of reverie, dancing with the locals for hours.

The next morning, which came too soon, we drove high above the city and gazed at the mountain-meets-water view that many consider the most beautiful on Earth. And later, we rode a bus close up to the poverty-invested favelas, which from afar cover the green hills like guano from giant birds. My travel article on the wonders of Rio could be capped by a sad description of begging urchins, one of the saddest sights in the world.

Perhaps to clear this experience from our minds, our day ended at the skyscraper headquarters of H. Stern jewelers. The vast first floor display room sparkled with a rainbow of gemstones: topaz, aquamarines, citrons, amethysts, jasper, jadite, and tourmalines, mined from nearby Ouro Preto, the charming colonial town.

We wandered the aisles, trying on baubles. After some deliberation, I bought a pale aquamarine, which I still have in my jewelry box, waiting for just the right setting, which I suspect now might never happen.

I must have spent more time than I realized hunting for this little gem, as the rest of the group had meanwhile walked back to our nearby hotel. I continued gazing, almost hypnotically at the prismatic flashes of purple and blue, green and yellow. So pretty.

Suddenly, a hand tapped my shoulder. "You're one of the journalists, right?" I nodded, taken aback.

"Would you come with me?" It was a young woman in black. "Mr. Stern would like to talk with you."

"Mr. Stern? H. Stern? There *is* an H?"

She smiled. "Yes, his name is Hans. We walked to the elevator, which rose and emptied into a gated hall. The gates parted and I walked another hall to a small office, and there stood H., in his 60s or maybe 70s, small and wiry, with a winning handshake.

"Come sit down." He gestured to a comfortable chair. "I like to talk to visiting journalists."

He in fact interviewed *me*. We talked about American history, presidents, and travel. The only topic we didn't seem to cover was jewelry. After maybe half an hour, when Hans tired a bit, he brought forth a little box containing a tiny gold arm with a fisted hand, the symbol of rebellion for the former slaves of Brazil.

"Take this gift please, Lea, and remember what a nice talk we had."

When I returned to the hotel our group leader was beside herself.

"We figured you wandered somewhere and got mugged!"

"No. I had an interview. With . . . H. Stern."

"There *is* an H?" people asked in unison.

"Yep." I told them about the conversation and showed them the pendant.

The next day, when we had some time off, I walked around the beaches, gazing some more at the tanned bodies, as beautiful as Brazilian gems. One of my friends went back to the H. Stern showroom, supposedly to look for jewelry, but really I think, to see if she could get an interview with H.

Sure enough, she was tapped on the shoulder by the woman in black. As she told it, the woman asked if my friend was with the press trip.

"Yes, I'm a journalist." She waited, expecting her invitation to go upstairs, to chat with H. and receive her gold pendant.

"Oh, how nice," the lady in black said. "Yesterday Hans Stern had a lovely talk with one of your colleagues. Please send her my regards." ꙮ

worth hundreds of dollars, and sold for a dollar. Unfortunately, I was the seller. I had no idea, and marked the price in a rush.

These informal, bargain sales are popular all over the world. One of my favorite pastimes when I lived north of London was visiting the weekend jumble sales in churches. You can sometimes find a valuable antique among the mothballed sweaters and used toys.

Outlets

Outlet shopping yields major discounts, but requires serious strategizing, akin to battle. Stores can be at opposite ends of a huge complex, so you need to plan ahead—mark outlets in clusters and leave plenty of time. Also, you may find some incredible sales that you weren't prepared for. Who can resist 80-percent off! Budget that in.

Outlet prices may be reduced but you can get in trouble on your own, especially when you feel you're finding good deals at luxury stores, and wind up spending more than you should. When you're dealing with an upscale outlet, carry a list—of needs and budget—and stick to it as much as you can.

I'd spend a full day at this, with a nice time-out for lunch. That way you won't rush and you'll have a fine day of exercise as well as shopping. Plan for transportation back, if you don't have a car. You'll probably have lots of packages, so if it's possible, see if the reputable stores can help you get the packages together, or send them on to your hotel. If you do this, pay by credit card to cover the loss or damage of any parcels. For a selected list of outlets, see "Resources" at the end of this chapter.

V.A.T.: What You Need to Know

Because you have to deal with taxes and customs on your own, I want to give you a heads-up. Value Added Tax, or V.A.T. is set by individual countries, but is quite high by U.S. taxation-for-goods standards (approximately 18 percent). As a tourist, you are entitled to a refund of this tax under the "Tourist Tax-Relief Program" provisions of the European Union. Look for "Tourist

Program Refund Offices" in European airports and other entry sites into European countries. My friend Paula complains that she usually collects her V.A.T. documentation—but doesn't bother to send it in. Take care of this as soon as possible to reap your entitlement!

After shopping at European stores, inquire on premises from customer service about the EU tax-refund program. If available, obtain, on the spot, a preliminary refund receipt (called a "check") and a refund envelope together with an application for refund (V.A.T. Refund Application Form; V.A.T. Form 10). The original bill and the purchase cash receipt must be attached to the preliminary refund check, and you must be able to present your valid passport.

On your way out of town, border customs will review your purchases and documents, possibly affix a seal or sticker to your luggage, and stamp the refund receipt/V.A.T. application with an official customs stamp. A refund will not be processed without this stamp. If you're traveling through several EU nations, request this review and stamp at your last point of EU exit.

RESOURCES
European Shopping
European shopping center award winners. A list provided by the International Council of Shopping Centres (ICSC) derived from their annual conference, comprising—in their humble Shopping Centre Industry opinion—the award-winners of Europe. *www.icsc.org*

Made in Italy online. While online shopping may not be what you had in mind, this well-organized site is a good review lesson for touring Italy and its merchandise, events, and happenings—including what's hot and what's not. Where to go and what to buy! *www.made-in-italy.com*

Shop in Northern Ireland. Prepare for the real Irish deal with this shopping directory. *www.shop-in-northernireland.net*

Outlets

Mississippi casino district. Tunica, Mississippi, the site of the Casino Factory Shoppes, a 40-store outlet center. *www.tunicamiss.com*

New England for visitors. An "all about" site, literally hundreds of links, include outlet-shopping guides, malls, and Filene's Basement, of course. *www.gonewengland.about.com*

Orlando shopping. Shopping hot spots (Mickey-related, and not), and extensive Orlando links. *www.go2orlando.com*

Outletbound. Search for U.S. and Canada outlets by location, store, brand, or product category. *www.outletbound.com*

Pennsylvania Dutch Country outlets. Quaint Lancaster County, Pennsylvania, horse-drawn buggies, modestly dressed women, bearded farming men (not the other way around)—and shopping. More than 200 stores. *www.800padutch.com*

Smokin' shopping in the Smoky Mountains. In Sevierville, Pigeon Forge, Tennessee. More than 100 name-brand shops in a pretty mall. *www.smokyvacations.com*

Vermont shopping. Directory of Vermont Shopping, including handmade, boutique, outlet stores, factory stores, and everything in between—in short, everything in Vermont that's for sale. *www.vtweb.com/wheretoshop*

chapter 12

Blending In: Traditions, Taboos & Tipping

The world may be a global village, but hooray for the eccentricities of its villagers. As a solo traveler you're able to concentrate on these cultural differences to the fullest, but you should also try to understand them, for your comfort, ease, and safety. In certain cultures and situations it *is* acceptable to stand out (see Chapter 13, Meeting People). That said, the ideal is to blend in, not call attention to yourself, and to be aware and appreciative of each unique custom and tradition.

Thailand has lots of ancient customs, as it's never been colonized. For a minute or so, the country literally stops—cars, pedestrians, everything—when an anthem is played in honor of the king, who is considered a god. I befriended a young Bangkok crowd that was appalled when tourists continued walking forward rather than sidling up to the statues of Buddha. My new friends were also put-off that Americans touched each other so much, especially on the head. At first I thought their complaints were ridiculous, but after a couple of months, I started to share their disgust. I kept my feet sideways and my hands in my pocket. I had blended in.

While in the Philippines on a video project, I was having trouble getting permits to shoot on location. Nothing seemed to work. Finally, my driver mentioned that I had to ask the town elders first. When I spoke with respect, and presented—with much fanfare—certificates of appreciation I brought from an office-supply store, with names filled in and a Polaroid photo of the elder and me attached, even the toughest old guy would smile and give permission. I had broken through the cultural barrier by understanding a custom. I had blended in.

Even in familiar cultures, differences abound. On the leafy street in the London suburbs where I lived for a year, men mowed their lawns in suits, and the politeness was overwhelming. When I backed my car over my neighbor's rose bushes, he said, "So sorry. Were those in your way?" I felt like a boor, and started making gratuitous apologies myself, as much a change for me as walking sideways in Thailand.

HOW TO BLEND

Americans are stereotyped as friendly, informal, and outgoing. Twist this a bit and we can also be considered domineering, loud, and insensitive. "Yo, Gunther, what's up?" just doesn't fly everywhere. We tend to shake hands, grab forearms, hug and kiss on departure, use first names on first meeting, flash money and jewelry and cameras, and talk loud and fast—in our own language. And often we don't realize this is not everyone's way. Many places find this behavior overbearing and disrespectful, not friendly.

Before you leave home, study the customs, history, contributions, and achievements of the area you're visiting. Know the names of the president or head of state. And when you arrive, inquire and adjust with respect to what you find. Create a cultural cheat sheet based on your research, printing out relevant material and carrying it with you as you travel, to remind you of local customs. And keep a file for future reference.

And even after all this thoughtful preparation, you know what? You're still not going to get it totally right, because other cultures may take offense at what you think are innocent gestures. And in some cases, these gestures may even be involuntary. In the Atlas mountains of Morocco I inadvertently grimaced when I saw a slab of meat covered with flies. The butcher must have spied me, and ran out of his stall—brandishing a knife in the air. I walked swiftly away, head down, like a bitch with her tail between her legs. I have no idea if he would have followed through, and I certainly didn't wait to find out.

In Russia men greet and part with kisses, whether they're gay or straight. Get used to it, and try to assimilate, if possible. At a minimum, don't make a face—or assumptions. Also:

Learn local dress customs and dress codes. If there's a world costume it must be T-shirt, jeans, and sneakers. But not always. Covering shoulders, legs, arms, cleavage, and head may be necessary, depending where and when. Long skirts or pants, and a shawl or long-sleeve shirt will suffice.

Shoes may be forbidden in Muslim mosques and Buddhist temples, Japanese homes and restaurants (place shoes together neatly, facing the door), Indian and Indonesian restaurants, and many museums where you're provided with slippers. To prepare, wear shoes that slip off easily—and get a pedicure.

Have a handle on food and drink etiquette. When you really, really don't want to eat the oxen eyeball with mango coulis offered by your host, smile, take a teeny-tiny bite and try to swallow without chewing. Wash it down with liquid. Dare I say you might enjoy the experience? No? As a last resort, "I'm allergic to eyeballs," might do, or "I don't eat facial parts for religious reasons." Oh, and don't ask if you don't want to know.

In the Far East, keep your rice bowl by your face, and keep your teacup full if you don't want more. Leave some food in the dish to show how generous your host is. Notice how chopsticks are placed, and try to copy. Don't offer to split the bill—either offer to pay all, or accept your host's treat.

"Right hand only" is the mantra when cultures eat with their hands (left is for personal hygiene). Also, try to learn the local

continued on p. 192

Fire Down Below

Even in a country of solemn beauty, absurdity remains, to remind us, with a crooked smile, that perfection is impossible. I remember one trip where that point was made, definitively.

On break from a video shoot in the Philippines, I visited Bali, flying in without a reservation, on a moonless night. To avoid the crowded coast, the cab driver suggested the center of the island. I agreed, the room I chose looked fine, and I fell into bed. Awakening early, I found at my door a tiny offering of carved fruit on a leaf, and I breakfasted in a pavilion overlooking a lotus pond in the middle of a former Hindu temple.

I hired a wide-faced, serene young driver, and in his small van, we explored the island, stopping at villages, where we observed artisans, each specializing in a different art form. I bought a mask and a painting. We drove narrow roads past sinuous rice paddies clinging to hilly, green terrain, and trekked to the rims of plunging gorges filled with palms and orchids. As we drove, my driver explained about Hindu customs, and asked about mine. Divorce? Is that good? Phoning a machine to get a message? Good? Credit cards? Good? We were both exploring, and learning, in harmony.

Beauty enveloped me. The locals bathed discreetly under waterfalls, and swayed as they walked, goods balanced delicately atop their heads. The percussive gamelan rang in the air, like wind chimes, and at night, each village presented a different traditional dance. Grace and art and gentleness yes, and all that I had hoped for. But, absurdity was lurking.

I visited a temple where women were preparing offerings— carved fruit or flowers arranged into a fragile work of art. Nearby, we spied a line of people heading toward a clearing, carrying offerings in silver vessels. A cremation ceremony was in progress, as many were each day on the island, some of them major spectacles, with food hawked and biers built high above the crowds. Strangers joined mourners, and the long ceremonies ended with the ashes thrown into the sea.

I remembered cremations on biers along the Ganges in Benares, India. There, the air was thick with smoke, and the river the color of death. Against a pastel backdrop of 18th-century buildings, Hindu priests sat under umbrellas, and mourners washed in their holy, ashy waters, and crowded along the riverbanks chanting prayers for the dead. Here in Bali, this cremation before me seemed as natural as the wind: an old woman had been placed on branches on a knoll under a grove of trees, and her family and friends were tossing petals, 'til her body was covered like the ground under a dogwood in late spring.

I stood back on the grass, already wearing a traditional black-and-white sarong tied around my waist—the custom for tourists who enter Balinese temples, or attend ceremonies. The mourners acknowledged my respectful presence and garb, and beckoned me forward. And then . . . a couple of moments I will never forget.

The wood was lighted, and as the flames crackled, I felt sharp, painful sensations, and realized I was standing on a nest of fire ants. I hopped away, too late, as the insects had already crawled up my legs, biting and stinging as they climbed. I jumped around, scratching and rubbing myself in a contained frenzy, all the while trying not to disrupt the solemn cremation.

The mourners, confused by my presence and sudden activity, couldn't help turning from the pyre and staring at the sight of a Caucasian woman, shaking and wiggling up and down and side to side in some sort of strange ceremonial dance; they seemed to regard my struggling movements as my way of showing respect to the lady going up in smoke. They continued to stare as I writhed around, slapping at the ants, hopping on one foot, then the other.

I didn't want to embarrass them, and they didn't want to disrespect me, so I kept moving, finally trying to rub the itch away by rubbing my legs together, as if I were trying to start a fire, an irony not lost on me, even in my intense suffering.

I finally managed to dance my way back to the van, led by my convulsed driver, his hand covering his grin, while my ill-fitting sarong practically unraveled around my splotched legs. At last! I could take off the damned sarong—and scratch!

The mourners turned back to their smoldering beloved. They must have thought I was one of the weirdest strangers they had ever seen, and that I certainly had an unusual way of paying respects. ❧

toast—it will please your imbibing companions. Later in the evening you can teach each other the really good ones. And if you remain somewhat coherent, you'll be able to remember it for an appropriate wedding, years from now.

Think before you shoot. Throughout the world people and entire cultures will either expect you to ask permission before you photograph them, or would expect you to know that for personal or religious reasons, you shouldn't even bother to ask. Think how you might feel if someone felt the right to capture your image while you are scratching your head or at other personal moments—especially if you felt the camera held negative karma. If something or someone is especially interesting, you can always ask permission, politely, by hand signals if not by words, but be prepared for a negative response, and accept it. No sneaking around. And if someone holds out their hand, or bargains for money in exchange for their image, that's an individual decision with no easy answer.

In the San Blas Islands of Panama, the indigenous women sew *molas*—intricate patterns on red cotton. Couple this with a backdrop of turquoise waters and tropical flowers, and you've got the potential for exceptional photos, a fact not lost on the canny native women. On a press trip to these islands, a well-known photographer was snapping away, and the colorfully dressed women obliged readily, posing with their children and at their work. When it was time to fly back to the mainland, one of them demanded $70 dollars from the photographer. He was shocked. She was adamant: $70.

"No way," he stated.

She made a noise. "Click, click, click."

Seems she was counting and noting the camera clicks (pre-digital), and in his zeal he hadn't noticed. The photographer tried to bargain, but the lady made it clear that our small plane wasn't leaving until he paid up. So he did, cursing under his breath. Lesson learned, I hope.

By the way, if you do get the green light to take pictures, carry a Polaroid—some of those you will photograph have never had a picture of themselves, or their children. What a gift!

HOW TO TIP

Relax. There are no set rules on tipping—just guidelines that sometimes quite intentionally come across as gospel, which is why you should consider their source: are they coming from a tourist office, restaurant, or other party with a vested interest? Or are they coming from an impartial source, like me?

Offering gratuities for services is a social custom we learn to live with, like taxation. We may not like it much, and in a perfect world of living wages and inner motivation for good service, we wouldn't need it. But in this far-from-perfect world, consider tipping a necessary travel expense. Making all tipping decisions by yourself, and constantly handing out money, can become tiresome. Remember, there are no absolutes here; the goal is a feeling of fairness and comfort on all sides.

Tip Tips

Ponder these tips that I've culled over the years.

Know how, and whether, to tip. Depending on where you are in the world, you could be branded a rube or worse if you either tip in the wrong manner or tip when it's not appropriate. Consider that in China it's considered illegal to tip, but gifts like cigarettes and T-shirts are welcome. Tips are not customary in Iceland, nor are they the norm in Fiji, but if you're at a Fiji resort you should consider making a donation to the "staff fund." Romanians don't tip, but while in Romania, foreigners are expected to: 10–12 percent in restaurants and not much elsewhere, unless you hire a driver for the day. And in the Czech Republic, Austria, and Hungary, your waiters will expect you to hand them tips directly.

For guidelines about tipping around the world, see the "Tipping Guides" at www.fodors.com.

If in doubt, shell it out. Once you're clear on whether your destination welcomes tipping, you'll be the sole judge of which of your hundreds of encounters are tip-worthy. Daunting? Yes, but it isn't rocket science. Jiminy Cricket's words, "always let your

continued on p. 195

Chinese Checker

From Macao, the Portuguese island off the China coast, I ferried to spend 10 hours with a group in the province of Canton—barely enough time to get the teeniest inkling of that southernmost region of the world's most populous country. It was 1984, and China was emerging from a cultural torpor.

The living dioramas around us combined a mix of old and new, past and present. As our bus approached a mountainside it appeared covered in ants; workers by the thousands were breaking the stone with hammers and chisels. I thought of projects like the pyramids, seemingly impossible human accomplishments, built by hard work, selflessness, and patience.

Our first rest stop was the region's new hotel, a Holiday Inn, shown off with great pride, especially the gift shop. The toilets there were less dismal than the pits we would encounter at other places, although the seats were sticky black lacquer.

Although it was a Sunday, quiet students sat straight up on benches in the school we visited, concentrating on the book before them, without an adult monitor. I compared the scene to the spit-ball laden high-school study halls of my past, even during school hours, with monitors and comfortable seats.

Farmers in cone-shaped hats and loose pants plowed behind water buffalo, and ducks waddled in lines across the flooded rice paddies. Outside of the city I saw almost no cars, and few bikes. People trudged along roadsides in olive drab. At a rural market, covered bamboo cages were filled with squawking, squealing animals, eggs were sold one by one as if made of alabaster, and a few meager household items lay on the ground, for sale or trade.

A wiry old man with a wisp of beard walked right up to me, within an inch of my face, and stared, unblinking. His eyes went from my hair to my toes. I was an exotic thing, and he looked impassive but curious. I stood still for this inspection for a minute or so, sensing his hot breath. Talk about in your face!

I don't know if the man approved of me or not, but no offer was made, and I went back to my suite in Hong Kong that evening with a feeling of relief, wonderment of the past, and a touch of rejection. ❧

conscience be your guide," should sustain you in most situations. But consider tipping anyone who makes your life easier by performing a service, physical or otherwise: good concierges who make phone calls on your behalf are trained to make it seem effortless. It isn't.

Tip according to the quality of service. In cities, tipping is expected, and generally more than in remote, or rural areas. If service is just plain lousy, you could leave a note, along with a paltry remuneration. ("My tip: Improve your service!" is cheeky but may be appropriate in some situations.)

Poll the locals about tipping customs for different services. It's impossible to know anyone's motivation, so asking at least three people is ideal to get a baseline. Also consult local materials and guides, again considering the source.

Make sure the tip is not already included. You may have to read the fine print, or ask. At resorts, on cruise ships, on tours, in restaurants, take special heed. And note if there is a staff box for tips, usually at the reception desk.

Add on. When a service charge is covered in restaurants, add an amount bringing the total to between 15–20 percent, usually appropriate anywhere in the world. In other situations, even when tips are included, handing off a small extra amount to someone who has been exceptional is always appreciated.

Round up. For a satisfactory taxi or carriage ride, round up to the equivalent of the next dollar, and give no less than 15 percent. For tips on managing the taxi fare itself, see Chapter 8, Getting There, Getting Around.

Don't forget the easily forgotten. Room-service waiters, maids, maître'ds, wine stewards, parking attendants, and the frequently taken-for-granted concierge often provide the best service of your trip, and should be compensated. At resorts and on cruises, check on specific, often listed, tipping guidelines.

Keep the change small. Carry change and small bills, in local currency if possible. And learn the currency. Even though 2,000 Bolivares may sound like a lot, in Venezuela it's less than $3.

Don't write a blank check. Don't hold your hand out with foreign currency and ask someone to take "whatever's appropriate." I did that on a short taxi ride on my first trip to France, and wound up with a palm emptied of about $50.

And at a minimum, smile and say, "Thank you." Just because you're cheap doesn't mean you can't be nice about it.

Dealing with Pressure

Tips are sometimes more like sustenance. While in India in the 1980s, four men rushed to carry me on a hammock slung between them up to a famous cave, for a quarter each. And they waited an hour for me to come out and carry me back. It was all they could do to earn money, and that wasn't a tip or a bribe—it was a wage. I was told to tip the amount asked for, and no more, which was difficult. Why so low? Was that fair? There was no easy answer.

But sometimes a tip seems pressured. The tip glass, once the province of sushi bars and piano tops, is now ubiquitous at take-out counters throughout the galaxy. Contributing to all is silly, while contributing to some seems arbitrary. Same with restroom attendants: If you're availing yourself of the proferred paper towel when you prefer to take it yourself, tipping feels forced. My rule of thumb is that if you feel manipulated, even tacitly, don't do it. But be prepared for consequences. I remember a lady, sweeping a toilet floor with a filthy broom in Belgrade, who swiped my feet with it when I didn't tip her.

In some countries, the concept of gratuities is something between a game and an occupation. In Egypt, this quasi-tip is called *baksheesh*. I couldn't walk a block or two around Cairo without some young man asking, "Are you from California?" to initiate conversation, then asking if he could "guide" me. One fellow lifted me up an incline before I realized he was doing it, and then demanded a tip. I was harassed by many

"helpers," until a distinguished-looking older man in a suit rescued me from their clutches and got me safely to the museum
steps.

"Thank you so much," I said, relieved.

"My pleasure," he said. And then he held out his hand for
baksheesh.

Gifts

Unless they're really expensive, gifts for workers should be
given in addition to cash tips, not in place of them.

I often pack small, lightweight items and clean, used apparel
and/or goods (nothing with rips or stains, and nothing intimate),
and leave them in the room for the staff. Shirts, shorts, caps, belts,
makeup, pens, pads of paper seem appreciated. Leave a note, saying something like "This is for you. Thank you." Sans note, maids
have run after me with the items, and one discarded cap was
wrapped and delivered to me at check-out. When visiting a host,
if you're not aware of gifting customs, ask the concierge for advice
on an appropriate gift for the occasion. Whether you then tip the
concierge for the gifting advice is your call.

LEARNING THE LANGUAGE

I've traveled throughout the world with excellent English, work-
able Spanish, dismal French, and laughable Italian, but I try my
best to learn a few words of each local language, and have been
rewarded with appreciation. Even in France, where I might get
corrected, but earn points for trying.

In a charming, highly recommended trattoria in Amalfi, I
ordered my dinner using my best "Learn-Italian-in-Ten-Minutes-
a Day" vocabulary. And then the waiter started talking to me, in
Italian. I fumbled with a few key words, and he spoke some
more, in Italian. The conversation somehow kept going. He didn't
let the small problem of my lack of Italian vocabulary, grammar,
and syntax get in the way. I wound up in the kitchen with a
delighted *nonna* (that's grandma to you non-Italian-speakers!)

continued on p. 201

The Translator

Four years of Spanish at Miami Beach High and a crash Berlitz course had left me with vocabulary that could get me to a train or a toilet, and such basic verbs as "I am" and "I have" in present and future tenses. Not enough to update hotel listings throughout Guatemala for a guidebook. So to get my creaky Spanish going, I enrolled for a week of language immersion in the colonial city of Antigua, the former capital. The school where I would study and sleep was a hacienda, surrounding a tiled courtyard. My dark little room was crammed with carved furniture.

I was the only student that week in April. La Duena, the school's owner, invited me to dinner the first night at a restaurant in a seedy colonial building. Her dark hair was pulled tightly back, and her face heavily lined. She smoked constantly, pausing only long enough to sip an ice-laden rum drink. She picked at her food as she talked about her family coming to Central America two hundred years before, and settling in the hacienda. My tutor was her favorite, a poor village girl named Maria, whom she claimed spoke Spanish as if she had emigrated from Spain.

I met Maria right after breakfast the next morning, at a round table by a fireplace, a petite young woman with delicate indigenous features and mocha skin, wearing a white blouse and black skirt. Her attitude made her seem invisible.

"Hola. Me llamo Maria. Y tu?" She used the familiar voice before I had said a word.

"Come sit down," I said in halting Spanish. "Me llamo Lea. Would you like a cup of coffee?"

"Taza de café," she corrected me, gently. "Solamente Espanol, no? Pero no café a mi, gracias."

"But you must be thirsty . . . Hace . . . .Hace . . ."

"Hace sed," she finished, and smiled. I prepared her coffee and added a biscuit despite her protestations. As she guided me through simple conversation, I learned that she had taken the bus two and a half hours to arrive at the school from her little village, leaving her feverish infant son with her mother, with the electricity turned off half the day. She was anxious, but not looking for pity.

That first day we walked around Antigua I carried a phrasebook—

groping a bit for the best words, writing notes as we walked. Maria opened up to me quickly. She said that her husband had illegally crossed the border into California and worked as a gardener. He sent money, periodically, but she did not seem to know if he would ever return, and if she cared, she didn't show it.

Her manner was as delicate as the jacaranda blossoms falling about us. But her shy smile hid a wicked sense of satire. I could talk to this peasant woman in stumbling Spanish and be safe. Better yet, I could laugh with her.

When I got back to the hacienda, La Duena was waiting to meet me. "How did it go"? She now spoke in Spanish only.

I told her, as best I could, how pleased I was with Maria, and that she and I were having actual conversations.

"Good," she said. "But remember, she is not your friend. She works for me and is doing her job. And I have a rule not to feed the tutors. Not even coffee."

I pondered her statement. "Well," I finally said, in English, "I will serve her coffee as an act of courtesy. She is my teacher." La Duena looked at me as if I had slapped her, and said nothing about it again.

As the week continued, our ritual became established. Maria would meet me at the morning table, where we spoke—over coffee—about our previous afternoons and evenings. Her routine was predictable (as was mine—studying Spanish). She tended to her son, worked in her garden, read until the electricity was turned off in her village.

Each day we would walk somewhere new in Antigua, and discuss just about anything, and then I would end the session by taking her to lunch at her favorite place, the Chinese restaurant by the plaza. She would always order the same thing: chow mein. She would gingerly taste my moo shu pork or General Tso's chicken, but preferred her staple dish. And then she would take the bus back to her son.

Day by day, our simple questions and answers turned into banter, then to jokes and even ironies. She even taught me a little verse about the fortunes of life: "Quando yo tenia dinero, me llamaban Don Tomas. Ahora, que no lo tengo, me llaman, Tomas. No mas." (When I had money, they called me Mr. Tomas, but now that I have none, they just call me Tom.)

She did not speak much of her husband and I did not ask. I was divorced then, and I assumed we were two women on our own indefinitely, who did not discuss men. Maria and I could have been best friends had we been born nearer each other, in a world where class and circumstance and geography did not separate like-minded souls.

The next-to-last day Maria brought me a sheaf of onion-skin papers. "My poems," she said. "Would you read them?"

I glanced at the first one, words of longing, and was touched that she shared them. "Are you sure you want me to"? I knew that this work was her heart and soul.

"Yes, I am. You are a writer. You can read the Spanish. I would like your opinion."

That night, in my carved bed, with my phrasebook by my side, I read Maria's poems. She wrote of tenderness and lovemaking, of ecstasy and longing and loss. Passionate words. The fact that I was able to comprehend them was almost secondary. I was comprehending her.

When I saw Maria the next—last—morning, my eyes welled with tears as she walked into the room—so small, and now, I knew, so talented and full of emotion. I was sad that this was our last time together, but my tears were joyful, too, because despite her difficult life, I knew now that she felt love. She had found that which even the privileged seek above all.

I hugged her. "Maria, your poems are wonderful."

"You think so?"

"Yes, yes! And best of all you have experienced love. I'm so very, very happy for you"

She looked down for a few seconds, as if she were searching for words. She, the translator, unable to speak her own language. When she finally looked up, it was her eyes that were spilling tears.

"No," she whispered. "I have never been in love. The poems are only my dreams." ❧

who was rolling meatballs. And she started talking with me. It was the best conversation I never had.

On the other hand, in Thailand, with its difficult, many-toned language, I learned one easy word—*kwai*, and used it as often as I could, to say "water buffalo." Over the weeks I kept pointing out all the water buffalo we would see. "Look at that kwai." "There's a big kwai." "Kwai, kwai, kwai." After a while the gentle young Thai man accompanying my group couldn't stand it any longer. He turned to me, and said, in a soft voice, "Lea, could you please stop! You keep saying, 'Look at that prick!'"

Kwai indeed means water buffalo, but evidently I was saying it as *kuai* (the aforementioned organ) when I should have been pronouncing it *kwhy*. And if you find yourself in Thailand you'll want to leave even less margin for error, stretching the "a" sound, more like *kwhaai*. As I learned, close doesn't count.

Even English-speaking countries can give us trouble. As George Bernard Shaw so quotably said, "England and America are divided by a common language," and the accents people apply when speaking English often make it harder to understand than Finnish and Hungarian laced with Tagalog.

Nonverbal Communication

Actually, I don't usually find the inability to speak a local language a terrible problem. You can often follow people's hand gestures, body language, and tone of voice—and they can do the same. Some languages, such as Italian, incorporate gestures with verbal communication.

One rainy day when I was driving in Poland, I had to ask for directions to a village. I stopped a man walking along, showed him my map, made gestures that showed where I wanted to go, said the village name, and hoped for the best. The man spoke in Polish, and I couldn't understand a word he was saying. I just watched his hands and his body. He was pointing me to another road. I took it for a while, then I asked someone else at the next village, again following his gestures. I was cautious and sought directions more than I probably needed to, but I got directions without ever understanding a word.

When we can't speak, we tend to compensate. So be expressive, use props, watch others carefully, and don't panic. You can usually get by. A rare exception for me was in Tokyo, where the pace made Manhattan seem sleepy, and the crowds were daunting. I couldn't read the signs, and I couldn't understand most of the English spoken by helpful people, because their accents were so heavy. I was pushed along with the flow of people at rush hour, and squeezed into a crowded subway car. I wound up taking the subway twice around Tokyo because I had no idea where to get off. A young Japanese woman who had attended college in Boston finally set me straight. So that was a worst-case scenario: a couple of round-trips. You can get through these problems with aplomb, and you sometimes have to, when you solo.

Gestures, especially those involving the face, can be subtle but communicative. There doesn't seem to be an obvious pattern. (I'm considering Botox just to make sure I don't convey "Come to my room cutie," with a miscued smirk.) Here are some familiar gestures and what they mean in various destinations.

- Raised eyebrow, in Peru = "Pay me."

- Winking, in Australia = "Improper!"

- Grasping ears in India = repentance; in Brazil, = appreciation

- Earflick, in Italy = "I'm gay."

- American "okay" signal in Colombia, when over nose = "I'm gay."

- Nose thumb, in Europe = mockery

- Nose wiggle in Puerto Rico = "What's going on?"

- Pulling on eye, Europe and some Latin countries = "Be alert."

- Nose tap in England = secrecy; in Italy = a friendly warning

- Cheek screw in Italy = praise

- Cheek stroke in Greece, Italy, and Spain = "attractive"; Balkan area = "success"; elsewhere = "ill" or "thin"

☞ Fingertips kiss, in most places = "beautiful"

☞ Chin flick in Italy = not interested; in Brazil ="I don't know."

☞ Circle around ear or head tap, many destinations = "crazy"
   And you thought *speaking* the language was tough?

RESOURCES
Etiquette Info
Manners matter. Do you know that if a Chinese national smiles, nods enthusiastically, and says, "No problem," you can expect major roadblocks? In China, the American-favored direct approach is inappropriate. The Executive Planet site provides excellent culture guides, lucid sketches, and quick tips on international "do's" and "don't ever's." *www. executiveplanet.com*

Tips and tests. Review international-etiquette articles and take a pop quiz on your manners know-how. This brief, to-the-point Web site is fun, and you can definitely learn. I did. *www. harcourtcollege.com/management/students/bus_etiquette*

Language Instruction
Learn at 30,000 feet. Living Language, part of Random House (as is Fodor's) publishes swell books, audio cassettes, and CDs that cover 20 different languages. A favorite product of mine is their "In-Flight" line, an hour-long recording, ideal for replaying when you literally want to tune out. For a free sampler, check out www.fodors.com/language. *Living Language, www. randomhouse.com/livinglanguage*

Learn Chinese in China. Or learn Japanese in Japan. Or study them both in your living room. Instruction options are plentiful abroad and online. Connected to facilities around the world, this group is one of the most comprehensive coordinators for learning a language on location. *www. mystudyadvisor.com*

Learn Italian in Italy. In Rome, Florence, or Siena you can take a class that generally begins every two weeks. Either participate for a few days or earn a "diploma," and get U.S. college credit in some cases. Small classes and individual instruction are offered. *Scuola Leonardo da Vinci, www.scuolaleonardo.com*

Learn Spanish in Mexico. Classes begin each week in Guadalajara. Individual tuition is available, and vacationers are specifically included. Cultural programs permit maximum exposure and practice, including salsa, karaoke, or guitar lessons, lectures, and social activities. A multimedia lab offers e-mail access. U.S. college credit possible. *Instituto Mexico Americano de Cultura, www.mexonline.com/imac.htm*

chapter 13

Meeting People

Going way, way back, some of the most extraordinary people were solo travelers. Moses and Jesus wandered alone in the desert—although both quickly formed group tours. And Marco Polo and Columbus were, after all, pioneers on the cruise circuit. Even though you can't expect to find a prophet or savior on a hike, or an explorer on a cruise ship, you just might find a nice doctor in the sands of deserts and beaches, in cities, and on the seas. And most of them are seeking friendly connections, just like you are.

Even if you truly enjoy your soloing, you'll probably still want people around, at least some of the time. You'll likely crave some companionship, discussion, and laughter, and perhaps more. As a soloist you have loads of choices, and breakthrough ways to get together with others for friendship or romance while traveling.

I usually am content seeking friends on the road, and leave the romance for when I'm in my own, familiar territory (it's hard enough then!). But I've enjoyed flirtations and romantic times while traveling, and we'll definitely address that issue.

My book-group buddy Susan remembers a little incident on her trip to Milan that says a lot about people. In her words:

"After visiting *The Last Supper,* I looked for a place to grab lunch, and found a trattoria (no English spoken). After eating, I walked back to the center of Milan when I realized that I didn't have my new camera with me. I dashed back to the trattoria, holding my breath (try to do that and run at the same time!). Luckily, my camera was still there.

"When I returned from the trip, I developed the film. I didn't recognize one of the photos, and thought it had gotten mixed up with mine by mistake. Then, by placing the photos in order, I realized the unknown photo was the staff at the trattoria, smiling and waving. Obviously, when they found the camera, they snapped the shot. What a warm surprise, and a great memory!"

Susan's photo represents the way much of the world feels about you when you're on your own. People may not like our politics or may be more restrained than we are, but for the most part they're out there, smiling, waving, and hoping to please you. The trick, of course, is to meet the good folks and skip the ones who mar our trips with a glare, insult, or worse. More than a hundred countries later, I don't have foolproof methods, but I'm happy to share my best tips for meeting people.

How to Meet People

Whether you're in Baluchistan or Isfahan or Little Rock you can meet folks at unexpected times, without a smidgen of planning, on a bus, or a plane, or on a park bench eating a bologna sandwich. Maybe you'll converse with someone staring at a Warhol painting on a museum wall, or walking out of a movie. Maybe you'll bond with your guide, or a shopkeeper who shares your interest in mid-20th-century silver teapots.

Open yourself to these kinds of connections to enrich your travels, while simultaneously trusting your instincts and always placing safety first (see Chapter 14, Safety & Health). Regardless of our ingrained savvy we tend to let our guard down once we meet someone nice on the road, and some not-so-nice-types know this. That said, get out there and enjoy one of the best aspects of soloing!

Be approachable. If you don't put your arm up, the taxi won't stop. Likewise, if you want company, send your message by eye contact, smiles, and questions. Be curious, look presentable and friendly, and you're on your way, sometimes more than you realize. I usually keep a low profile when I travel, but in Japan, newly separated, I must have opened up in a way I hadn't before. Body language, eye contact, innuendo, a more vivid scarf—I'm not sure why, but I noticed a tremendous amount of attention. I have since learned to heighten my "aura" or tone it down depending on my mood.

Chat it up. Just as job hunters tell everyone they meet that they're looking for work, there's no harm in chatting up even the most unlikely conversationalists. Hang out in your room and the only people you'll meet are the maid and the minibar checker. Get out and stay out for a while and you can always initiate a conversation, or at least ask a question in a line, in a lobby, at an ATM, ordering a beer at a brauhaus, or a burger at Burger King. Or with the person next to you at a U2 concert, in front of you waiting for the loo (we women, of course can make lots of friends that way), at a crosswalk, on a bus, in a bookstore—anywhere, anytime, the world offers friendly, chatty people, fascinated by your choice to travel solo.

Follow it up. Once you have somebody's attention, don't just stand there. Keep it going. Ask engaging questions to elicit preferences and opinions. Avoid simple yes or no questions, straight requests and trite comments or compliments; they don't lead to chats. Some good openers:

"Where would locals eat?"

"I only have a day. What can't I miss?"

"What souvenir best represents this region?"

"What's the best place to . . ?"

Try to have a joke or amusing anecdote at the ready (borrow some from this book if you like). And avoid potentially controversial topics such as politics or past relationships, and certain sure-to-bore topics that focus on you, such as your health problems or work.

Network. Networking is a truly acceptable part of business, and many of you are excellent at it. Why not apply it to travel? At a New York dinner party I was seated next to a famous architect. I saw him a few more times at parties over a couple of years, but he was only an acquaintance. Before traveling to Argentina, I got in touch with him, as he had designed many buildings there and had lived in Buenos Aires. He was most gracious and impressed that I would be soloing, and provided an incredible line-up of his creative friends without my even having to ask. The owner of a great Buenos Aires hotel gave me a tour of the suites, invited me to tea and talked for hours about the country. Restaurant owners gave me special service and drinks and food on the house. And people who worked at the architect's office there took me around for a special drive, highlighting his buildings. All because I politely asked for help.

Friends of friends, business contacts, or shopkeepers all might know people who they suggest you meet. Think a bit. Going to Mexico? How about the guy who owns the local Mexican restaurant? We know more people from other destinations than we realize, and most people will be happy to connect you.

Sometimes networking happens when you least expect it. On a press trip to Venezuela I met Rocco, a correspondent for an Italian paper who lived in New York. He had pasty white skin and a little black mustache, and unfortunately resembled a former German dictator. While the rest of us swam in tea-color water through a narrow canyon, Rocco was in a long-sleeved shirt sitting in a raft, paddled by natives. He was rebuffed as a misfit by most of the group, but the two of us got along swimmingly, pardon the pun. We sat next to each other on bus rides and at dinners. On the flight home, he confided that he was a cosponsor of a major Italian jazz festival, and asked if I wanted to attend for a week, with a guest. Because of that unexpected connection, my guest and I met and lived among many blues and jazz greats, including BB King and Wynton Marsalis, and enjoyed a magical week of music and celebration.

Rocco even invited us to the home of his friend, a famous celebrity photographer, in Rimini. We stayed overnight, savored home-cooked seafood and pasta, laughed unendingly, and peeked at outrageous outtake photos, too X-rated to be sold. The whole experience came about because I had been friendly and used my contacts. And by the way, Rocco may have been a misfit in the Venezuelan jungle, but he seemed way cool in his own environment.

It's good practice to bring along the business card or contact information of the person back home who's putting you in touch—in case you find yourself having to prove who you are. And as a good-will gesture, when someone offers you travel contacts, ask if there's something you can bring back for them. Even a photo of you and their friends might be a cherished memento.

And reciprocate. Share some of your treasured contacts with others. It helps make the world go round just a bit better for other solo travelers.

Travel to "friendly" countries. Some places are known for friendly, outgoing people. In my experience, U.S. midwesterners, Greek Islanders, Southern Italians, Filipinos, Australians, Canadians, and people from many southern African countries have been among the friendliest. And if you travel in countries where there's a historical connection or political connections to our country, it will help. Conversely, I avoid traveling solo where governments or people have shown major hostility to our way of life. (See Chapter 14)

Go long. The more time you devote to travel, the more time you'll have to meet people, so if making connections is a priority, plan for longer trips (even if it may mean fewer ones).

Where to Meet People
Over drinks. My friend Joseph tells me that the bartender at a restaurant in Paris didn't speak English, but even so, by the third night he had Joseph's favorite drink poured and ready. Words

aren't always needed. Sitting at a bar is an easy way to meet people, but be careful if you're not interested in romance—a bar meeting may connote an intimacy you aren't seeking.

Over food. Eating together is often a way of showing friendship, but can be awkward. My friend Diana was in Ho Chi Min City, Vietnam, at a sidewalk table. When it started to rain an elderly French teacher invited her to his table under a tarp. The teacher insisted on ordering a special dish he called "soft-boiled baby chicken in a spoon." Appalled, but unable to hurt the kind teacher's feelings, Diana came up with a classic comment: "I'm allergic to fetus. You enjoy it, and I'll enjoy your pleasure."

I wish I had been that quick. I had mentioned to an Irish friend that I liked local crayfish. He called ahead to his friend's pub, and when I arrived there, a giant crayfish—the last of the season—was awaiting on a plate. Unfortunately, I had just eaten lunch, and it was 3 PM, but the owners were watching, and I stuffed the crayfish down my throat, bite after endless bite, because I appreciated the gesture and didn't want to disappoint them. By the way, in other Irish pubs I chatted up Fred Astaire's daughter and Liam Neison's mum (who looked like him, in a scarf). You never know who—or whose kin—you'll meet in these friendly establishments when you're on your own.

On projects. If you're away on business or taking a class you'll have to discuss, assist, or commiserate at some point with kindred souls. And some of them will be characters. I'll never forget Estrella, a government official in a Central American country, who was assigned to host our press group. Estrella was, let's say, well-endowed all over, and kept that way by ordering double portions of everything for herself—and all of us, at her expense. I roomed with her, and one night she mumbled something about her former lover, "Rohere More." I didn't understand what she meant until she showed me a newspaper clipping from years past, a slender Estrella romping topless on a Cannes beach with 007 himself. You just never know.

In transit. Locals who meet lone travelers on boats and buses often start conversations, and some of them are legit. Just keep

QUICK TIPS TO ATTRACT PEOPLE

Dress uniquely. Vivid flowers lure bees, and vivid clothing will have people buzzing around you. Create your own come-hither look. You know your comfort level, so stay within it, and be sure showboating is appropriate for your destination.

Share suggestions. People like to check out hotel and restaurant recommendations and other advice. Carry a Fodor's guide, of course, to attract questions, pipe in if you hear others talking, and have a helpful tip handy.

Carry useful items. Popular reading material is a magnet. Traveling with paperbacks rather than heirloom first editions means you can offer your book to someone after you're done. Weather essentials also increase your popularity. A big umbrella, sunscreen, and bug spray are tops.

Walk a dog. An excellent conversation starter. Plus, you'll have company even before you start making human friends—and exercise (see Chapter 6, Traveling with Pets).

Offer to take somebody's photo. Or, ask that they take a photo of you. A camera provides one of the easiest and best ways to meet people. With that in mind, permit me the following digression: When the William Jefferson Clintons moved to Chappaqua, my husband and I were invited to a welcome-new-neighbors pot-luck supper. (The Clintons brought a casserole and two secret servicemen.) Nobody wanted to be uncool and take photos, but when the first camera came out, a dozen others followed. When my photo-op came, my hubby couldn't seem to click the camera button on our disposable, so there I was with the president's arm around me for what seemed like a minute, while clueless hubby kept trying to take our photo. Finally, President Clinton asked, "Can I help with that?" and he went over to my husband and wound the film forward, then came back and put his arm around me, and my husband took the photo.

People always ask why I'm laughing so hard in that snapshot.

your wits about you. A nice lady on a Greek ferry invited me to stay at her abode—a rented room, but it was awful and grimy. Because we had become "friends" on the ferry it was hard to extricate myself from the deal, but I managed.

On the same trip, my guide Dmitri invited me for a stopover at his grandmother's house. We had coffee and Greek pastries and a tour of her home, with precious family photos that were more than 100 years old. Another Greek guide brought me to meet her husband and children, and to enjoy homemade pastries and jam made from grapes grown in her garden.

These guides worked for reputable firms, and I don't know that I would have accepted their invitation otherwise. I have accepted many offers and declined just as many. Judge each case, and trust your instincts.

Special-interest travel. Nothing brings people together more than shared interests. A sports enthusiast can hike or ski or play tennis with people of the same skill and knowledge level. Civil War buffs can reenact together, chatting about Manassas and Gettysburg. You start off ahead, by being interested in the same things—a great way to converse and connect.

Anyplace where people congregate. Make a list. Mine would include hotel lobbies, transport stations, hairdressers, libraries, bookstores, malls, coffee shops, museums, concert halls, and houses of worship. You can meet different types of people depending on where you hang out, so choose carefully. Take Ali: I met him in a Turkish bazaar. He seemed kind and studious, and invited me to his tiny apartment where his father, wife, and children treated me as an honored guest. When I left, I realized my bracelet was missing, and cursed my naiveté at trusting him. The next day, a package was delivered to my hotel: Ali had walked miles out if his way to deliver my bracelet, which had fallen off my hand behind his couch.

Over the Internet. Today we have an instant world community and immediate company. The key, of course, is finding the *right* company.

Your Web browser will lead you to travel forums—travel-driven chats and bulletin boards. As you surf, you'll find a broad fee structure, ranging from none to hefty. No-fee travel forums typically include promotional links to travel related products, services, airlines, hotels, and tours. Fee-charging forums usually yield quicker, more direct personal connections among members, and typically the stiffer the fee the more exclusive the forum. All reserve the right to boot offensive or abusive users off at any time, a good way to filter out jerks.

One free forum is our very own fodors.com, which allows users to scroll through chats and postings without registering. Active participation (posting or responding to queries), however, requires registration, a fairly painless process. Once you've registered, you can read questions and comments, and look for people going somewhere you'd like to go. Perhaps you'll be in Switzerland, and your postings will be about trying to get people together while you're in Bern. You might even suggest a detour to join others who will be nearby.

If you have a planned itinerary, try to post a notice on a travel-related Web site's bulletin board ahead of time—at least a week, but ideally a month before your meeting date. Request what you want, and where you'll be and when. Be clear, but not too specific. Something like, "I will be in Singapore on March 14. Anyone want to meet for lunch?" Go from there. Don't tell where you'll be staying, or use your real name or personal information. You might get lots of answers, but as you don't know the people, remember: meet in a public place.

Before meeting someone, you might want to let others know where you are. And be prepared with a way to back out if it doesn't feel right. For example, if you're in a bar you could tell the bartender to rescue you with word of a call if you give a signal, and have a taxi at the ready. Then you could excuse yourself: "Sorry, but my plans have changed and I didn't have time to let you know. I have to go." If the other party persists, keep your excuses short, and be civil. And if civility fails, remember that being nice is not your first priority in this situation. In the end,

continued on p. 215

An Aspiring Actor

Traveling solo is a big plus when it comes to seeing a concert or event, or show, and chatting comes easy with those around you. Sometimes, you get to talk to the actors too.

I long ago purchased a matinee ticket for a well-reviewed drama, *Indiscretions*, brought over from London to Broadway. The writing was intelligent, Kathleen Turner was at her sexiest, and much was made of the adult, thought-provoking theme.

The day was warm and bright, and as I stood outside the theater, I spied a slight young man, maybe in his early twenties, smoking outside the stage door. He was in a grubby T-shirt and jeans, short, but with nice features.

"Got a ticket to the show?" he asked.

"Yes, last minute. Are you in it?" He didn't look like an actor.

"In it down to me bum."

"Oh, you're the one winds up nude?"

"Today *and* tonight. Think you can stand it?"

Since he was kidding, and flirty, I felt comfortable enough to kid him back. "I'll try not to laugh too hard, if you don't."

"I never laugh onstage. Too busy shivering. It's damn cold in there." The young actor explained that he was trained in England, this was his first time on Broadway, and how excited he was to be in the American production.

"Oh I'm sure this will be the first of many times you'll be on Broadway." I couldn't remember the reviews about him, but figured a polite word of encouragement was appropriate.

"Hope so. I love it here. New York's amazing."

We chatted a bit about America, the movies versus Broadway, and he said he wanted to do both. I admired his ambition.

He finished his cigarette, and turned to go back into the theater. "Well, I guess you'll be seeing me again. Soon."

"All of you." Such a cutie; I couldn't help it.

He smiled shyly, and waved off, and sure enough there he was onstage less than an hour later, emoting and disrobing, and doing both effectively. I wished him success, but had my doubts.

I didn't have to worry. Jude Law did very well for himself, indeed. 🕊

trust your gut. Which leads us next to perhaps the highest-stakes meeting-people topic of all.

ROMANCE (OR DON'T TAKE A CHANCE?)

You'll never know when you'll meet a nice man or woman on the road—but I doubt few relationships have developed as fast or as unexpectedly as one of mine did. At a major event in New York, honoring Scotland, I was seated next to the Mayor of Edinburgh, an utterly charming politician who had been that great city's top executive for dozens of years. His wife was seated at another place in the ballroom. The mayor and I had been chatting amiably for several minutes, when introductions and remarks began, and I suddenly was blinded with light.

"We are honored to have with us the mayor of Edinburgh, and his lovely wife," said the speaker. I slowly realized that the spotlight was on . . . *me*.

"Wave!" whispered the mayor, chuckling under his breath. So I produced, in my best Queen Elizabeth–style understated manner, a kind of windshield-wiper swipe befitting a mayoral wife. I didn't catch the look on the real wife's face, but boy did my fellow writers have a laugh.

Romantic relationships on the road can be as illusionary as that one, and I usually have avoided them. But the allure is ever present. Because you're away from home and no one is going to judge you, there's a temptation to take chances you ordinarily wouldn't. You trust, perhaps, faster than you do in normal life, especially if the person has a cute accent. But these things don't usually last longer than the time spent cajoling, and although the moon may be high and words may flow like a waterfall at snowmelt, intensity does not equal longevity. Just as you need to sometimes cut things off even before they start, you have to be just as firm about curtailing them once they do. For every "hola" be prepared to say "adios."

Where to Find It

If you're a female mammal, chances are you've been pinched in Italy. If you consider this kind of attention romantic, then just go to any piazza and smile at the passing guys and you'll find "romance." In Greece, there's a rite of passage for young males, testing to see how far they can lure Western female tourists. These earnest young studs hang around the Plaka area, the ancient section of Athens by the city center, waiting for women of all kinds, to practice their playful flattering—and maybe even score. "Come with me to see the sunset over the Parthenon," is one of their popular lines. They think of it as harmless flirtation, but if you take this sort of subterfuge as "romance" you're bound to lose—something.

Where should you go if you're itching for romance? Airline lounges, the tonier hotel lobbies and bars, and top tourist attractions attract solo grown-ups on the prowl—as do warm weather destinations with lots of nightlife. Honolulu, San Juan, San Francisco, New Orleans, Miami, Las Vegas, New York, San Antonio, San Diego, and Santa Fe are among the American cities with plenty of action, according to my single friends. To that list, from personal observation and a few well-placed questions, I'd add the international cities of Paris, Venice, Rome, Barcelona, and Hong Kong.

Romance & Risk

For the best dramatic example of the perils of romance on the road, rent *Summertime,* a mid-1950s movie starring Katherine Hepburn as a lean and fortyish spinster (that's what they called single women in those bad ol' days). In an unforgettable scene at an open-air café on the Piazza San Marco in Venice, she waits for her new lover, a Venetian shopkeeper, played by Rossano Brazzi. (I have never, ever seen a shopkeeper who looks as good!) Violinists are playing, couples are chatting at tables, sipping Campari, and there sits our Kate, bravely holding back the tears in her trembling but stoic Hepburnesque way. He—of course—never shows up. That scene conveys all the angst and stereotypical loneliness of looking for love on the road, but the message—at fade out—hints that it was worth it.

Real-life romance as a soloist isn't always dramatic. You may meet someone on a tour, and enjoy each others' company and a bit of flirtation without falling in love. Maybe there's some companionship, or even more.

In another movie, *Lost in Translation*, the look on Bill Murray's face as he cabbed to his hotel in Tokyo is in turn a sometimes all-too-classic look for a solo traveler: "What am I doing here?" I too once arrived solo in Tokyo. The neon lights of the Ginza seemed brighter than Times Square, the Japanese calligraphy was daunting, but the difference between the Murray character and me is that my face wasn't on a huge monitor over the street as I arrived. And nobody was meeting me. Yet, like Murray, I made a romantic connection—fleeting and memorable, in Japan. One of the only places I ever did. I knew the man's background and felt safe about it, and had a fun week. He went back to his life and I to mine, and we never heard from each other again. Was it worth it? For me, yes.

But there's always risk. Wherever you go there are seasoned opportunists as well as garden-variety jerks ready to test the effectiveness of their lines and stories. Let's face it, if you're a woman, you're already capable of deflecting lewd remarks and amateurish come-ons. You can minimize the risks of unwanted attention by keeping the following five points in mind.

Be careful. Some people are on the lookout for gullible travelers. They seek money or easy sex, or they may be already attached. These people are often charming and full of insincere words.

Be conservative. If the culture is carefree, that attention-getting blouse might be just fine. But blend in as much as possible, and respect the typical woman's role in that region. Observe how men and women interact on the street, and conform to those norms.

Stay in public places. Stay out of cars and other private spaces until you're really, really sure. You already know not to fall for lines like, "Come weez me, I have an original Picasso in my apartment," but be as aware of other ploys, especially ones that might get you into a private area. You can kiss someone on a park bench by the Danube or in Piccadilly Circus rather than in

Woody's Muse?

Many years before DVDs made director-interviews no big deal, I attended a movie festival in Tarrytown, New York, 40 minutes north of Manhattan. Judith Crist, a film critic for *New York Magazine*, coordinated the event at a sprawling, former estate on the Hudson River. And the guest film director at the weekend I attended was Woody Allen.

I was a young contributing editor at a local magazine, assigned to cover a story on weekend escapes. I excitedly arrived that first night, pen, notebook, and tape recorder at the ready, and with the other writers did prep work on Woody and his films, prior to his arrival the next day. At this early stage in his career he had only made a few comedies, and they were hilarious. The one he would be previewing that weekend was *Everything You Always Wanted to Know About Sex But Were Afraid to Ask*.

The film aficionados seemed intent on playing a practical joke on Woody. A favorite idea was buying several hundred (tiny) orders of coleslaw like he had ordered for his band of rebels in *Bananas*. But that idea lost out to all of us wearing the Groucho Marx eyebrows/glasses/nose that he had used for brilliant comic effect in *Take the Money and Run*. An eager volunteer was dispatched to wherever those sorts of things can be found, and actually came up with dozens of the disguises, passed out solemnly the next morning at breakfast. Glancing at the getup in my steamy, postshower mirror, I looked like Groucho after a botched sex-change operation. Oh well, anything for a good story.

We all bent down and donned the bushy paraphernalia when Woody first greeted us at a podium, and he looked more frightened than amused at the sight—who wouldn't have been? But then again, that seemed to be his expression throughout the weekend. He also appeared shy, courteous, and overwhelmed by the fawning, eager Woodyphiles.

His new film was a series of vignettes linked to the sexual theme, and the surreal discussion dealt with the problem of costuming actors who played sperm, and the difficulty of finding a sheep pretty enough to wear a nightgown. He showed a scene he never used, of his then wife, Louise Lasser, as a black-widow spider catching a fly (Woody) in her net just before eating him for dinner. Better left out, we all agreed. A most unusual film, not destined for greatness, but stimulating to discuss.

I spent most of the time listening in on conversations, and taking notes, wriggling my way close to Woody to overhear any of his words. He noticed me after a while, and seemed relieved when I told him I was writing for a regional magazine. If I spied him walking alone, I ran up and asked him as many questions as I could before anyone else horned in. He wanted to be Ingmar Bergman and do serious films, he said, and hated every city except New York and Paris. He was always wary, and never alone—if I could help it.

A year or so later, I saw his newest movie, *Starlight Memories*, now best remembered for Sharon Stone's debut in a tiny role with no dialogue. The plot was a parody of a put-upon-celebrity at a weekend function set near New York City, and Woody played the lead. Hmm. And look, there on the screen was Judith Crist, playing a guest at the function! Hmmm. And oh my, my, there was a young woman who hounds the Allen character with questions throughout the weekend, and when he opens the door to his room, she is in his bed, talking away!

Could it possibly be? I was insulted as I did not, nor did I want to, wind up in his bed. I was a budding journalist, not a groupie!

Now I'm not exactly saying that I was the inspiration for that young woman—I mean Woody has lots of fans, and I didn't go near his room. But I can't help thinking that as I was taking notes, so was he. Mental notes. From the other side, with our false noses and our goofy, unrelenting questions, he certainly didn't have to exaggerate much to find all the absurdity a director could ever want. ❧

their Volvo. And as for their room, I wouldn't; and as for yours, make sure it's devoid of valuables—and I still wouldn't. How about a cozy corner in the lobby?

Downgrade your looks. Just by being on your own, you've upped your availability aura, and many people will assume you're eager to connect, passionate and exciting. If you've reached your threshold for getting attention, don't be afraid, literally, to get ugly. Wear a cap over your hair and no makeup. Or repel to the max; I know someone who used eyeliner to put a cold sore on her lip! Less extremely, you can carry and show pictures of your family or home, or make an insta-wedding ring by flipping over your ring and placing it on the proper finger.

Break it off. If you're on the verge of an uncomfortable situation, break off contact and get near other people immediately. If your efforts are met with resistance, don't be afraid to shriek, flail, or fight back with whatever means and will you have at your disposal.

RESOURCES

Destination Web Sites

Destination-specific Web sites offer travel forums with various postings (essentially time-delayed chats), chats (live postings), and bulletin boards (slightly different, and discussed below).

To go about a search, use keywords: "Travel Chat," "Travel Boards," or "Travel Bulletin Boards or Postings," together with your destination (Italy, the Caribbean, or Australia. Or try a more narrow focus and search specifically for Rome, Barbados, or Sydney, for instance). Destination-specific sites also supply details about special attractions: sites worth a look-see, current attractions, events, and entertainment. Once you know your travel target and are at the pinning-down-the-itinerary stage, or if you're still selecting your destination and are curious about others' experiences, and/or the availability of travel mates for coffee or more, destination-specific sites can be one-stop clearinghouses.

Social Web Sites

Chat forums continue to evolve as a social networking mechanism, and travel forums are emerging as some of the hottest focus chats. Among these are:

Craigslist. Now in every major U.S. city, craigslist categories include personals (both strictly platonic and romantic) as well as travel. *www.craigslist.org*

Friendster. Probably the most popular social Web network, including a large travel forum. *www.friendster.com*

Lifeknot. Make friends with shared interests; free registration. *www.lifeknot.com*

Zorpia.com. This site provides a photo storage and journaling service and works according to a point system. Travel is a prominent topic. *www.zorpia.com*

Bulletin Boards

Backpack Europe on a budget. Readers initially select from a variety of topics, including "travel mates." Messages are dated and include a link to a broader description of the invitation, as well as an e-mail response link. Simply clicking on the "post a new message" link enabled me to post my own travel-mate note and response link ("going nowhere no time soon"; FYI, I got few responses and almost no serious ones). Visitors to this site can join the live chat simply by registering for free. *www. backpackeurope.com*

eTravel.org. Discussion topics have included travel companions; general travel chat; visa, passports, permits, and documents; travel news; travel gear; and health and medical. Date posted and reply links are included. *www.etravel.org*

Companion-Matching Sites

Same-sex or opposite-sex travel partners are a few keystrokes away. Whether you're looking for a platonic roommate to help you avoid a single supplement (see Chapter 2, Planning & Saving) or looking for something more, proceed with caution. Online services don't track the success of their matches, so "undesirables" can remain on the service and avoid detection. Free sites are riskier than others, since potential undesirables are less likely to release their information to these companies.

Even with careful screening there's no guarantee. But then, there never is. Herein lies the adventure. Here are few of the better sites.

Solo Travel Network. For a fee, so-called E-Members receive online newsletters every other month with info about solo travel. Most subscribers are women, and many opt to travel—but not room—with another person. *www.cstn.org*

TravelChums.com. A free service based in New York, TravelChums has more than 11,000 members—many of whom fill out profiles with photos. Members contact each other through the site's internal messaging system, and avoid disclosing contact information until they're ready. Many don't fill out profiles, and instead log onto the site's message boards, divided into global regions with multiple discussion topics. *www. travelchums.com*

Travel Companion Exchange. For about $300 a year, subscribers receive a newsletter and profiles of prospective travel partners, based on a questionnaire. When I was writing a travel column I researched an article about this pioneer group, and was a member for a while to receive info—although I never traveled with other members. Services are delivered by mail, and Web. Most of the several hundred subscribers are fairly upscale senior citizens, looking for companions of the opposite sex. *www.travelcompanions.com*

Vacation Partners. Prospective clients can fill out an 80-item questionnaire, and for a small fee you list your name in a database; for about double the fee, you get profiles of four prospective travel companions, whom you may contact directly. The pool of potential travel partners is more limited than at the other paid services. *www.vacationpartners.com*

Singles Travel Agents/Tour Operators
Several travel operators assist singles in coordinating trips and events that other singles attend.

Marion Smith Professional Singles. The scoop on parties, including ones catering to tennis buffs. *www. marionsmithsingles.com*

MatchTravel. As its name implies, this is a looking-for-romance site. Fairly upscale, trips range from Berkshire weekends to hiking Mt. Kilimanjaro. *www.matchtravel.com*

Singles Travel Company. Affordable globe-spanning tours mainly for travelers under 40. Same-sex roommates available to avoid the single supplement. *www.singles-cruises-tours.com*

Singles Travel International. Tours with soft to moderate activity levels. Same-sex roommates are guaranteed, or single accommodations are supplement free. *www.singlestravelintl.com*

chapter 14

Safety & Health

Remember the good old days when our biggest health problem was traveler's diarrhea? When our major safety concern was pickpockets?

Welcome to the new millennium. AIDS, SARS, Ebola, and al-Qaida are only a few of the dread terms that have emerged recently to thwart our travels, and indeed, our lives. Yes, the world seems scarier than it was a few years ago, especially when we venture alone.

We all have a different tolerance for risk. My son "Rand the Risk-Taker" has undertaken pretty hairy ventures, including entering Syria under the guise of being a barber rather than an American writer. Luckily he wasn't asked to cut anyone's hair, or he might still be there. When I ask him why he takes so many chances his answer invariably is, "Mom?!? Guess!"

Well, yes, I once traipsed alone to the Syrian border, just to see some incredible Roman-era mosaic floors in Antioch, Turkey—but my choices are calculated. I do what feels right, think carefully before deciding, and I'm not afraid to say, "No way." Life is a balancing act, and believe me, I try not to fall on my face. But I will not let unreasonable fears keep me from a full, exploratory life.

Most of us feel less vulnerable when we're herded around in big groups between airports, hotels, and tourism sites. But that's an illusion: alone, you have more control over your health and safety. Your profile is lower and you're much more in charge of your own itinerary. On a press trip I flew in a plane that looked like a banged-up SUV with wings (I swear, there were bandages on it!), but if any of the six of us balked we might still be on that isolated island off Panama like a reject group from *Survivor*. So I took a deep breath and boarded with the others, praying to the luck gods and wondering why I didn't work at a nine-to-five desk job. (If I were alone, I'd have built a raft!)

Simple rule: If you're not comfortable with something, if possible, don't do it. Break away if necessary (See Chapter 16, Breaking Away).

On the down side, when you're alone, no one will wake you up so that you take your antibiotic in the middle of the night; you'll have to awaken yourself, even if you head feels like a water-filled balloon. No one will walk five blocks to the pharmacy to get your meds, or hold your hand when you walk down a dark street. You'll have to figure out ways to adjust, and some of them are simple: wake-up calls, alarms, paying for delivery of the medicine, and not walking in the dark. So be as comfortable as possible, and don't give in to unreasonable, fixable fears. Be clear about your aims and your risk-tolerance, gather info before you go, and be resourceful when you get there.

This chapter will take a hard line on safety and health, and face some unpleasant truths, but travel isn't just about lying on a palm-fringed beach with a piña colada. Jellyfish sting. The sun burns as well as tans. Jerks kick sand in your face, and even steal your camera. Or that piña colada may give you traveler's diarrhea, just like old times.

SAFETY

For just about any answer to a safety question, *The Safe Travel Book,* by Peter Savage, remains the classic guide for the international traveler. It warned of terrorism in 1988; today I'm struck by its prescience, and agree more than ever with a blurb I wrote for the back of the first edition: "Offers practical suggestions for just about any travel-safety problem. Useful and timely." I hope my suggestions are, also.

Protecting Yourself & Your Stuff

As a solo traveler, you don't have the luxury of saying "Watch my purse" or "My pants don't have pockets, will you carry this?" Nor will you have a protector to make you feel safe, or a companion to give you driving directions. This is potentially one of the biggest downsides of solo travel, but it doesn't have to be. Not if you're prepared.

Don't present an easy target. Fanny pack, camera, and guidebook, oh my! Yes, you're a tourist, but you can downplay it. Keep your purse and backpack closed until you reach a private or at least semiprivate place. Only use luggage tags that close over your name and address or, better yet, only display your cellphone number. Avoid standing on a street corner struggling with a map. In general, avoid any gesture that gives way to distraction or befuddlement.

Don't carry valuables in your bags. My friend Moira carried a big wallet filled with cash and credit cards, and when a trio of greedy girls surrounded her in Spain I figured she'd had it. Luckily they grabbed her makeup bag instead. Most of us are seldom as lucky as Moira: your knapsack, fanny pack, or purse should not be your go-to place for currency or important documents. Use money pouches snapped on the inside of your clothing, or money belts that can be worn against your skin and ride comfortably under your clothes.

Don't wear expensive or expensive-looking jewelry. Big cities and third-world and Mediterranean countries are known for street crime, but your jewelry can tempt anyone, anywhere. Find another way to accessorize.

Stay away from, or on the edge of, crowds. I remember a scary situation at a jazz festival in Assisi, Italy. The crowd was drinking heavily, and suddenly a group of young men started walking toward those of us who were entering the piazza. We were pushed against a wall, and if a kind and feisty nun hadn't scared off the men and led us to her convent above the piazza, this book might not have been written.

Don't be nice all the time. Trust your suspicions if you think someone is out to harass you, or worse. Learn how to say, "No," and, "Get lost!" in the local dialect. Don't be afraid to say, "Gotta go. Big Bubba is waiting on me," or even "I've already called the police." Safety trumps truth.

Don't tell everybody everything. Although you may normally tell people you're traveling alone, and wouldn't feel funny about joining certain people, change your actions if there's even a hint of suspicion. Also, don't give your hotel name, home address, or other personal information to strangers.

Give up your goods when you see a weapon. In Stockholm of all places, a guy with a knife came by my VW pop-top camper and said, "Give me your bread!" I wasn't sure if he meant whole-wheat or money, and decided rather than be witty, I'd hand over what I had. I didn't like the looks of his bread knife.

Be nimble on the street. If you feel unsafe walking day or night, there's no shame in demonstratively altering your course, even if you think it makes you look foolish. Duck into a cab or restaurant, attach yourself to a group, or sidle up to a couple. I have walked (alertly) in the middle of the street, preferring that danger, when I've sensed someone is following me. Know precisely when the sun sets in your destination so you're not literally caught in the dark.

Watch yourself at ATMs. These ubiquitous money machines are magnets to pickpockets. In Rome, near the main train terminal, my husband was taking money out of an ATM, and I was diligently guarding him, my eyes scanning the streets to be sure no one was lurking about. I was pleased at my carefulness, and was shocked when he came over with the money, but no wallet;

KEEP YOUR NUMBERS TO YOURSELF

A corporate attorney sent the following note to his employees, with useful suggestions for travel, as well as the rest of the time.

▸ Order checks with only your initials and last name on them. If someone takes your checkbook, they won't know if you sign your checks with just your initials or your first name, but your bank will.

▸ When you're writing checks to pay on your credit-card accounts, don't put the complete account number on the "For" line. Instead, just put the last four numbers. The credit card company knows the rest of the number and people in the check-processing channels won't have access to it.

▸ Put your work phone number on your checks instead of your home phone. If you have a PO Box use that instead of your home address, or use your work address.

▸ Never have your Social Security number printed on your checks. You can add it if it's necessary, but if you have it printed, anyone can get it.

seems while I was busy looking out, a pickpocket had sneaked behind him and in a few seconds, removed it. We spent the next day on the phone and at the American Express office.

Bring minimum cards. The inconvenience mounts with each one lost. Unfortunately my husband had not emptied his wallet before traveling. The pickpocket could not only charge on several credit cards, he could charge groceries and use our library!

If Your Wallet Is Stolen

Make copies. Keep photocopies of passports, credit card numbers, and traveler's checks at home (preferably with a friend) and in your luggage—anywhere but on your person. If you're robbed or burgled, these backups will make it easier for you to procure the new documents. Keep the toll-free numbers of your credit-card companies with you. And here's a radical idea: memorize your credit-card numbers. If you're only carrying two, and that's as many as you should need, it's not a big deal.

Report it. File a police report immediately in the jurisdiction where your item was stolen; this proves to credit providers you were diligent, and is a first step toward an investigation (if there ever is one). A police report is also a money saver: many organizations will waive card- and documentation-replacement fees if you provide them with a copy of the report.

Other important phone numbers are those of the three national credit-reporting organizations, which, once contacted, will place a fraud alert on your name and Social Security number. The alert conveys to any company checking your credit that your information was stolen, and they must contact you by phone to authorize new credit. Equifax: 800/525–6285; Experian (formerly TRW): 888/397–3742; Trans Union: 800/680–7289. Also: Social Security Administration (fraud line): 800/269–0271.

Terrorism, Political Situations & General Safety

Perceptions of terrorism and political upheaval can foil the solo traveler and, not incidentally, the travel industry. Get the facts before planning—or not planning—a trip, and follow this advice.

Reach out. When traveling solo, especially in potentially volatile areas, make sure someone outside of your trip knows your itinerary completely, including updates and changes, and stay in touch with that person on a regular, prearranged basis (e-mail that person at least every other day, if possible).

Register with your local embassy or consulate. An embassy is a patch of home soil, a haven of information and protection. If officials know you are in the country and where to reach you, it will be easier for them to help in an emergency situation. If you're staying longer than a week, or if a situation gets dicey, registering is worth it to help you feel more secure. Make sure someone you trust has your power of attorney. Leave photocopies of your passport with the embassy. They will gladly hook you up with your family.

My friend from Buenos Aires, Liana, was hurt in an auto accident. In her words:

"I was living in Bangkok and one day while crossing the street I saw a car coming toward me. I was badly injured, and the police came immediately. We all went to the regular police, where the driver defended himself. I was asked to sign a paper, but insisted in seeing the tourist police, who are more fair to tourists and can speak English. I wound up in the hospital for 11 days and was in a cast for three months, and because I had registered with my embassy, they sent Argentinians to visit me, and help. I felt good that my country was caring for me. If it weren't for the embassy, I would have not been able to talk in my own language, and feel secure."

Another fine use of your embassy or consulate: natural disaster. I was in a typhoon in the Philippines, and managed to get through it, as most of the locals did, with a minimum of fuss. People just went out to work when it subsided, as if nothing had happened. But I had the phone number and address of the American Embassy, just in case.

Use awareness and instinct, supported by observation and local information. The likelihood of being involved in an act of terrorism, a political upheaval, or kidnapping is remote—but try to make it even more so.

On the last day of my month-and-a-half stint in Manila, rumblings of a coup were in the air. Because of the political unrest, I stayed at a hotel near the airport, and my driver had to maneuver the car onto the sidewalk to avoid the flag-waving crowds. The next morning I was out of there. The coup fizzled, but I was wise to stay as close to my escape route as possible.

Heed travel alerts. Call the U.S. Department of State, 202/647–5225, to make sure the country you're considering is safe. British, Canadian, and Australian foreign-service reports are also excellent for the latest advisories. Or go to the destination's English-language local newspaper on the Internet, (see www. thepaperboy.com) for state-department warnings and travel procedures.

I try to keep my travel plans as normal as possible and not change them for over-hyped reasons, but I know when I personally would back off. The key word is "comfort level." The summer after the Chernobyl nuclear melt-down in Russia, in the mid-1980s, I traveled to Europe when there seemed to be fewer Americans than Easter Islanders! It was safe, but the perception lagged. I read the facts, took advantage of the bargains and uncrowded sites, and felt fine about it. You may not have. However, today I would not want to travel in the Middle East, and I doubt if most of us will ever see Afghanistan, Iraq, Iran, North Korea, or Albania. Such is life.

Be tactful. Alas, in many parts of the world where we used to be praised for our citizenship, we should now think twice before volunteering it. If things get dicey, try to change the subject, and make a point of separating yourself from politics, with a soft, firm voice and a smile. Good jokes sometimes work, so have a few ready. And you can always ask questions about travel, which people seem to love, and which gets them off the subject of you.

If that doesn't work, listen patiently, even if the discussion gets nasty. Then excuse yourself sweetly and get the hell out of there. That has happened to me a couple of times, most recently in Manchester, England (our political allies are often the most vocal). I have strong opinions, but feel it wiser to keep them to myself until I get home.

If I sense rabid anti-Americanism, and I can't extricate myself, as a last resort I'll mention casually and quickly that I'm from Ottawa! I consider this subterfuge a safety precaution rather than a fib, especially when I'm alone. If you try this yourself, just be sure you know a little bit about Canada.

HEALTH

Sick? Ick. When you don't feel well, travel turns a stranger's gaze upon you; nothing's more rotten. Traveling with someone, it's different. In Vienna, with a headache and nausea, I missed a night out and a taste of a sacher torte, but my young and dutiful husband brought in a doctor and bought me remedies from the pharmacy, and a sacher torte from Demel's, for later. I felt safe.

On a trip in Acapulco, new hubby and I were both dreadful with dysentery in our hillside casita overlooking the bay with its own little pool just outside the bolted door. Someone arrived twice a day to throw fresh hibiscus petals into the pool, which floated like soggy pink potato chips. Goodies to eat arrived through a slot in the door, which usually prompted one of us to drag ourselves out of bed in our tiled and darkened room to retch. I had barely enough energy shuffling to or from the bathroom to open the shutters and gaze a couple of minutes at the sunset we were paying through the nose to view. But we were together in adversity and there was a castaways feeling to our malaise. And after a couple of days we paid our bill and moved along.

Alone, you'll really be calling on your strength, judgment, and resources. I had just arrived in Guatamala City on a three-week research trip, preparing to critique maybe 100 hotels throughout the country for a travel-trade publication. My itinerary was set, my driver hired and ready. But on the first night, I didn't feel well, and stayed up all night watching the same Steven Seagal movie until the morning, when I wrote a note, and flew back to the states. It was a close call, but a good one. I had a (successful) operation, and was back six weeks later.

But it was hard for me to pull out. I didn't want to screw up the plans, and disappoint people. I wanted to keep on my schedule. You may be the same way, but if so, get over it. Health is more important than losing a deposit, or anything else.

Before You Go
Find out from consulates or travel boards what immunizations and documents you need, and follow up with your doctor.

See your doctor a few months before you leave. Tetanus, hepatitis, cholera, yellow fever, and typhoid might be among the diseases for which you need shots; tetanus and cholera shots sometimes produce a strong reaction, and some inoculations

continued on p. 236

Fear & Joy in Java

A day in Jojakarta, the historic university town in Java, was all I had. I hired a car and asked for a driver who spoke "the best possible" English, which meant he could—maybe—understand a bit. I knew to bring along a guidebook.

My driver was an earnest young man in a tie and jacket who talked openly of his new son and of his vasectomy. "I will make sure he can go to college and become a doctor. But I cannot have more children." He paused. "Our country is responsible about birth control and family planning."

A man with a plan in this fourth largest of all countries. He explained that the economy was improving rapidly, that Indonesia was modernizing, and although he would have liked many sons, he would sacrifice to bring up his one. He drove me slowly around, pointing out the downtown and the university, and dropped me off at an open-air palace, a seraglio complex, where Javanese rulers had lived through the centuries.

"I will pick you up in an hour," he said. "Right here in front."

Walking through the pavilions, on cool surfaces open to the heavy air, I heard the percussive, bell-like sounds of the gamelan, as dancers in diaphanous gowns streamed forth, legs and arms twisted, their dark slanted eyes darting in studied poses.

Most of the hour passed as I watching the ritual dances, and when I wandered to the gardens, I noticed the sky had turned heavy and pewter. Suddenly rain pelted, and within minutes gutters spewed torrents. I sat on a slick stone bench under a ledge in the courtyard, and realized I was alone, except for a bearded man in a white robe, sitting on the bench next to mine, also staring out to the gardens and the monsoon rain.

I couldn't move. I would have to wait it out, as the waters slammed down like sabers, and the angled roofs of the seraglio became waterfalls. The robed man and I never looked at each other. The hour I was to meet my guide had long passed, and I was sure he had returned to his son.

No one knew where I was, and my mind started to spiral. The man on the bench could rape me, rob me—kill me, and no one would ever know about it. My kids would think I was lost at sea. Years from now they would tell their children stories of their lost grandmother, who traveled alone in the late 20th century, who one day traveled too far into the unknown. I would become a lesson.

Darkness deepened as the afternoon waned, but finally, *finally* the rains stopped, and I ran, dripping, to the front of the seraglio, delighted I had survived, but worried now how I would get back to the world. I was shivering, and for once, lonely. I looked around, desperate.

My guide was waiting! I have never been happier to see a man. I took him for tea at the first shop off the road, and the smoky brew revived me, and loosened his tongue. It was getting late, but he talked on and on, and I was grateful for each word, even though I still wanted to visit Borobadur, the main reason I had come to Java.

"It's closed now, but you shouldn't miss it," said the guide, who sensed my disappointment, and once again was going to rescue me. "If you give the gatekeeper 10 dollars you'll have the place to yourself before it turns dark."

We sped through the puddles and soon arrived at a plain dominated with a towering mound of Buddhas. At the gatehouse, after some discussion and a proffered bill, the gatekeeper brought an iron key, big as a carving knife and as heavy, and opened the gate with ceremonious clanking.

"Twenty minutes only," he said.

I clambered up a spiral path lined with hundreds of massive statues staring impassively, as if to ignore my scramblings. I climbed circle after circle, in what seemed Dante's version of Nirvana, stopping to gaze at the fields surrounding the huge monument that had become a hill unto itself.

The wind blended into my heavy breathing, as if the Buddhas themselves were sighing, en masse, along with me. The clouds that had drenched the earth that afternoon were now miles away, reflecting the sun's fading rays in mango and guava.

Alone again, still damp, darkness fell about me as completely as the rain had, but now I was without fear or loneliness. The forces of humanity and nature were too glorious for words. I was blissful. ❧

require a series a month apart, so leave plenty of time. Also consider a flu shot, and ask whether a pneumonia shot would be prudent. Consult your doctor about how you might want to tailor your med kit for your intended destination. Discuss any health issues that you've been putting off. Likewise, make appointments with other medical practitioners, such as your dentist or optometrist, if you haven't seen them recently.

Get referrals. To find a doctor where you'll be, ask your doctor for recommendations ahead of time or join a group such as Intermedic or International Association for Medical Assistance, which has listings of English-speaking doctors throughout the world.

Know what your plan covers. Determine whether your regular medical insurance covers you while you're away from home. If not you should consider extra coverage, which might include trip insurance.

Bring your meds. Get an updated prescription and make sure you bring enough of it; best to take an extra month's supply, just in case.

Carry medical documentation. If you have special health problems, collect pertinent records, including names, dosages, allergies, and blood types. Carry your doctors' names, phone, fax numbers, and e-mail addresses, if possible.

Learn about helpful resources where you'll be. Besides doctors, others who can help if you're ill include staff at the nearest American embassy or consulate, who can provide a list of doctors, concierges, and local police.

Learn the emergency number for the area you're in. And learn how to ask for a doctor in the local language.

Dealing with Common Health Problems

ACCIDENTS
You may already have experienced an accident with no one around to help. I've wrenched my back and had to stay put for

hours, hoping someone would knock and I could scream, "I've fallen and I can't get up," just like that lady in the old TV ad. Be extra careful when you're traveling.

A young friend—who wishes to remain nameless—was traveling in Vietnam and in his youthful joy jumped 30 feet off a boat into the water, dislocating his shoulder. Now this sad circumstance is scary and painful anywhere, but when you are in a foreign country, on a boat, it's especially unfortunate. He was transferred to a truck in terrible pain, and bounced along so hard on a rutted road that his shoulder popped back into place!

The bottom line is, don't take foolish risks. Think before acting out.

JET LAG

Our body's reaction to the disruption of its biological clock— our normal pattern of eating, sleeping and waking, has been dubbed "jet lag." If you fly between time zones, and are fatigued to begin with, you're prone to get it. All kinds of complicated suggestions use melatonin and Argonne Lab diets, but I find them confusing, and if misapplied they can leave you worse off. There are simpler ways to minimize the headache, fatigue, and general malaise.

☞ Get extra rest before and after your flight.

☞ Break a really long flight into segments, so that you can recuperate. You could fly from New York to Los Angeles, Los Angeles to Hawaii, and Hawaii to Australia, rather than from Los Angeles to Australia.

☞ Drink lots of nonalcoholic beverages, and eat lightly.

☞ Try to sleep on the plane and then stay awake during daylight hours at your destination.

☞ After a transcontinental or transoceanic flight, reward yourself with a gentle day. Nap a bit, and try to stay up so that you go to sleep early evening, local time.

FATIGUE

When you're dragging, your whole travel experience suffers, so be really good to yourself. Sound sleep—enough sleep—is imperative. To rest well, carry a mask, ear plugs, and even your own pillow so that if your room has sheer curtains and is above a club you can still rest easy. Try to get at least as much sleep as you would at home. To relieve stress, wear loose fitting clothing and comfortable shoes. Your entire body will benefit and you'll avoid blisters, athlete's foot, and corns. And if you haven't fully joined the 21st century, make sure your luggage has wheels.

DIARRHEA

With a bad bout of the runs, you may have only about 10 minutes to get to a toilet—a nightmare situation if you're in the middle of a rock concert or on a ride at an amusement park. I remember once on a bus in Italy, the driver had to stop somewhere between Bologna and Venice for a guy to relieve himself on the side of the highway, with cars honking and all of us averting our eyes. Not a pretty sight.

Eating moderately and watching what you eat and drink are best. If you do get sick, over-the-counter Immodium, Pepto-Bismol, Lomotil, or prescription Ciprofloxacin or other doctor-recommended prescription medicines are important allies. During the bout, drink many fluids, eat bland foods and try to get some rest. Dare I say: This too shall pass.

FOOD POISONING

If you're unlucky enough to get food poisoning, don't self-medicate—get to a doctor or to an emergency room. With food poisoning, discomfort turns to pain, nausea to full-out retching. If in doubt, seek help right away.

Prevention is the best foil for food poisoning. Be wary of street food, even if it looks and smells fabulous, which it often does. For several months I had to feed a crew in Southeast Asia, and I learned how to judge. Is the food fully cooked? Is fruit unpeeled? Is there refrigeration? Hot water to clean things? Is it a popular place, serving typical fare? As a precaution, carry your own food and water. Granola bars, peelable fruit, peanut butter, crackers, herbal-tea bags, a hot-water immersion gadget, and small bottles of water are staples.

NAUSEA/MOTION SICKNESS

Did you know that if you drive you're less likely to get motion sickness than if you're a passenger? And if you feel seasick, you should breathe some fresh air, then rock and roll with the motion, resting in your bed. Bonine and Dramamine are popular anti-nausea pills, but some swear by a patch of scopolamine, put behind your ear a day before you go. Others feel that pressure-point bracelets avert nausea, but you'll have to wear them ahead of time. Ginger—fresh or candied, or even gingersnaps, ginger-bread, or ginger tea are refreshing antidotes. Powdered ginger is available at health-food stores; include it in your med kit.

COLD & FLU

A bad cold or flu can knock you out when you have to keep going, and if you don't attend to it, can hang on for weeks. Rest, drink liquids, use antihistamines for symptoms, aspirin or Tylenol for fever, and don't push yourself. See if you can rest in one spot at least 'til the worst is over.

I remember when I wasn't feeling great and had only a couple of days in Singapore. On the first day, I took a bus-tour overview, and suddenly felt terrible. At one point, at a stop, I simply went over to a garbage can and threw up, then got back into the bus. (No time to spare, and I knew I'd never see these people again.) Next day I felt worse—achy, tired. I took meds, but instead of staying in bed all day, I taxied to a park wrapped in a pashmina like a mummy in coral wool, propped myself on a bench overlooking a pond, and spent much of the day listening to birdsong, and watching the children play near the pond. The next day I was revived and on schedule.

INFECTIONS

A simple infection can flare up in the most inconvenient places, even from a paper cut. Use Bacitracin or other antibacterial salves and bandage, if needed to allow for healing. Wash your hands all the time, with soap and hot water or antibacterial gel to avoid possible infections. And use your head—don't hang around where germs are rampant. To avoid yeast infections, most common in humid situations, wear loose cotton clothing, especially skirts rather than slacks, bring medication and avoid antibiotics. If you're traveling to places where it's difficult to get antibiotics, ask your doctor if you can bring along a basic, all-purpose med.

INSECT BITES & RASHES

Flying insects, spiders, mites, fleas, and ticks can cause itching and more serious problems, and you'll see lots of these critters as you travel. Try to avoid them rather than confront them. I once found a scorpion in my shoe and recovered from the shock by promptly sitting down on a huge palmetto bug. Don't do that if you can help it!

Sprays and creams with DEET should keep the bugs away. Also, avoid scented toiletries, and do wear loose-fitting long-sleeved shirts and pants with socks. Check your body for ticks right after walking in tall grasses or woods. As for poison ivy, oak, sumac, and other contact rashes, if you're prone to them keep a lookout and carry some prescribed antihistamine and cortisone-based cream.

SUNBURN

Sunburn can get severe enough to hold up your travel. This one is easy: wear 30-level or higher sun block to prevent it. Don't forget your neck area, nose and lips—vulnerable areas often forgotten. And as solo travelers, we can always ask the concierge to cover our backs with sun block. Do not be fooled by cloudy days, and at great heights or in the tropics be sure to wear a hat as well. I wear T-shirts to the beach or snorkeling, which may not be sexy, but on most trips, I'm not interested in calling attention to myself anyway.

DVT

Flying for several hours can cause deep-vein thrombosis, a potentially serious condition in which blood clots form in the leg or pelvic veins, usually within two weeks of a flight. Symptoms include cramping, intermittent leg pain, redness or swelling in a calf, shortness of breath, and chest pain. The Coalition to Prevent Deep-Vein Thrombosis (www.preventdvt.org), recommends these measures for all passengers on flights of six or more hours:

▷ Drink plenty of water and little or no alcohol; wear loose-fitting clothes to avoid constricting blood vessels; walk around the cabin and do simple exercises, like pumping your feet in your seat to increase blood circulation.

▷ If you're at moderate risk, with a history of the disorder or are over 60, wear compression stockings that help increase blood circulation from the legs to the heart by putting pressure on the legs.

▷ If you're at high risk, including heart disease, cancer, or clotting disorders, or if you've had recent surgery, talk with your doctor about taking medicine to prevent blood clots before flying.

HEPATITIS

This virus, which attacks the liver, is transmitted mainly through blood, but Hepatitus B can be more easily picked up through contaminated water or food, usually in less-developed countries, or in situations where sanitation is lax. A series of three vaccinations will help prevent this problem, but you'll need to start them six months before travel.

MALARIA

Malarial fever is caused by a mosquito bite, and the world is filled with swampy areas where these insects breed. Once you get the potentially deadly disease you can have bouts of fever, chills, and severe malaise for life. Cover-up clothing and sleeping under mosquito netting are wise preventative measures in endemic areas, such as parts of Africa or Southeast Asia, and you'll need to find out from your doctor at least a month ahead of travel if you need to start taking malaria pills. Several medications work well, depending on many factors, but the main thing is to take the prescribed pills on schedule, and to wash them down with lots of water. I had an esophageal ulcer for several months because I didn't do this, and felt as if I had swallowed a ball of fire every time I swallowed, for weeks.

RESOURCES

The U.S. Department of State, Bureau of Consular Affairs offers
two detailed and informative Web sites providing important
travel advisories and information.

Travel security advisories. American Citizens Services
Division provides "Travel Warnings & Consular Information
Sheets," including medical advisories, according to country.
Warnings range from advising on short-term conditions or
threats, to avoiding certain countries altogether. Links are
provided by country to every U.S. embassy or consulate in
the world, and a link to the CIA Factbook is provided for the
same information for U.S. territories. *www.travel.state.gov/
travel_warnings.html*

U.S. Transportation Security Administration. The Traveler &
Consumer Center provides Department of Homeland Security
alert status and addresses travel security by mass transit, air,
rail, vessel and, highway. Notices regarding checked bags, security measures to expect, and travel tips are regularly updated.
www.tsa.gov/public

chapter 15

Special Solo Situations

A traveler inhabits more than one category when she's on the road. Take yours truly: I'm a solo traveler as well as a woman traveler, a mature traveler (young in spirit), and a business traveler. You might be all of these things, or a parenting traveler, or a traveler with disabilities. Whether you cross one category or many, the following tips and resources will assist you during special solo situations.

Women Travelers

Let's face it, if you've picked up this book, you're likely to be in this category. And it's a time-tested one: The first women travelers may have been 4th-century Christian pilgrims, and the Catholic Church soon provided them with separate hostels. (Even today, convents offer cheap, safe, and clean accommodations for solo women.) Unfortunately, except for religious reasons or emergency travel, up until the last century most women soloists were considered loosey-goosey types, or oddball spinsters.

We've come a long way, traveling every way, and everywhere—and on our own! By the end of the 20th century, almost 250 million women traveled solo or with other women. Today, more of us from all age groups are traveling, and many travel alone, whether married or not—spouses or companions can't get away, have different interests, or may not want to travel. And many women prefer breaking away from their normal family routines just to interact with an all-women's group.

Some of us have no trouble being on our own. But what prevents more women from traveling alone? Women Traveling Together in Maryland reports that in a poll of more than 500 women, 68 percent of the respondents said they traveled alone at least once in the past three years, but 79 percent of these wouldn't have soloed if they could have found a companion. Besides security fears, popular reasons for joining a travel group are companionship, and the desire to avoid the single supplement by sharing a room.

Alone or with others, or only with women, the great news is that you're doing it. You'll be able to match your spirit, stamina, pocketbook, and sense of fun with a women's travel resource. Women's tour groups and adventure trips can take you to top resorts around the world on a discounted "group" rate, or whisk you overseas—all on tours exclusively for women. Women's tour coordinators and adventure-travel operators are sensitive to the single supplement issue and provide roommate matching, or sometimes no, or low, supplement fees.

Business Travel

Whether you're spending a week at an ocean-front suite researching the hula in Maui, or addressing a group on fender-bender prevention in Detroit—in January—it's business. For many of you, work-related travel is the only time you'll be soloing, with a chance to indulge in the pleasures of being alone. If you're already packed and on the road, it's simple enough to turn an extra day or a few stolen hours into a minivacation. This might require adding time to the front or back end of your business plans, or extending days or evenings, so you need to plan and use your time efficiently. I like to wrap business time around a weekend for maximum effect.

For more than a decade I conducted writing workshops for corporations around the country, and a business-travel routine that worked for me whenever possible was half work, half fun. I purposefully mixed enjoyable down time with necessary work time. In Los Angeles, I shopped in Little Korea and Rodeo Drive and poked around the La Brea tar pits after my workday. In Houston, after intense days of lecturing, I slipped into jeans and dug into five-napkin ribs and chicken at the best local barbecue joint, eventually line-dancing and even mechanical bull-riding (Bull, 1; Lea, 0).

Ask your hotel for favorite tours that can be accomplished in a few hours, and canvas your destination's visitor information Web site for worthy activities that accommodate your schedule.

Under-Thirtyish Travel

Can I hedge on a heading, or what? The under-thirtyish set is everywhere, especially in summertime. Study-abroad programs, free time, flexible lifestyles, appropriate fearlessness, and a "no-biggie" approach is this age bracket's norm—a backpack, a rail pass, and a few weeks or months to see the world.

You can find most under-thirty soloists in trains and hostels, budget hotels, cafés and bars, public transportation, museums, and popular sites in-and-around universities, including cyber-cafés. I married for the first time in my early twenties, and hardly traveled solo until after I divorced, but I often talk to young travelers on my trips, and I'm thrilled at their love of going it alone. Young travelers should seek student and youth discounts whenever buying tickets; major rail transport, such as Eurail, usually offers special youth passes.

Mature Travel

Travelers are considered "mature" at different ages in different places, so lots of us might qualify for special treatment depending where we travel. Nowadays mature travelers—with hard-bodies and not-so-hard; and tons of time and funds and not-that-much but just enough—fill the world's beauty and hot-spots. Whether on bus tours or cycling, on foot or in the back of a stretch limo, they bring appreciation, experience, seasoning, and yes, passion to their travels.

continued on p. 248

Alone on a Cliff

Two weeks after I reserved a cabin on an island off the coast of New Brunswick, Canada, for a romantic getaway, my husband was diagnosed with an incurable brain tumor, and three months later he was gone.

The next spring, when I got a call from the owners, I had forgotten all about the cabin reservation. My house was up for sale, my husband's estate was being challenged, my funds were free falling, and I would be turning a Major Number in a few weeks. To hell with it, I decided to get away from everything and go to the cliff by myself. I loaded my black Miata, the one my husband had gifted me. I brought few clothes, but I did haul Mel Torme, Bach, the Eagles, Dvořák, Leo Kottke, and our favorite Alsatian wine, chocolate, biscotti, and vinegar potato chips. At least I would enjoy our music and food.

I kept the top down the whole way on the drive from Westchester County, and overnighted in Augusta, Maine, in a Motel 6 as darkness fell, around 9 pm. The only available room had a broken bed, but I slept in the other one, opened the windows to erase the smell of smoke, and fell asleep with "The Mole" on TV, wondering what I was doing.

Arriving by ferry on Grand Manan Island the next day, I drove to the western side and parked the car in a clearing. The young cabin owner, who ran a local kayak company, met me there in an All-Terrain-Vehicle and drove me over a rutted dirt road, into thick woods. The cabin was set on a little-used hiking trail, along 30-foot basalt cliffs towering above rocky beaches, covered twice a day by the highest tides in the world. The view overlooked the setting sun, and a weir where fisherman trapped herring in purse seiner boats. The structure was handmade with pine trim and floors, powered by the sun, augmented by a generator. Using the in-house-out house earth toilet, I empathized with my cat, left behind with my son.

At first I felt like a child, playing house. I picked daisies and a blue flower called cow vetch and plopped them in a glass by the windows. I cooked veggies and chicken in the little kitchen. But by the third day, when I walked 25 minutes back to my car, and then drove to check my e-mail at the kayak office, I must have seemed starved for company.

"Want to take our dog while you're here?" asked the sympathetic cabin owner. So Sole, their chocolate lab, joined me on the cliff. She offered a chance to hear the sound of my voice without feeling like a fool, and patiently waited for me to arise, romping near me along steep paths, chasing butterflies on our morning walk. She leaped and pawed and licked me when I stirred sardines into her kibble. And she stared at me as if she understood more than I did.

Along the cliffs I passed streams and waving meadows of grasses. Waves crashed below in the fierce tides, and herring gulls and bald eagles and osprey wheeled and screeched. As the days passed, sounds became simple and pure, and more intense: the lapping water, wind, birdsong, the generator, a foghorn from a nearby lighthouse. A red squirrel scurried on the roof each morning about 6 AM, waking me so that I could see the dawn. My CDs seemed superfluous. The cabin's satellite TV remained unused, the cell phone hardly used, the hot tub stayed covered.

I read, wrote, slept on the deck, and watched some sad/funny movies—*Patch Adams* and *Phenomenon*, but fell asleep before the end of both. One night I awoke in the cold light of a full moon in the skylight, and fell peacefully back to bed.

Piece by piece, life's complications stripped away—jewelry and makeup, and deodorant. Then, showers—now every other day, when I walked through the woods to get to my car, and then drove into the island to shop and check e-mails. When I couldn't find my comb, fingers sufficed. I stopped looking in the mirror. I'd go to sleep naked, and often stay that way long into the mornings. I ate tea and grilled cheese when the rain hit the windows, and the bay and sky disappeared in a fog. From the deck I watched the sun set in silence, as sweet-eyed harbor seals bobbed their heads by the weir. At night kerosene lamps and candles glowed, and as Sole looked on, one night I danced in the firelight to *The Best of Dusty Springfield*.

The two weeks passed, sometimes like sludge, but steadily, as if in the silence I could hear every beat of time. Fishermen trapped the herring every other day, and I'd watch their rhythmic movements through binoculars. An old man came by kayak to collect dulse, the sea-weed strewn on the shore, and watching him, I spied the carcass of a minke whale beached by a far cliff. A few hikers passed along the ridge, but none stopped. Once, during a downpour, a middle-aged couple looked toward the cabin and I wondered if I would let them in, or if they thought it was unoccupied, but I didn't have to make the choice, as they kept going in the rain. For just those few minutes I felt my vulnerability.

Why, I wondered, did I go on this solitary inner journey, farther than I had ever traveled, but within myself? To wash away pain? To prove my fortitude? As a child I found my own company precious, and now, on the rim of an island on the eastern edge of the continent, I felt perhaps that same magic. Here I had escaped from hypocrisy, greed, and loss. So I pondered and cried and rested and remembered, and grieved.

Alone on the cliffs of Grand Manan Island overlooking the misty Bay of Fundy, I didn't feel any lonelier than I did anywhere else. I felt peaceful. I missed my husband, but I felt his presence in my memories. On the last night in the cabin, snuggled under the duvet, drowsing to the tug of the tides, I patted Sole, and I knew I was ready to move on. 🐾

We're used to great-looking, young-old baby-boomers, going everywhere and doing everything. But the best old solo traveler I remember was Gillian, a white-haired, long-limbed English lady who walked the Lake Country of England. She was a sweater-set and sensible-shoe woman with a silver-tipped walking stick who sketched and wrote in a leather journal, and sipped tea and nibbled gingerbread, and whose healthy look seemed beautiful with age. Gillian had met Virginia Woolf as a young student, so she had to be in her late eighties when I conversed with her one fine early fall day. She had been a hiker all her life, and was now, as she put it, a "meanderer," who planned her day between inns that were a village apart, and along green and fertile back roads. Her Irish setter accompanied her on her meanderings. She was one happy old lady.

Whether or not you're on a strict budget, discounts are available for senior citizens in transportation, lodging, fast food, entertainment, cultural sites, and incidental expenditures. You usually need to ask for these discounted rates, or look closely to see if there's a notice about them in fine print. This info is not always volunteered—sometimes because people don't think you qualify (so bring adequate identification).

If you're retired you may have all the time you need to travel, but perhaps you're alone now after traveling as a couple or family for most of your life. You may feel uncomfortable about soloing. Although it's hard to break old habits, I encourage you to try to adjust to your new situation. Like it or not, many fellow travelers seem to love it when older people show spunk, and will gravitate toward you with warmth and kindness. Maturity is your full-bloom, ready-to-drink-it-in, now-or-never prime time—and it doesn't get any better. So if you're able to go forth late in life, give thanks and then make up for lost time and enjoy every wonderful second.

Travelers with Disabilities

The human spirit is the last thing to go. I've seen people in wheelchairs, and in those chair scooters that zig and zag, at the rim of the Grand Canyon. I've also traveled alongside women with oxygen tubes in their noses and men with heart monitors attached to their chests, creating flower arrangements in Kyoto, exploring the Great Wall of China, and even voyaging to Antarctica. They inspire us.

I traveled frequently with an adventurous man who had trouble walking. We roamed the world, yet I doubt my friend would have done as well completely alone. I spurred him on, fended off the questions, carried his luggage when needed, and made sure he was safe. It's great if you can go it alone, but based on my experience—depending on the type or extent of the disability—physically challenged soloists should consider traveling with others, and if disabilities are more severe, a group. But whatever the choice, the key is to keep traveling.

Solo-Parenting Travel

I flew alone with my son from New York to Honolulu when he was eight months old. He was a big, bouncy baby, who used my lap as a trampoline, but tense and tired as I was, I managed, like loads of us do, to get to my destination in one piece.

Today, more than a quarter of all U.S. households with children are headed by single parents who are typically between 30 and 50 years old, and who vacation once or twice a year either by flying to their destination (about two-thirds of them) or driving. Special travel agencies and parenting magazines cater to this booming travel market, which includes noncustodial single parents traveling with kids, half-couples soloing with kids, single grandparents traveling with their grandkids, and friends and relatives who often travel alone with children.

These hardworking solo caregivers seek both family-oriented activities and separate activities with other adults. My biggest gripe is when suppliers insist that there be two adults in a room before the "kids stay free" part of a package kicks in. The problem is not easily resolved. Resorts set prices assuming—needing—two full-paying adults. A room that's $150 per person based on double occupancy is really $300. Period. So use the same savvy you'd use when trying to dodge the single supplement, and don't be afraid to ask for a break, particularly during off-season or marginally off-season travel times, when many rooms will otherwise be empty. Bypass the reservation clerk (who's not empowered to negotiate), and get to the front-office manager or sales director to try for a reduction on your single supplement, or your child's rate. You might score at least some concession or compromise.

If you're soloing with a child, you may need written approval from the other parent to travel, even domestically. And your child should carry personal identification as well as information about locating you, your destination, and where you are staying with them.

RESOURCES

Women Travelers

AdventureWomen. Tours for women over 30. *www. adventurewomen.com*

Adventurous Wench. Mostly women-only trips, and you've gotta love the name of this outfit. *www.adventurouswench.com*

Sacred Journeys for Women. Tours to sacred sites. *www. sacredjourneys.com*

The Woman's Travel Club. Loads of free tips and—with nominal membership fee—eligibility to travel with the club. *www.womenstravelclub.com*

Women Traveling Together. Tours and retreats. *www.women-traveling.com*

Under-Thirtyish Travel

Contiki Tours. Trips for the 18 to 35 set. *www.contiki.com*

Paddywagon Backpacking Tours of Ireland. Literally a slew of backpacks and travelers piled onto a vividly decorated bus touring the Emerald Isle. *www.paddywagontours.com*

TrekAmerica. North America adventure camping trips for those 18 to 38. *www.trekamerica.com*

STA (Student Travel Agency). Large international student, youth, and budget-travel organization with links for young travelers to low airfares, inexpensive and discount accommodations, and travel packages. *www.statravel.com*

Mature Travel

If you prefer to solo but not alone, growing numbers of tour coordinators serve the over-50 community, and those listed here are sensitive to the single-supplement burden: minimizing it, mitigating it, waiving it, or offering roommate-matching services.

Elderhostel. Excellent learning vacations for travelers over 55. *www.ElderHostel.org*

Grand Circle Tours. Caters to over-50 solo/single crowd with trips to international destinations—some with no single supplement. *www.gct.com*

Saga Holidays. Packages international cruises for soloists 50 and over, many with no or low single-supplement charges. *www.sagaholidays.com*

Sea Kayak Adventures. Targets the mature traveler and offers fully guided individual or small group ventures for up to six days on Mexico's Sea of Cortez. *www.seakayakadventures.com*

Travelers with Disabilities

Access-Able Travel Source. Good general source with travel agent and tour operator links and a chat room. *www.access-able.com*

Gimp on the Go. Dynamite searchable database of accessible sights, theaters, hotels, and restaurants. *www.gimponthego.com*

The Guided Tour, Inc. Trips for developmentally and physically challenged travelers. *www.guidedtour.com*

Society for Accessible Travel & Hospitality (SATH). Organization raises awareness about travelers with disabilities; free tips and resource links. *www.sath.org*

Solo-Parenting Travel

Quality Time Travel. Vacation specialist for solo-parent families, books group, and individual trips. *www.qualitytimetravel.com*

Single Parent Tours. Weekend and weeklong trips and getaways across the country. *www.SingleParentTours.com*

Single Parent Travel Network. Solo parent family travel bulletin board, tips, and deals. *www.singleparenttravel.net*

chapter 16

Breaking Away

If you glean only a few ideas from this book I hope this is one of them, because it can truly improve your life, whether you're on the road or not.

Soloing is not an all-or-nothing proposition. Even if you always travel with other people, there are times when breaking away from them is possible and preferable. A few minutes spent ditching the group, even if that group is comprised entirely of your beloved spouse, can maximize your travel experience. We used to call this "doing your own thing." That's still what we call it.

Breaking away can mean the difference between a great trip and a disaster. I can't tell you how many couples and groups argue, harangue, nag, annoy, and even cancel because they can't fathom spending time alone for part of the trip—or even part of the day. And that's a shame.

It's a simple idea, really. And we apply it at home and through our daily lives all the time without bothering to think about it. But for some mysterious reason most people don't seem to apply the concept of breaking away while traveling. Perhaps out of fear, habit, loyalty, or the uncommunicated suspi-

Butterflies Can Tell

The Amazon River is a swelling, branching force in the Peruvian jungle, midway from where it first sweeps from a trickle in the Andes, and rushes toward the Brazilian rainforest. The rusty gingerbread buildings of Iquitos frame piles of rotting bananas and flocks of swirling vultures, and at night, the sky lights up like bombs over Baghdad, the humidity released throughout the night with booming thunder.

The first night there my journalist friend Marilyn and I were noting an iguana walking on the bottom of the empty swimming pool when an elderly workman overheard us talking, and asked me a one-word question I still can't believe: "Scarsdale?"

This leathered, indigenous man in worn trousers had probably never even been to Lima! And then he asked an equally astounding question. "White Plains?"

Was this a put-on? Why did he know those commuter towns in Westchester County, north of New York City, used as clichés by comedians for years? And what was most incredible, and even more unsettling, he was right: I lived just minutes away from these places!

"How did you know where I was from?" I finally asked.

"Way you talk," he answered shyly. And then I decided that through the years, hundreds from my area must have come here, and this gifted man's ear, trained to discern the most delicate jungle sounds, was acute enough to venture guesses about accents. It was a game for him, and in my case, he hit a bull's eye.

Marilyn and I were still talking about the experience when the next night our press group moved farther into the Amazon jungle, a camp by a tributary, lighted by kerosene lamps, with cold showers and boiled water. Our native guide was Leo, a tall man in his thirties, with wire-rimmed glasses and gleaming muscles. He walked us through the jungle and explained the flora.

Leo announced that, those of us willing to get up at dawn would be treated to a canoe ride with him down a tributary, to observe hundreds of awakening birds, insects, and animals. We all planned to enjoy this special trip, but the night was long, and filled with dancing and laughter.

Groggy-eyed and dragging, I managed to show up by the canoes at sunrise. And I was the only one.

"Good," Leo said. "There will be more birds. They will not be frightened away. You are smart to come alone."

Indeed, there were birds, and Morphos butterflies, big as birds, which swarmed above my head, maybe 20 at a time, their iridescent, blue-violet wings like Tiffany glass in the rising sunlight.

"They like you," Leo said. "They know you care. Butterflies can tell."

I have always been enchanted by these showy insects; I called them "flutterbys" as a little girl. But I had never, ever seen anything like the Morphos. At breakfast, when we got back to camp, Leo told everyone what we had experienced, and the other writers seemed especially sorry they hadn't awakened to see the butterflies. Leo piled it on.

But one piqued lady dashed the fantasy. "Lea's wearing a red shirt. Butterflies are attracted to red."

"So that's why," I whispered in Leo's ear. "You were just pleasing me."

"Yes," he said, "but I think that the butterflies did know that you came on your own to see them. You went out of your way, they went out of their way."

I believe Leo. Sort of. And about a month later, I received a pictograph he drew of our trip down the tributary, illustrated with blue butterflies everywhere. And that was probably the most wonderful thing of all the surprising wonders of that trip. ❧

cion that our companion will be lonely, we stick to each other, even while grumbling and fussing as we go—when we'd be much better off on our own for a little while. Let's see if we can change this. And let's start with our definition.

"Breaking away" means that when you're traveling with others, sometimes you go off on your own, where you want, doing what you want—and your travel partners can do the same. You all agree to be fine with that arrangement, whenever it may come up. That's it.

To make it work best, agree on this concept, and talk it over ahead of time. Discuss all aspects, so no one feels guilty or abandoned when someone asks for a breakaway. It's simply a time out. No big deal.

You can use the word as a noun: "I want a breakaway to a spa tomorrow, Millie." Or as a verb: "I'm going to break away from the group and have a pizza for breakfast. You all do whatever."

The benefits are enormous. For a time you can do what you want. You'll be refreshed and enthusiastic—as will your partner(s)—when you reconnect. You won't have wasted time or money on things you don't care about. And best of all, you can practice solo traveling, so when you're ready for more, you'll be able to jump right in.

How a Breakaway Leads to a Happier Ending

Picture if you will: You're on a one-week trip to Brussels with Hector, your significant other. You and he share a love of fine dining, history, and museums. But you're an architecture buff. You love to walk and stop at art nouveau buildings, admiring the ornamented doorways, the swooping lines. You walk slowly, often stopping, gazing happily. Hector couldn't be less interested. A building is a building to him. Watch how the day goes with these two different endings.

WITHOUT THE BREAKAWAY

Hector: "Why are we stopping. We stopped 10 times already. What is it with you?"

You: "I like stopping. You know that."

H: "Yeah, but enough already. I count, you know. Ten times!"

Y: "Why is it when there's something I like, you always make a fuss? I'm pretty sure I was quiet while you were in that bookstore forever."

You see where this one is going, and it would be just as unfortunate if, to please Hector, you walked at his pace, right on by the interesting buildings. Later that night, you'd sleep on the other side of the bed, and neither of you would even be sure why. Now consider the alternative.

WITH THE BREAKAWAY

Hector lingers over tea and chocolates, you kiss, and then you head out on an architectural walk. He reads the local paper, spends a blissful two hours in the bookstore, and meets you at lunchtime near the Grand Place for mussels. Or, you take an architectural tour while he visits a museum and ogles the Bruegels and Rubens. You both share experiences when you meet by the Mannequin Pis and walk to a café for an artisanal beer. You go to bed early, on the same side.

Scenario #2: On the Road with Laurel

You have three weeks of vacation time. Your best friend Laurel has 10 days. You love traveling together, but you can't decide where to go. You want to go to Spain, but don't have enough time in 10 days to see Madrid, Andalucia, and Barcelona.

WITHOUT THE BREAKAWAY

You compromise and do Spain in 10 days. You miss out on 11 days of travel and either skip places you want to see or rush through them. Or, you wind up not going to Spain at all.

WITH THE BREAKAWAY

You leave 11 days ahead of Laurel—a mini solo trip to the parts of Spain you most want to visit and that Laurel cares least about. She meets you in Madrid and you continue on to the parts of the country—Madrid and Barcelona—that you both want to see. You are both happy. You both filled your travel time completely. You plan your next trip together.

Scenario #3: The Group Tour

You're on a group tour to Italy, but have already visited Rome several times. You'd rather go to the nearby Ligurian coast and visit ancient Etruscan burial mounds.

WITHOUT THE BREAKAWAY

You stick with the group. You miss Liguria. You are angry at yourself for being meek. You missed the mounds, so you scarf

continued on p. 260

Marrakesh Fantasy

Marrakesh that June evening long ago was soft and mild enough to wrap around your shoulders. The slipping sun fired the clay-baked city the tint of wild roses, and in seconds it seemed, the black desert night was strewn with sparkles. It was the last night of a press trip, the strange combination of hard work and hedonism we travel writers attempt to balance on these junkets, with hours crammed from early morning to late night.

The day before we had been to Agadir, and walked the beach beside covered Muslim women and topless tourists. We lunched at a hunting lodge, where pigeons were bred to be shot, and the pool was set into the 1,000-year-old walls of the ancient town.

At sundown we were driven so off-road that "hijacked" came to mind as the bus stopped in the middle of sands and scrub. A tiny, abandoned settlement had been morphed into a restaurant, where former souks were now banquettes with low tiled tables, set around a square crossed by waiters with brass trays. While we dined on couscous, swordsmen in white robes flashed silver daggers, and they pulled us up to dance among them, to ancient instruments. A belly dancer dispersed the fragrance of jasmine with every undulation.

Sightseeing in Marrakesh on that final morning centered on the central marketplace where jugglers, snake charmers, scribes, and soothsayers staked their few feet of space. One man set up a table marked "dentist," and spent the day pulling teeth next to a band of acrobats. In the afternoon, thundering horses raced on open fields, back and forth, and standing on the sides we cheered them on—so close to the action that we were covered in dust.

At dinner, rested and clean, we reclined on woven pillows in a room of soaring, carved-cedar ceilings, dining on pigeon in pastry leaves, dribbled with oranges and pistachios. A musician strummed, and water splashed from a turquoise-tiled fountain.

Another tough day of research.

After dinner, we viewed special entertainment a couple of rows behind King Hassan and his entourage; the dancing, juggling, and magic proceeded late into the evening. Moroccan ladies ululated vibrato approval, and warmed by wine, I tried to duplicate what I heard: Carol Burnett's Tarzan call on fast-forward.

As the crowd dispersed, I strolled along a souk-lined corridor, back to the press van, enjoying the shadows and atmosphere. I like quiet reflections on my own, a frisson of risk and solitude in a world packed with schedules and guides.

Suddenly, horse's hooves echoed in hollow cadence out of the darkness. Atop a chestnut stallion sat a mustachioed horseman in a short suede cape—skin gleaming, teeth white as sugar. I imagined a romance novel cover: *He Came Out of the Moroccan Shadows, and She Was Never the Same.*

I stepped aside, but the horseman caught my gaze. He pulled the steed to a halt, tilted his dark head, and his black eyes literally twinkled, perhaps from the starlight above, or the torchlight in the corridor, or—could it be, I half hoped, *The Fire Within Him.*

I stood motionless and he gestured to me. What I interpreted: "Come up and sit behind me." I read even more: "Come away with me into this soft Moroccan night of roses and breezes and stars. Come away to a land where I will make your dreams come true."

Holding romantic promise for a second, I smiled, rather fetchingly, I thought. My imagination kicked in, big time. Should I ditch the press trip and head off with this guy to his tent? Should I give up my life as suburban wife and mother, 40 minutes north of New York City? Would it be worth it to leave good bagels behind, not to mention my sons?

After what seemed an eternity—probably five seconds—I looked into those black eyes high on that horse and shook my head, shyly, side-to-side.

The horseman shrugged as if to say, "I gave you your one shot lady. Your loss." He prompted his steed's flanks past me, as I stood, looking back at him, waiting for him to turn his mount, rush back and sweep me up into his saddle, despite my protestation.

But all I saw was the horse's swaying rear, and his. The moment passed, and reality returned. Now I figured he probably headed back to his apartment, removed his cape, and watched the Moroccan equivalent of *Queer Eye for the Straight Guy.*

I never wrote about this fleeting memory, but remember it more clearly than anything else that happened on the trip. As years pass, it becomes ever more precious, ever more a romantic moment from a time of innocence. 🐾

down a Mounds from the minibar, as well as a bag of licorice, some chocolate-chip cookies, and a canister of peanuts. Now you're angry, sick, poor, and a pound heavier.

WITH THE BREAKAWAY

You ditch the group. You take a day off from the Rome segment and visit Liguria on your own. You decide to stay overnight at a small hotel in the region and enjoy the local cuisine. You rejoin the group as they are heading for Florence, happy, full of tales, photos, and memories—and with no regrets.

Scenario #4: Jan's Story

My friend Jan tells of a trip to Sydney with her husband and a group of married friends. They had only a couple of days there, and after arriving, some of the group expressed a desire to eat at a famous restaurant. Jan had no interest in this, and there was much debate, but she went along with the crowd. The elaborate luncheon took the entire afternoon, and overstuffed Jan had no time to visit the opera house as she had planned, or even take a walk on the beach. She figures she missed out on what interested her, and because Australia is so far away, doesn't intend to return.

BREAKAWAY WITH A TWIST

Jan later divorced, and not just because of that trip! But she vows that the next time she's traveling and there's a group decision that she doesn't care for, she will announce proudly—"I'm breaking away!"

Tips for Breaking Away

Figure out timing as best as possible, but allow for surprises. Make the most of them, and be flexible. You may have to change plans that allow for you or your partner to enjoy a breakaway.

Plan for contingencies. Agree on a spot to meet up at a clearly understood time. And prepare if your partner is late—with cell-phone numbers, or alternative plans, like reuniting at the hotel for dinner if you get tied up and are unable to communicate.

Carry reading material, or something to do. In case there's a spontaneous breakaway by your traveling partner, you can always find a nearby bench and enjoy yourself.

Split up once in a while for meals. One of you likes fancy restaurants and the other doesn't? Lunchtime is the easier time to dine alone and it's often less expensive—so the fancy diner can enjoy haute-cuisine restaurants and then join her travel partner later for dinner at the hot-dog cart.

Consider shopping breakaways. If one of you shops with abandon while the other doesn't enjoy it as much or for as long, let the shopper check out the stores while the other walks the time off, has a coffee and people-watches, or does his own thing.

Ditch the group freely. The same concept that works well with travel partners applies to groups. If you join one, you don't have to stay with it all the time (it's your money). You can start and finish in Paris and leave on your own for Provence while the group stays north. Or just choose the activities you enjoy, and dip in and out. Or choose your own restaurants whenever you want. Just be sure to let the group leader know your plans.

Break away serially. Come earlier, leave later, and just be with others during part of your trip. If you're traveling for a long while, have several people break away serially, and you can have company the whole time. Or join someone for a while, then break away while they continue traveling. On ultralong research trips of several months, I switch travel partners when one can't afford the time I have. It works beautifully. I've been in Brazil with one travel partner, and when she left I joined another in Argentina; I did the same, leaving one partner in Poland before traveling on to Sweden, and joining another.

Lea's Favorite Breakaways

IN FRANCE

I was traveling with close friends, a married couple, and after several days of staying at expensive lodgings, decided I didn't

continued on p. 264

Passages

I am with someone I've been dating for more than a year, and we have been on a two-week road trip in India, from Bombay to Agra. I amuse him, and sometimes he amuses me, but I plan to leave him when I return home. For days we have talked about personal things with our driver and guide. They are happy in their arranged marriages. We are both divorced after failed "love" marriages. "Ah," says the driver, "you expect everything and are disappointed. We expect little, and are pleased."

In India, cars dart about like schools of fish. Overloaded trucks, huge and silent as beached whales lay on the shoulders every few miles, and old men, camels and donkeys meander across the highways in the dark of night, cars grazing by, headlights dimmed. The road is a dismal carnival. We pass a bear on hind legs chained to a tree, and a dead man lying like road kill, and we keep going. I close my eyes much of the time.

On Independence Day in New Delhi this January the air is clean, and the sky, eye-blue. We are near the end of the journey, guests of the tourism board at a daylong extravaganza of marching men, elephants, overhead jets, bands, and floats. Hundreds of thousands of spectators have steadfastly walked miles to the parade route in their white celebration dress, and they line the wide boulevard, dozens deep.

We are in a black limo, the windows opened, and we wend at a walker's pace through the swirling whiteout of people. The mass seems so large that a satellite might have picked it up as a snowfield in India. Miraculously we avoid hitting anyone, too hard. The masses seem to ignore us, except for a few who ominously thump the car.

I am overcome with feelings: fear, that we could become victims of this avalanche, a mob turned suddenly sour at the sight of us. I feel awe at the mass of stoic people, seemingly content in the midday sun; sorrow, for the poverty; guilt for being relatively well-off; misery for being here with someone I don't like much.

The man I'm traveling with stays in the car, but I break away and make it to the edge of the huge boulevard, to an island of folding seats in a sea of standing souls. Across the way, behind a bullet-proof screen, I see the handsome prime minister, Rajiv Gandhi, and his Western wife, Sonia. Our rows of seats, facing theirs across the way, seem to be the only ones along the entire parade route. The guide escorts me to my

place, and I experience close-up the panoply of booming guns and waving politicians, streaming jets flying low above the crowds, ark-fulls of
costumed villagers and animals. I am uncomfortable with the disparity
of sitting while so many are standing, but not so uncomfortable that I
give up my chair.

Our stay lasts perhaps an hour, but the ride back to our nearby hotel,
parting the throngs at a walker's pace, takes another hour. "Did you like
the parade?" asks the guide, thin and scholarly, in his sing-song voice, as
we halt along.

"Magnificent! Oh yes," we concur in the offhand tone used by conde-
scending first-worlders.

"You had a wonderful seat, Lea."

"Yes it was. Thank you for arranging it."

"You know, you were sitting next to a star. More popular to us than
your Elizabeth Taylor!"

I thought back to the minutes before. A movie star next to me?
Nobody glamorous was near me, or I would have noticed. The guide
sensed my hesitancy. "She was on your right."

Aah, yes. The large lady in an iridescent pinkish sari. I thought
she was a local writer. She never glanced at me. Who could possibly
know she was a star in a country of half a billion avid fans—a Bolly-
wood legend?

I did not know much on that sunny day in New Delhi: that the Prime
Minister across the boulevard would soon be assassinated, and his blond
wife would for a short while take his place, and 20 years later be elected
herself, only to turn the position down. And I did not know that it would
take me another year to leave the man I was with.

What I did know, more with each trip that spun me farther around
the globe into cultures that unsettled and challenged me, was that I
would not find easy answers to disparities and ironies. Like the Indian
roads—dark and full of the unexpected, life would continue to throw
surprises my way, and I would continue to deal with them, best I
could. ❧

care to spend so much money on my room. I stayed at an inn in a Provencal town, while they stayed at a deluxe manor house. They felt sorry for me, until I mentioned that the room I slept in was the same one that Napoleon had stayed in on a visit almost 300 years before. That was a thrill I still remember, far more than any other accommodation on that trip—although I figure that the mattress had been changed at least a couple of times in-between our stays!

IN ITALY

Bobbi and I both loved Mel Torme and antiques—but would we love Lake Como? We were ready for our first major trip together. We soon discovered we were both "oohers and aahers"—there's a silly disconnect when one is and one isn't—so scenically, we were on course. But she's a shopper and I'm a museum goer, and she's a simple-food lover and I'm a fine-diner-once-in-a-while-at-least. I usually gave in, because I wanted to please—but neither of us was pleased.

In Trieste, finally, I decided to break away. She wanted to window shop. I preferred to see an ancient church at the top of a hill. When she balked, I suggested, "You shop while I go up to the church. We can meet at three for tea in this shop."

She didn't like the idea, but got to roam around the arcaded shopping area and schmooze with the shopkeepers, and I climbed the hill and visited the church. And when we met afterwards for tea, we had lots to talk about, we both felt satisfied, and we actually enjoyed our break so much that we broke away every chance we got.

IN HAWAII

On a trip to the Hawaiian Islands with a boyfriend, Mark (yes, I was single a long time between marriages and I don't *always* travel solo) we were staying at famed golf resorts. The only problem was that he would be on the golf course about five hours a day. I thought of options: nag, or seduce him so that he didn't play; do other things while he golfed; split time—half doing what he wanted (golf), half what I wanted (anything but golf); or learn to play, fast!

We arranged that I stay in his golf cart while he played. Fine for him; he got hugs and praise, and had fun playing and showing off. I brought a novel that I never opened. I enjoyed the golf-course scenery, framed by mountains, but it was a foursome, plus me, so the experience was extremely slow. By the time Mark putted out on 18, I was bored out of my mind, and annoyed with him and everything else in paradise.

The next day, on the island of Hawaii, I broke away. While he golfed I flew in a helicopter over a volcano. We missed each other all day, enjoyed ourselves doing what we wanted, and had an ultraromantic reunion that night, replete with orchid petals. He was actually envious of me, and told me that he returned to the island many years later to take that helicopter ride.

IN INDIA

The Taj Mahal, in Agra, India, is a landmark people wait a lifetime to visit. Mine was midday, when crowds and hawkers were spoiling the beauty of the experience. I wasn't satisfied, and wanted to return early the next morning. My traveling partner preferred sleeping.

So the next morning, before 6 AM, I decided to break away. I hired a cab to wait for me, and visited the Taj, by myself, at dawn. The marble building was tinted pink in the rising sun. No one was around. Birdsong was the only sound I heard, except for my own quiet breaths. Those private 15-minutes or so with that bejeweled monument to love were simply exquisite, and I was back in bed by 7:30.

IN NEW YORK

My first husband and I visited a holistic spa in Suffern, New York, about an hour north of New York City. It was a time of touchy-feely therapy, and the spa offered optional nudity. I was researching an article and we had no interest in that aspect—I thought. The first day, I luxuriated with a facial, and when the session was finished and I went outside, there was my husband, walking around naked.

I guess you could say he had a breakaway, but he didn't warn me at all, and I felt not only clothed, but shocked and hurt.

Remember, prepare your partner if you break away, even if you aren't planning to be nude.

IN SICILY

On the first day of a vacation that was supposed to be as friends, staying in separate rooms, Charles opened the door to "our" room in Taormina—with a queen-size bed awaiting. The entire trip became a breakaway.

About the Author

Lea Lane is an award-winning writer of travel articles and features for magazines and newspapers. She was managing editor of the newsletter "Travel Smart," has written about traveling solo in the *New York Times* and the *Miami Herald*, and wrote a travel column for Gannett newspapers, "Going It Alone." Lane is a contributor to dozens of guidebooks, including Fodor's *Greece; Naples, Capri and the Amalfi Coast; Belgium & Luxembourg*; and *The Thirteen Colonies*. She has authored books on cruises and bed-and-breakfasts and inns, served as a host at fodors.com, and has appeared regularly on The Travel Channel and other TV and radio shows as a travel expert.

Lane grew up in Miami Beach, earned two and a half college degrees, and didn't travel much, or even see snow 'til she was 22. Besides writing about travel, she has been a high school and college teacher, a corporate VP, an actress ("Nurse 1," in a low-budget indie), an off-Broadway producer, a (produced) musical playwright, a counselor for foster children, and a romance and mystery novelist. She is the author of *Steps to Better Writing*, and using her book, trained more than 1,000 people in corporations and government to improve their writing skills.

She lives in South Florida, and in upstate New York, near her family—when she isn't exploring the world as a solo traveler.

Notes

Notes

Notes

Notes

Notes

Notes

Notes

Notes

Notes